Theorizing *Twilight*

Theorizing *Twilight*

Critical Essays on What's at Stake in a Post-Vampire World

Edited by MAGGIE PARKE *and* NATALIE WILSON

McFarland & Company, Inc., Publishers
Jefferson, North Carolina, and London

Natalie Wilson is also the author of *Seduced by* Twilight: *The Allure and Contradictory Messages of the Popular Saga* (McFarland, 2011)

Library of Congress Cataloguing-in-Publication Data

Theorizing Twilight: critical essays on what's at stake in a post-vampire world / edited by Maggie Parke and Natalie Wilson.
    p.   cm.
    Includes bibliographical references and index.

ISBN 978-0-7864-6350-3
softcover : 50# alkaline paper 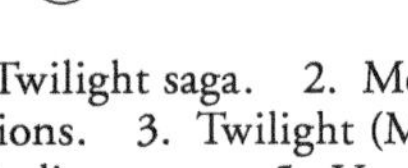

1. Meyer, Stephenie, 1973– Twilight saga.   2. Meyer, Stephenie, 1973– Film adaptations.   3. Twilight (Motion picture : 2008)   4. Vampires in literature.   5. Vampires in motion pictures.   I. Parke, Maggie.   II. Wilson, Natalie, 1971–
PS3613.E979Z8855   2011
813'.54 — dc23   2011024220

British Library cataloguing data are available

Front cover design by David K. Landis (Shake It Loose Graphics)

Manufactured in the United States of America

McFarland & Company, Inc., Publishers
Box 611, Jefferson, North Carolina 28640
www.mcfarlandpub.com

To my family, immediate and adopted, across three continents and twelve time zones for your encouragement and enthusiasm, and to anyone who is passionate about the whys, whats, and the hows of popular culture.

— Maggie Parke

To Naomi, Shane, and Graham, who support my theorizing with enthusiasm, and to my blog readers, who continue to inspire me with their *Twilight* analysis.

— Natalie Wilson

Acknowledgments

The editors would like to thank the fans of *Twilight*, and those that let us discuss this popular moment in history academically, in an encouraging atmosphere, and without mockery. We would particularly like to thank our contributors for their prompt return of drafts, optimistic attitudes, and brilliant perspectives on the various issues that surround *Twilight*. Thanks also to our friends and families for putting up with many untold hours of hearing about Twilight texts, movies, and fans.

Natalie Wilson would like to thank her non-vampire clan that has been so supportive of her work on vampires and werewolves, especially Rachel Karlin, Patty Wilson, Pamela Redela, Heidi Breuer, Lezlie-Lee French, Sarah Wraight, Sheryl Lutjens, and Simon Bacon. She would also like to thank the "Forks Cougars" who shall not be named lest Edward or James tries to hunt them down, but who know who they are. Finally, she would like to thank Shane, Naomi, and Graham—you all may not be ab-tacular wolfy shapeshifters, but I am glad to be part of your pack just the same.

Maggie Parke would like to thank the *Twilight* film's creative team who invited her into their encouraging circle, the Ph.D. NIECI Junta, Blue Sky, Thandi Gilder, Taylor Brady, Richelle Geist and the whole McDowell clan for encouragement and sanity-saving, and also her helpful voices of reason: Samantha Rayner, Ashley Benning and Warren Rochelle. She would lastly like to thank her family: Ann, Bill, Tom, Sarah, Amy and Tripp for their endless support and firm grounding in a land entirely devoid of vampires and werewolves.

The editors would also like to thank each other: for persistence, patience, and a positive trans-continental working relationship! This manuscript made its way back and forth from Wales to California via email, Skype sessions, and Google docs. We are thankful for the technology that supports such a collaboration, and for each other's determination to see the project through!

Table of Contents

Part III. *Twilight* Through an Intersectional Lens: Patriarchy, White Privilege, Heteronormativity, Rape Culture, Religion

Introduction

Twilight. It's no longer just a time of day when the sun is setting and the moon is rising. Now, the mere mention of the word brings on shrieks of delight, sighs of derision, and pronouncements of which "Team" one belongs to. The word can send fans of the saga dashing to the nearest online fansite, cause others to roll their eyes in mockery, and for a few, it can cause questions to arise about all manner of topics from gender, race, sexuality and religion, to film production and popular culture. That's where this collection of essays comes into play.

The idea for this work began over coffee, as so many ideas do, but this coffee was sipped in the Sheraton hotel in Dallas, Texas, during TwiCon, the first and largest *Twilight* convention (and the only fan created convention) in July of 2009. Maggie Parke, who conducted her Ph.D. research on the set of *Twilight* in 2008, was the chair of formal programming at that event and organized the academic panels and paper presentations, and Natalie Wilson, who recently published the first academic monograph on the saga (*Seduced by Twilight*), was a presenter there. It was an inspiring and unique experience. Presenters and panel members were able to share their ideas with fellow aficionados, fans, and critics of the saga. They could exchange ideas enthusiastically with fellow fans and scholars in a non-threatening location where mockery had no place, but open discussion and serious interrogations about the implications and pervasiveness of *Twilight* was encouraged.

After hearing numerous exciting papers that looked at the *Twilight* phenomenon through different lenses, and realizing how much there was to say in relation to the saga, the editors felt that there was a need for this work to exist. Other *Twilight* fans should be able to read essays about their favorite works in a smart, researched, but accessible way, and extend their realm of interaction with and interpretation of Meyer's works. Plus, as there is not much existing scholarship on the saga, and the editors had a collection of ideas and topics from which to choose from, they wanted to share the perspectives of other authors with the *Twilight* fandom, academic community, and popular audiences. Wilson, who attended and presented at the earlier (and much smaller) Summer School in Forks Symposium, came to TwiCon with hopes she might meet more possible authors to contribute to a *Twilight* anthology, and with Parke, they had the resources to do so.

In December 2009, the editors sent out a call for papers to those they had met at Summer School in Forks and TwiCon, and also invited open submissions via various list-serves. After receiving hundreds of abstracts from everyone from unpublished college students all the way to renowned researchers and retired professors, the editors chose those that best covered new territory in terms of academic discussion on *Twilight*, and that could fit together in a cohesive collection. This is by no means a definitive text on *Twilight* criticism; this is simply one of the first thorough works out there to look at *Twilight*, the phenomenon surrounding it, and the cultural and popular effects and implications of the saga through well-written pieces composed with an emphasis on accessible tone — you don't have to speak Academia to understand the essays that grace these pages! Any fan of *Twilight* will find something of interest within these pages. On the other hand, the editors also wanted to avoid the overly casual, light and fluffy tone (and sometimes celebrity photo-laden pages) that has shaped some of the existing texts discussing the saga. The editors aimed for a middle-ground between dense academese and frivolity and hope that the essays contained herein are entertaining but enlightening, thought-provoking but user-friendly.

The Dawn of Twilight

For the vast, phenomenal impact that it has had, *Twilight* started from surprisingly modest roots. As is now the stuff of common knowledge, and the dreams of first-time authors the world over, what started out as a dream has morphed into a mega-franchise. The saga is the story of an easy-to-relate-to heroine, mature beyond her years, who transplants herself to the small town of Forks, Washington, to live with her single father. In this rainy, Pacific Northwest location, our human heroine and vampire hero, Bella Swan and Edward Cullen, begin a tortured and impossible love story that provides the central conflict throughout the saga. There are other conflicts that shape the saga as well: the Cullen family consider themselves "vegetarians" as they do not feed off of humans, and this separates them from other vampires who are the main, threatening force in each of the books; first with James and the nomads in *Twilight*, through to Victoria, the Newborn Army, and the Volturi — the ancient, royal-like ruling clan in the vampire world. Additionally, the Quileute wolves and the Cullen vampires have an uneasy truce, one that is threatened by Bella's (more than) friendship with Jacob Black. Additionally, the saga presents us with what we have termed "post–Vampires" — or vampires that re-work traditional conceptions of this supernatural figure.

Within six months, the first book of the saga was written, edited, and Meyer obtained a book agent. Then, Little, Brown and Company negotiated a three-book deal with her (Stepheniemeyer.com). *Twilight* was released in October 2005, with *New Moon*, the second book, coming out in August 2006; *Eclipse*, the third, in August 2007; and *Breaking Dawn*, the final book, in August 2008. The movie-making process of bringing *Twilight* to the screen began even before the first book was released. Greg Mooradian, a producer on *Twilight*, was the one who found and optioned *Twilight* in 2004. While the book was still being edited by Megan Tingley at Little, Brown and Company, a New York book scout brought Mooradian the raw manuscript. Mooradian said that he was "drawn into the epic, forbidden love story" (personal interview 2008) and that he believed in its potential for the screen, thus illustrating his personal attachment, and seemingly fan-like appreciation for the project. He took this passion for the story and pitched it to multiple studios, which apparently impressed the executives at Paramount, and presumably those at MTV and Summit, as it was these three studios that at one point or another had access to putting *Twilight* onscreen, and thus spawning the subsequent phenomenon now known the world over.

Twilight, with its small but strong online following, has developed into the four novels that have dominated numerous best-selling charts, *Twilight* (T), *New Moon* (NM), *Eclipse* (E), and *Breaking Dawn* (BD). In addition to the four central texts of the saga, there is also Meyer's novella, *The Short Second Life of Bree Tanner* (BT), bonus chapters of the novels on her website, and a draft of the unpublished *Midnight Sun* (MS) which charts the same tale told in *Twilight*, but from Edward's perspective. In the summer of 2010, Meyer published the first of three installments of a graphic novel interpretation of *Twilight* with the promise of parts two and three to come. In 2011, Meyer finally released her *Official Illustrated Guide*, a guide that had been slated for initial release in 2009. With the release of the films from Summit Entertainment, as well as regular *Twilight Conventions* around the world, the reach of the *Twilight* universe if far and varied.

The saga, at the time of publication, has sold 116 million copies worldwide in nearly 50 different languages. As of July 20, 2011, the *Twilight* books have spent 302 weeks on the New York Times bestseller lists. Additionally, the films and actors have been consistently the most searched for actors on IMDB since summer 2008.

Scholarly interest on the saga is also growing. Existing analysis of the series includes texts that read the saga in relation to religion (such as *Touched by a Vampire* and *Spotlight: A Close-Up Look at the Artistry and Meaning in Stephenie Meyer's Twilight Novels*), texts that take a particular disciplinary approach (such as *Twilight and Philosophy* and *Twilight and History*), and texts that, like the present volume, offer an inter-disciplinary approach to the saga from fields such as women's studies, film studies, cultural studies, and literature (such as *Bitten by Twilight, The Twilight Mystique,* and *Bringing Light to Twilight*). To date, there is only one single-authored monograph penned by an academic, and that is Wilson's *Seduced by Twilight.* Many non-scholarly or "popular" approaches to the saga are in circulation, from "love guides" (such as *Everything I Need to Know About Women I Learned by Reading Twilight: A Vampire's Guide to Eternal Love*) to unofficial guides to the series (such as *Twilight Companion: The Unauthorized Guide to the Series* and *Love Bites: The Unofficial Saga of Twilight*). There are also a number of biographies of Meyer as well as Meyer's much awaited *The Twilight Saga: The Official Illustrated Guide* (released in April 2011).

With all of these existing texts, you may be asking yourself, do we really need another anthology on *Twilight?* In short, yes. Though the saga is often interpreted as a simple love story made appealing via the inclusion of uber-hot vampires and werewolves, the series, like all texts that capture the public imagination, is far more complicated, symbolic, and ideological than is often acknowledged. When texts spark a zeitgeist — be they *Buffy the Vampire Slayer* or *Harry Potter* or *The Hunger Games* — they do so for a reason. Yes, they are often carefully marketed and packaged as transmedia products, but even so they must tap into cultural trends and concerns in order to become part of public discourse and to infiltrate our cultural desktops, so to speak. *Twilight,* from its spawning of thousands of blogs and fan sites to its five film adaptations, to its launching of several actors' careers, is not merely a blip on our socio-cultural screen. It, like all texts that garner widespread popularity, acclaim, and disdain, deserves serious attention, academic and otherwise.

This anthology seeks to take part in the growing field of "*Twilight* academia" by proffering analytical arguments about the saga that expand upon, re-work, and further existing scholarship. The first section, "*Twilight* as Pop Cultural Artifact: Pilgrimages, Fan Culture, and Film Adaptations," examines the cultural implications of the *Twilight* saga, investigating the fandom, the franchising of *Twilight,* and why fans are so enamored with the "neutering" of the vampire that Meyer enacts. In "The Vampire Capital of the World: Commerce and Enchantment in Forks, Washington," Tanya Erzen assesses how fans participate in and resist *Twilight* consumerism and celebrity-worship, and how the social and political economy of the fandom both generates and forecloses possibilities for more lasting forms of community. By incorporating interviews with fans, fan site-creators, Twi-bands, *Twilight* business owners, and interspersing the analysis with participant observation at events like Twicon, Creation Entertainment conventions and *Twilight* tours, this essay demonstrates that fans have a complicated relationship to the commercialization of *Twilight*.

The second essay, "Fanpires: Utilizing Fan Culture in Event Film Adaptations" by Maggie Parke, discusses new practices of fan management in event films through an investigation into recent popular event film adaptations, comparing the *Twilight* adaptation process to other major event films such as such as *The Lord of the Rings* and *Eragon*. Parke explores the filmmaker's treatment of fans, discussing how fan participation with new media platforms assists in box office earnings.

The third essay, "The Hero and the Id: A Psychoanalytic Inquiry into the Popularity of *Twilight*" by Heather Anastasiu, argues that *Twilight* has gained such immense popularity because it vividly portrays unconscious desires and provides readers a platform for vicarious participation in a therapeutic hero's journey. Exploring the novel's potentially positive psychological potential, this essay delves into the psychological underpinnings of the saga that contribute to its mass appeal. Colette Murphy, in "Someday My *Vampire* Will Come? Society's (and the Media's) Lovesick Infatuation with Prince-Like Vampires," offers an investigation of the ways in which *Twilight* employs many of the same strategies of fairy tales, from classic stories to Disney adaptations. Detailing how vampires have transitioned from blood-sucking demons to figurative Prince Charmings, the essay uses the concept of a "media virus" in order to interrogate why the saga reverberates in particular with a female audience raised on the idea of fairy tale love.

The final essay in this section, "Team Bella: Fans Navigating Desire, Security, and Feminism," by Ananya Mukherjea gives voice to the intellectual work various under-represented groups are enacting via their engagement with popular texts. Given that the fans Mukherjea interviewed for the piece are primarily from working class or lower middle class backgrounds with diverse racial, ethnic, and religious identities, and mostly either young women or young gay men, this essay offers an important contribution to the field of fan scholarship, revealing that the examination of popular culture and its resulting fandoms discloses a great deal about social inequalities and systems of power.

The second section, "Once Upon a *Twilight*: Fairy Tales, Byronic (Anti)

Heroes, Post-Feminist Romance, and Growing Up in a *Twilight* World," focuses on how fairy tales and literary tropes such as the Byronic hero inform the saga. With an emphasis on growing up female in a patriarchal world infused with romantic tales, the section investigates how the series taps into our culturally constructed notions of age, gender, love, romance, and sexuality. While there has been much ado over the age-appropriateness of the series in relation to the targeted readership, few critics have examined the themes of aging, parental authority, maturity, and coming-of-age as components of Meyer's construct of age in the saga. Ashley Benning addresses this omission in her essay "'How Old Are You?' Representations of Age in the Saga." Reading the *Twilight* series as a bildungsroman, the paper addresses issues of age and age relations both within the world of the novels and in the fandom. The next essay, Angela Tenga's "Read Only as Directed: Psychology, Intertextuality, and Hyperreality in the Series," executes a fascinating folkloric reading, framing *Twilight* as modern day fairy tale replete with virginal red riding hoods and dangerous wolves. Proffering a psychological reading of Bella's character, Tenga contends that Bella problematically sees her life as an enactment of fiction, something she suggests fans also do in their response to the saga. "Torn Between Two Lovers: *Twilight* Tames *Wuthering Heights*" by Sarah Wakefield documents the ways in which Bella's admiration for *Wuthering Heights* plays a key role in *Eclipse*. Offering a close comparative reading of Meyer's saga and Bronte's novel, Wakefield shows that Edward, Bella, and Jacob are less extreme, hybrid versions of Heathcliff, Cathy, and Edgar Linton, arguing that this allows the love triangle to end happily for all three. Carrying on the inter-textual focus, Jessica Groper's "Rewriting the Byronic Hero: How the *Twilight* Saga Turned 'Mad, Bad, and Dangerous to Know' into a Teen Fiction Phenomenon" discusses the trope of the Byronic hero and Meyer's re-working of this literary type. The considerations of the gender messages within the Byronic hero trope as well as the Gothic genre offer new and intriguing reads of the social construction of gender and how that construction is solidified and/or contested in literature. The next essay in this section, Hila Shachar's "A Post-Feminist Romance: Love, Gender and Intertextuality in Stephenie Meyer's Saga," reads Meyer's text as a new form of post-feminist backlash and investigates how Meyer incorporates centuries-old ideas about gender into a modern narrative. Shachar compares *Twilight* to *Wuthering Heights* in order to reveal that Meyer's texts offers females *less* opportunities than Brontë's did. Then, turning to an analysis of why the saga is so alluring/addictive for so many female fans in this contemporary moment, Shachar widens her gaze to look at post-feminist backlash in wider U.S. culture.

The third section, "*Twilight* Through an Intersectional Lens: Patriarchy,

White Privilege, Heteronormativity, Rape Culture, Religion," includes the most overtly political responses to the series, exploring how social norms and hierarchies infuse the series in ways that problematically champion heteropatriarchy and violence against women. In "Maybe Edward Is the Most Dangerous Thing Out There: The Role of Patriarchy," Melissa Miller offers a unique exploration of patriarchy and the role it plays in the series as well as in society, insisting that both women and men are essential to the maintenance and/or subversion of patriarchy. Miller concludes that while popular media can help shape a worldview in audiences that reinscribes dominant positions of masculine power and authority, ultimately readers can still challenge and resist these norms, even in texts with such seemingly regressive messages as *Twilight*. Along similar lines, Ashley Donnelly's "Denial and Salvation: The *Twilight* Series and Heteronormative Patriarchy" examines the heteronormative world view currently dominating U.S. culture, arguing the *Twilight* saga echoes and perpetuates this view via its support of heterosexual monogamy. Reminiscent of earlier feminist theorizing that explores patriarchy and capitalism as mutually supportive systems, this essay reveals how patriarchy and heteronormativity are similarly constitutive. Theorizing this via reading *Twilight*, the essay offers a contemporary read of how popular culture legitimates "normal" marriage, rendering it compulsory for new generations of readers. In "It's a Wolf Thing: The Quileute Werewolf/Shape-Shifter Hybrid as Noble Savage," Natalie Wilson argues that Meyer's grafting of werewolf lore onto indigenous legend results in a racialized depiction that furthers the notion of indigenous people as Other and lesser. Documenting the differences between werewolf lore and indigenous legend, the paper suggests that Meyer relies on the trope of the werewolf as a horrific figure and grafts this onto Quileute legend, the result of which is a saga that plays into colonial notions of Native peoples as savage. "Violence, Agency, and the Women of *Twilight*" by Anne Torkelson turns its inquiry to the saga's female characters and reads the representation of sexualized violence in the saga as perpetuating the societal normalization of violence. Torkelson's essay offers an incisive critique of how rape culture is bolstered not only via the rape myths that permeate our sociohistorical moment, but also via romantic fiction such as *Twilight*. The final essay of the anthology, Lindsey Issow Averill's "Un-biting the Apple and Killing the Womb: Genesis, Gender, and Gynocide," documents the biblical themes that permeate *Twilight*, arguing that Meyer's work functions as symbolic re-telling of the Adam and Eve myth. Reading Eve as a Biblical feminist, Averill concludes that Meyer re-writes Eve, rendering her non- or even antifeminist. Detailing how the text erases the female power to create and clears the way for an un-sexed man of the mind and a subordinated feminized body,

Averill claims the saga metaphorically kills off the female womb/body in order to justify male vampire rule.

Taken together, these essays offer a deep exploration of the saga; one that teases out the implications of its popularity and asks readers to examine more deeply their own reactions to the cultural phenomenon that is *Twilight*. The editors and contributors sincerely hope these readings offer an enjoyable, thought-provoking exploration of the saga and its widespread cultural impact, and, more generally, that the essays start a conversation on what is at stake in representations such as those proffered in *Twilight* in our post–Vampire world.

PART I

Twilight as Pop Cultural Artifact

Pilgrimages, Fan Culture, and Film Adaptations

The Vampire Capital
of the World

*Commerce and Enchantment
in Forks, Washington*

Tanya Erzen

Amidst a tattered landscape of heavily logged forest punctuated by snow-capped peaks is Forks, Washington, a former timber town, which has been swept up in *Twilight* mania and invaded by *Twilight* pilgrims, eager to experience first-hand the setting for the novels. Although Forks is an actual place, named after the former prairie cleared by the Quileute Indians at the confluence of several rivers, for fans it exists as a manifestation of the world of *Twilight*. One woman who organized a trip for 250 members of the *Twilight*MOMS fan site describes it as "traveling into your imagination in real life." With a population of 3,175 (and 8.5 Vampires, as one sign reminds visitors), it seems fitting that Forks, four hours from Seattle, is one of the few remaining places in the U.S. that feels like a frontier untouched by modernity if not the ravages of logging. Situated so far west on the Olympic peninsula, the only indication that you are near a town is an outpost-like gas station that advertises Orange Crush soda with the promotional sign "Edward Cullen has a crush on you."

Stephenie Meyer, who hails from Cave City, Arizona, never actually visited Forks until the first book of the series was already in press. She chose the dampest, rainiest, most remote place she could imagine as the setting for her vampire romance without knowing the saga's success would transform Forks into a tourist destination, and the repository for fans' longings for romance and the supernatural. By random luck and some internet research, she happened upon a town surrounded by otherworldly scenery: the Olympic mountains form a ring in the center of the peninsula like a saw tooth wall. A travel writer remarked on the "dreary continuity" of the terrain when he visited in the 1840s, but the area has the most varied ecology and towering trees in the world, including the world's largest Douglas fir (Dietrich 65).

This essay discusses how Forks epitomizes the messy entanglement of commerce and enchantment, not necessarily as oppositional but as part of an ongoing negotiation of authenticity and experience amongst fans and residents. The analysis is based on interviews with the Forks High School principal, teachers, town officials, business owners as well as my attendance at Stephenie Meyer Day, experience on a *Twilight* tour and numerous visits to Forks pre–*Twilight* and during the tourist boom. My examination is in service of a larger set of questions about how enchantment is lived and communicated as a shared structure of feeling for fans. Fan pilgrimages, as performances, fantasies, and rituals of transformation — are sites for imagining and enacting forms of social intimacy other than those constrained by the everyday. As museum critic Barbara Gimblett writes of cultural heritage tourism, tourists travel to actual destinations to experience virtual places, negotiating questions of authenticity in relation to *Twilight* and the actual town of Forks (6). Throughout, I address how commodification does not necessary negate the enchantment of Forks, but provides emergent meanings of authenticity in relation to the construction of fantasy and the real. One resident, known locally as Hallelujah Bill, designed a t-shirt that sums up the complexities of Forks' logging history, and local vexation about tourism and *Twilight* fans. The shirt reads, "Forks, WA — Logging Capital of the World," a common slogan from the 1970s, and it features a logger, axe in one hand and struggling vampire writhing in a choke-hold in the other. Ha! Great!

Forks serves as a prism for fans' collective fantasy that they might momentarily live in the marvelous world of the books. In their pilgrimages to Forks, they indulge the idea that a supernatural world exists alongside our own. One woman on the *Twilight*MOMS trip summed it up, "I think I am a fan because I love the idea of being something more than the ordinary. I love how there can be beings that we didn't even know existed right in our own backyard." For many, it is not a stretch to imagine that the impenetrable curtain of green forest conceals vampires and werewolves. Unlike other fandoms such as *The Lord of the Rings* or *Harry Potter*, the setting of the series is in an actual town. A *Twilight* fan might tumble through a hole in the world they know and emerge into a better one; a world that is more exhilarating and fully felt than their own. The 2010 *Twilight* parody film, *Vampires Suck*, visually suggests this idea with images of an Alice in Wonderland–like hole in the forest. Yet, unlike the Hogwarts of *Harry Potter* or the Shire of *the Lord of the Rings*, the

Forks of *Twilight* is an ordinary town where fans can visit the high school where Bella and Edward met, perch on Bella's weathered red truck and straddle the treaty line between Forks — vampire territory — and the nearby Quileute reservation, home of the wolf pack where a sign reads, "No Vampires Beyond this Point." It's immaterial that the truck, classroom, and treaty line were assembled by the town of Forks and the Quileute tribe to satisfy the legions of *Twilight* tourists. The fans are thrilled to inhabit the places of their fictional characters. According to statistics in the local newspaper, in July 2009 alone, 18,000 fans trekked to Forks like supplicants to a holy site, more than the total number of visitors in 2008 (Dickerson A1). The former logging capital of the world is now the vampire capital of the world.

Yet the other side to the enchantment is how the economic complexities of tourism have also deepened fissures of mistrust and resentment in a town that prides itself on its self-reliance and isolation. There are claims by merchants and residents that only a select few have profited from the *Twilight* influx while according to the Sierra Institute, approximately twenty-percent of residents retain an income below the national poverty line. The tension between the fantasy and franchise is most evident in the local residents who outwardly express the sentiment of a town invaded and even violated. How does an insular town, made infamous by the spotted owl controversy that pitted generations of loggers against environmental activists, reluctantly and haltingly reinvent itself as a tourist Mecca? Even as *Twilight* fans congregate on the main street in town, local residents grumble about traffic and outsiders. Other locals have entered the fray with zeal, creating businesses and selling merchandise from *Twilight*-themed hotel rooms to the "Bella pizza." At the same time, those residents who have made a living on "Twi-tourism" inspire some ire and jealousy, resulting in law suits and accusations of tax fraud.

Touring for Twilight

As you enter the city limits, a rustic green billboard welcoming people to Forks looms ahead at a turn-out in the road. The sign was recently relocated by the city after visitors, eager for the requisite photograph, would scramble up the muddy hill where it rested. It was only a matter of time until someone broke their leg in the quest for *Twilight* proximity. The first sign that businesses are reaping what they can from tourism is the Pacific Suites motel sign that reads, "Edward Cullen Didn't Sleep Here." Get it? Edward doesn't sleep. By mid-morning, I'm gliding along in a shiny black van with "Be Safe" carefully stenciled on the back in the cursive script that Edward writes in. There are fifteen of us crowded into seats including two Mormon mothers and their fifteen-year-old daughters, a father-daughter duo from Spokane, and a harried dad supervising a group of three junior-high girls. With the economy in a moribund state, a mini-vacation to Forks appeals to cash-strapped parents and restless teens. They've each paid $39 for the Dazzled by *Twilight* tour although anyone could find the sights via the free map courtesy of the Forks visitor center. However, then we wouldn't have Travis, the burly tour guide who leans into the microphone and asks in a deep voice, "Do you twinkle? Do we have any Jacob fans on board?" There are a few enthusiastic shouts from the group of high school girls. Engraved on the back of Travis' seat in that same loopy handwriting a letter reads, "*Twilight* Fans, although tips are not required, if my friend Travis gives a good tour, they are greatly appreciated. Edward Cullen."

My fellow van pilgrims exemplify how *Twilight* connects strangers, families, and online communities through structures of feeling. The term "structure of feeling" comes from Raymond Williams who proposes the term to describe "pre-emergent" phenomena, experiences that are "active and pressing but not yet fully articulated" (128–35). The structures of feeling define a social experience for fans, often perceived by them to be private, idiosyncratic, and even isolating, but can also tie together disparate, even contradictory, experiences, bodily sensations, feelings, and thoughts. *Twilight* and other recent vampire books assume the supernatural as a facet of everyday life, and for fans, these structures of feeling spill over into everyday life so that the boundary between the paranormal and the everyday world is porous. For instance, many fellow passengers were disgruntled by the weak sun outside since it means glimpsing a vampire will be more difficult, despite the fact that *Twilight* vampires break with genre and sparkle in the sun rather than risk slow obliteration by it. "I ask myself," Annette Root, the owner of the tour, explains, "how can we bear to live in a world that is all fact, in which every answer can be tallied up like a mathematical equation?"

For some, Forks attracts them in as permanent residents, where they might merge their professional and everyday lives seamlessly with the *Twilight* fantasy. After his wife, Rianilee, convinced him to move to Forks from Las Vegas because of her obsession with *Twilight*, Travis worked as a correctional officer at the maximum security prison at Clallam Bay, the only other major employer in the Forks area, outside of logging. Travis formerly conducted tours of Hollywood, and when Annette offered him the position in the Dazzled by *Twilight* tours, he eagerly obliged. Travis, Rianilee, and their extended families of brothers-in-law, parents and children now reside in Forks and work for Annette's *Twilight* enterprises. Andrea, a spunky 17 year old from Staten Island, New York, who is traveling with her mother and aunt, regards the series as sacred texts to which she returns again and again for advice, pleasure, and to recall specific details. She's lanky and pale, her eyes hidden by oval glasses, but she's dressed in the jeans and t-shirt uniform of every high school girl on summer vacation. After composing fifteen pages of notes about why the film is inadequate in hewing to the reality of the books, she answers the trivia questions thrown at us by an increasingly rattled Travis with impressive ease: "What kind of math did Bella take in her final semester?" "Calculus." The tour we're on will take us to the main *Twilight*-themed sights in Forks, but Andrea wants to know where we can find the meadow where Bella and Edward first embrace, and the tour company is currently scouting for a site.

Our first stop is the Forks City Hall where Bella's father, Charlie, the Forks chief of police, combats vice and crime. Mike Gurling, the actual police chief of Forks, relishes his *Twilight* notoriety, and he frequently poses for photographs with tourists outside his police cruiser. Yet, he's absent today so the tour group clusters around a glass wall cabinet containing a *Twilight* diorama in the central hallway. While Andrea and others snap photos, the reality of police work intrudes abruptly in the life-size photograph and memorial on the adjacent wall honoring Officer Fairbanks, a young woman killed in the line of duty in 2008, the jarring tragedy intruding into our reveries. The tour enables fans to travel through the landscape of the books, but images like the memorial intrude and rupture the fantasy. If the fans are pilgrims, as many of them define themselves, their holy sites are constructed out of an artifice that appears flimsy at times, as the police station reminds us.

Normally, fans must content themselves to peer awkwardly through the windows on the wrap-around porch and take photographs of the notes left on the door at the Cullen house such as: "The Cullen family (and Bella) have gone to Fairbanks to check out the University of Alaska." The two-story bed and breakfast is owned by the Millers, who have gamely entered into the spirit of things by agreeing to re-model their home as the residence of the Cullens. However, as we're jostling for pictures, the door opens and they beckon us inside. The Millers have just acquired a seven-foot picture frame stacked with rows of high school graduation caps in dusky purple, blue and maroon hues, donated by fans, like the one that hangs in the Cullen home in the film. As we watch, a handyman is installing it on the wall. While the cameras snap, Andrea glances at the giant battered upright piano in the room, covered by framed photos of Edward and his vampire brothers and sisters. "This isn't Edward's piano," she comments. "Edward plays a black shiny baby grand." The Millers smile indulgently from the parlor. Is Andrea making reference to the piano in the books, or the piano in the film representation?

The failure of what Kirschenblatt-Gimblet calls "the performativity of objects," and their inability to hue to fans' fictional ideals is evident everywhere (12). The tourist sites are supposed to signal the authenticity of the home and our experience of Forks, and bolster our shared sense of temporarily visiting this fictional universe. Yet, the books, film representations and fans' own visions often conflict. At the Swan house, we're only allowed on the fringes of the yard. At the yellow, two-story Georgian style home, the girls point to the upstairs window where Bella slept and Edward slipped in the window each night to spy on her. A favorite fan shirt reads "Watch Me Sleep Edward." Bella's house, the scene of so many almost-seductions, appears drab and ordinary. "If I was them, I would have put a cut-out of Bella in the upstairs window," Andrea pouts, frustrated that the town can't quite muster the energy to reveal her *Twilight* world according to her exacting standards.

Just like the piano, on occasion, Forks, with its one main street and sagging homes doesn't measure up to the collective imaginings of the fans before arrival. The glossy film images, the fans' carefully nurtured vision culled from the books, and Forks itself collide awkwardly. The last film screened at the shuttered movie theatre was the *Little Mermaid* in 1989. To underscore its remoteness, Travis informs us in sober tones that in order to see a film, shop, or eat fast food the residents of Forks have to drive two hours east to Port Angeles or Sequim. To emphasis the isolation, he explains that it's 67 miles to McDonalds and Walmart and 62 miles to outer space from Forks according to local lore. "Oh my god," someone gasps. "How do you survive?" Summit Entertainment, which produced the films, deemed Forks too isolated for filming, and chose various sites in Oregon and Vancouver, British Columbia, instead. Boosters like Annette emphasize the vision in the books rather than the film sets: "The movie is Hollywood, the book is Forks. We're the real thing." Out of necessity, residents of Forks privilege the fans' perspectives over the glossy film version, situating themselves as the authentic Forks through the town's gritty and derelict appearance. As Cynthia Willis-Chun also notes, by claiming to be the "reality" of the fictional word of the books, Forks has reinvented itself as the authentic embodiment of *Twilight* (Willis-Chun, 2010). Yet, in doing so the town has banked its financial well-being on the fickleness of fans, and in some ways will never succeed in approximating their vision. Fans like Andrea have an ambivalent relationship to people in Forks whom she both envies for living in the setting of her favorite books and disdains for not being fans of *Twilight.* From her perspective as a temporary visitor, she expects local residents to participate actively in the fantasy, and there is some animosity when they refuse. Aside from the construction of the spaces of the books like the houses, the opportunities for *Twilight* tourists mainly include purchasing whatever is being sold: a Bella burger, a bumper sticker or a hotel room. Andrea and others complain about inflated prices and rapacious locals making money from their fantasy. The obvious necessity for residents to capitalize on the ephemeral vampire craze leaves fans like Andrea feeling swindled out of their own version of authenticity.

Capitalizing on the Vampire

Bella confesses that Edward frequently "dazzles" her, and he had the same effect on Annette Root, a sturdy woman with a bushy shock of red hair, who quit her sixteen-year career as a social worker and moved her entire family to Forks in 2008 from Vancouver, Washington, 250 miles away. In Forks, you can even buy real estate in your fictional universe, and Annette now operates two stores selling *Twilight* merchandise, a tour company and a performance space. Her ambition has made her the alternately reviled and envied mogul of Forks where you're considered a newcomer unless you've lived there for at least four generations. Annette shares a birthday with Bella, and her niece and mother-in-law brought her to Forks to celebrate while she was on maternity leave in 2007. When they arrived, Annette recalls her disappointment at the lack of real *Twilight* presence. She returned home crestfallen but also intrigued by some of the empty storefronts, and with some trepidation, she moved her family of seven to Forks and opened her store, which she calls "one step of faith after another." Other merchants soon followed by renovating their beleaguered businesses: the Chinese restaurant has *Twilight* discounts, the coffee shop was on the brink of bankruptcy until Catherine Hardwicke, director of the first film, dubbed it her favorite haunt, and the Native American art gallery renamed itself "Native to *Twilight*." The owner of Bella Italia, an upscale Italian restaurant in nearby Port Angeles, was baffled as customers continually requested mushroom ravioli until he caught on to the fact that it's the dish Bella orders on her first date with Edward. He estimates selling 4,500 $17 bowls of mushroom ravioli in 2009 and is figuring out how to sell it pre-packaged to the fans.

Just who is profiting from *Twilight* is a source of contention in Forks as merchant rivalry about who can carry and sell merchandise has escalated since Annette's arrival. Annette claims she has yet to draw a paycheck after several years, but her business is flourishing if her twelve employees and expansion are any indication. An article that appeared in the *Peninsula Daily News* claimed she owed the state thousands in taxes (Dickerson, A6). Annette refused to comment on the veracity of the claims, only stating that she was being unfairly persecuted as a successful merchant. Regardless of financial difficulties, Annette's newly renovated second store, which opened on the official Forks

"Stephenie Meyer Day" in September 2009, has an interior that is more disorienting than dazzling. Enchantment is the commodity of Forks' tourism, and this is evident in Annette's store where she markets directly to fans' captivation with the series through the merchandise and décor. The store is designed as a simulated forest, and through the murky light customers strain to view the plethora of goods for sale amid fake conifer trees, including one with "Bella loves Edward" carved into a heart on the trunk, an Astroturf grass floor, fountains, and a giant mural of First Beach at La Push. The store combines the claustrophobia of enclosed woodlands coupled with the commotion of frenzied buyers. Rather than hike or explore the adjacent national parks, fans enter a forest microcosm of the Olympic peninsula with shirts, sweaters, posters, mugs, bumper stickers, and jewelry crammed everywhere.

Annette wants fans to "touch the feeling" of *Twilight* magic in a bodily, all-encompassing way. She describes it as "an experience, a feeling, a sense of wonder or the *Twilight* vibe" that she wants to instill in fellow fans. "I don't want them to feel like they came in a store. And I don't care if they don't buy a thing. They come in, we chat, we hang out, you find out all these great things about people." Describing her work a sacred calling, Annette relishes the connections she's made to other fans and considers vendors and the tourists in her store lifelong friends. Concealed at the back of the warren-like array of clothing racks are what Annette calls her *Twilight* shrines, two eight-foot long glass display cabinets where she communes regularly. They are overflowing with objects such as Vampire wine bottles, Indian masks, a white chess piece, a frayed bumper sticker that reads "Smitten" and "I kissed a werewolf," shot glasses, tampons (to invoke blood), beads and wolf figurines. Annette describes the feeling of *Twilight* enchantment as a common sense of wonder for people who love and worship the same thing. Yet her unceasing economic expansion also financially exploits the *Twilight* vibe, emphasizing that enchantment can be bought, worn, eaten and simulated. She is committed to making sure they "shop, shop, shop while they're here." Annette is forging ahead with plans to expand the Dazzled by *Twilight* presence, including an upscale restaurant named Volterra after the Italian home of the reigning vampire monarchy. She has plans to cater *Twilight*-themed weddings, sell flowers, and add a site for the baseball field where Edward and his family play. Annette may be making money, but she is also living out her dream, which entails the "disneyfication" of *Twilight* (Bryman, 5). She admits that Disney is her favorite place in the world.

How do we adjudicate the real Forks among the representations circulating in various media: the "Real Forks" documentary film, heavily marketed alongside the *New Moon* DVD release, the proposed Forks reality show that would feature actual people in town (Annette was one of the finalists for the cast, but the production has gone no further) (Dickerson, A5), residents' assertions of an authentic logging past, or in fans desire for a bit of enchantment and escape, a brief sojourn into a fictional world, however much a simulacra it might be? Annette's tour avoids Leppell's shop, a former florist across from the high school, owned by Annie Leppell, one of the locals directly affected by Annette's successful businesses. The Leppell family owned the former chain-saw repair shop when logging instead of vampires was the basis of the town's economy, and they were one of the most vocal opponents when environmental organizations and the federal government halted clear-cutting to protect the local spotted owl population in the early 1990s. The controversy decimated the logging industry around Forks and still inspires deep rancor among residents. At one point residents erected a cross topped by spotted owls and posted defiant signs like "Forks against the world." This history illustrates why Forks is an unlikely place to welcome giddy tourists enamored of vampires and werewolves where the local identity is still bound up with a version of a hardscrabble, authentic logging past. Part of what repels people like Hallelujah Bill is the renunciation of this frontier identity for the label of vampire tourist town. Yet, rather than ignore fan tourism, Leppells' merchandise eschews the flashy look of Dazzled by *Twilight* and now does a brisk business selling hand-painted *Twilight* signs and Forks High School paraphernalia. Leppell's can cater to tourist desires and claim to be the "real Forks" while Annette is merely a recent interloper. However, they still have to provide the merchandise the fans want. When I arrive in the store, a pre-teen girl's exasperated mom points to the owner and exclaims, "Why don't you ask if they sell the t-shirt here?" It's a popular shirt prominently on display in Annette's store that reads "FORKS, Washington: Where Twilight Comes True." Twilight should be *Twilight*.

The Fog of Twilight

What is sustainable tourism? In the mind of many residents, the logging past evokes an economy and identity that designates Forks as unique and economically vital. Everyone needs wood and paper, but do they need *Twilight* goods? For many, the tourism seems built on a service economy consisting of fantasies that will only exacerbate the town's income disparities and inequalities. The local pastor of Calvary Chapel believes the community is in what he calls a "fog of *Twilight*," and that although a lot of money is spent by fans, most of the families at his church struggle as much as before. "I'm bracing for the shock when the fog lifts, the movies are over, the books quit selling, and our poor community goes back to dealing with the reality of having to sustain itself economically." The tourists have resurrected the town and its weary residents, and aside from the renovation of the high school, little is being done to build an infrastructure for Forks in the long run. Since Washington does not have a personal or corporate income tax, the economic activity of tourism benefits town services through a 2 percent motel and lodging tax that is standard throughout the state. How this additional *Twilight* tourism money will influence development in Forks remains an important question. Unlike other towns on the Olympic Peninsula, Forks has prospered in the recession, and their taxable retail sales have *increased* (Erb). This period of prosperity may taper off as the heavy promotion around the cycle of films ends. As if anticipating these concerns, Annette tells me something I've heard her repeat in other interviews and articles: "We came because of *Twilight*, we'll be back because of Forks. So many people came through the door saying, 'We didn't know Forks was a real place!' And then, 'We didn't know it was beautiful here!'"

Some business owners cling to the belief that once *Twilight* fans experience Forks, they'll be compelled to return as long as the locals cooperate. If they're "busy grumping because you had to wait at the stoplight, or you had to wait in line to buy gas, why would anyone want to come back to a town like that?" The fans that do seek out nature, do so only in relation to how they compare to the books, and without the *Twilight* veneer and value placed on the rainforest or First Beach at La Push, the appeal of being in the Forks area for the sake of outdoor adventure loses its luster. The irony is that while fans arrive in Forks searching for exotic vampires, werewolves and an enchanted experience, the extraordinary, surreal landscape outside beckons, if only they were to travel a few miles outside Forks and desist from shopping. Yet few fans seem interested in exploring the national parks and surrounding area because they're enclosed in the van or shopping.

The pastor's glum prognostication fades when confronted by the throngs of ebullient fans from Australia, Spokane, and Barcelona in the Forks visitor center, which appears at the far end of town just when the road seems to stretch to nowhere. Marcia Bingham, the practical and *Twilight*-literate director of the Forks Chamber of Commerce, is an energetic woman in her early fifties with short brown hair and a no-nonsense attitude. She presides over the center with her furry terrier dog and an array of employees. She's wearing a "Team Jacob" pin and is gesticulating to tourists next to a giant cut-out picture of Edward Cullen slouching against the main door. Outside the visitor center is the infamous replica of Bella's red truck. In 2006, a trickle of sheepish fans arrived at the center, guilty and embarrassed, offhandedly mentioning they were in Forks because of the *Twilight* books. Marcia quickly learned to "speak *Twilight*," and decided to render what she calls their "dirty little secret" unnecessary. She knew that Forks would be forever changed when a security person detained her in an airport because of her Forks, Washington, shirt, merely to chat about how much he loved the books.

To account for the 500–700 *Twilight* visitors per day, her volunteers keep a tally of the visitor log on a three-inch pile of wrinkled yellow notepaper that they add up at the end of the month. The log bursts with the all-caps enthusiasm of swooning fans: "Thanks for speaking *Twilight*!" "At last my wife can stop nagging!" The center provides an elaborate *Twilight* map of Forks, a four-page trivia test about the books, which the assistant manager, a former park ranger, completed after reading the books as research, and a five-day suggested itinerary in the Olympic National Park free of charge. Most of Travis' questions are borrowed from the visitor center package. The Visitor Center was forced to apply for a grant to print enough copies of their welcome packet, for which the Dazzled tour charges passengers. Inside the small room a banner over the fireplace reads, "Vampires Thrive in Forks." Two giant maps of the world and the United States have pushpins representing the origins of visitors. They are concentrated in the U.S. and Europe with dense clusters on Australia's southeast coast, and in Japan, but there are pins in Africa, Brazil, and throughout South America. Before the deluge, Marcia took photographs of fans for the visitor center website. They eventually reached 900 pictures and realized their server couldn't hold any more. A group of girls barrel through the door, and gleefully exclaim, "ohmygodohmygodohmygod" as they ricochet from one part of the room to another.

The young high school volunteer answering the phones informs a caller, "There have been a few vampire sightings," in response to a question about visiting the nearby Quileute Indian reservation. The sense of the supernatural is precisely what captivates the fans who arrive in droves, and Marcia and the others gallantly acquiesce. Marcia offhandedly remarks, "I live in a fantasy world here," as if it's a joke they're all in on, relishing the giddiness of inhabiting the world of *Twilight* even while the less exalted reality of Forks encroaches. One woman writes that day in the log book, "Just a couple of girls looking for a couple of vampires or wolf boys." The pleasures of engaging in the performance of warning and being warned about stray werewolves in the woods enable fans and residents to transgress the everyday and experience the leakiness between fictional and real roles (Stanley, 17). *Twilight* tourism defies neat boundaries between fantasy and franchise, the supernatural and everyday. As an affective experience, it makes one susceptible to escapism, enchantment and commercialization depending on one's identity as a fan, resident or business owner. Annette explains, "I do understand the difference between fact and fiction, but we all need a little magic and fantasy in our life ... we wanna pretend together. And we do, and I don't think there's anything wrong with that. I still do the dishes; I still scrub the toilet, just like everybody else."

The final tour stop is La Push on the Quileute reservation. In the books, Meyer identifies Jacob Black's house as a sprawling red bungalow where he repairs motorcycles. The van pulls up next to one of similar description with the fortuitous coincidence of being owned by a person with the surname Black so "B. Black" is written on the mailbox. Between the mailbox, motorcycle, and pictures of Jacob in the window (Andrea is pleased that someone finally got the details right), the illusion is complete. The fans tend to romanticize the tribes of the Pacific Northwest, purchasing earrings and jewelry and raving about meeting actual Native Americans. Some fans have privately arranged to have Chris Morganroth, a storyteller and member of the Quileute tribe, recount traditional legends for them around a bonfire at First Beach (Baron, A7). The remoteness of the reservation and the invisibility of Native Americans in general outside of their fantastical portrayal in the books or fans' cursory knowledge of American history imbues La Push with an enchantment that is sometimes tinged with vestigial racism and sentimentality, as Wilson explores further in this anthology.

On a promontory at First Beach, an arrestingly desolate stretch of coast strewn with driftwood, we glimpse the barren James islands, the rocky tips of the sea stacks considered sacred to the Quileute tribe. In the distance are the sheer cliffs where Bella recklessly plunges into the churning water in *New Moon*. Even Andrea, who eagerly craned her head out the van's window as we approached, appears dazed by the scenery. For the first time that day, we're outdoors for an extended period of time, without a house, restaurant, store, police station, truck or visitor center to distract us. However, the lack of *Twilight* infrastructure is a stark reminder that the Quileute tribe has fewer economic resources than Forks, and there are complaints that Forks profits at the expense of the reservation. The coffee kiosk with the title "Jacob's Java" is no doubt a harbinger of more *Twilight* tourism on the reservation, especially given that the tribe has hired a public relations specialist to cope with the barrage of requests for interviews and visits.

Like all pilgrims, we must eventually return home from our journey, outside of ordinary time and space. By the time we arrive at the tour office, it's finally drizzling, and Andrea still wants to find the meadow or anything that will approximate it. So, we set out with vague directions from Marcia and Annette, following a dubious trail leading from the drag-racing track across the street from the visitor center. Andrea's Ugg boots are not ideal for the terrain, and the trail is indecipherable and spooky. We double back twice, consult our map and consider abandoning the endeavor altogether, but there is a mixture of pleasure and absurdity in searching for a meadow in a fictional book abetted by the fact that we've all agreed to the fantasy together. And then, a lush expanse with a few late-blooming foxgloves and wildflowers opens before us. It is a meadow worthy of *Twilight*, and for a brief moment we are seduced by the fantasy of this imagined place, and it's possible that if we squint hard enough, we can almost glimpse a girl and a vampire lying entwined in the sun.

Yet, our expedition away from the tourist hype is fleeting and soon forgotten as we re-enter the town. The meadow may soon become one of the tour stops rather than a private discovery. After that, it doesn't seem possible that the *Twilight* phenomenon will sustain itself in its present frenetic incarnation for years, and Forks, being 62 miles from outer space and Walmart, isn't a convenient place to visit without a reason. The town is banking on the fact that Twi-tourism will continue until the final film installment of *Breaking Dawn* and then inevitably abate, especially because the majority of the fandom is now devoted to the films' celebrities rather than the books. A few former *Twilight* fans could trickle through in subsequent years, but the economic boom won't outlast the popularity of the series or films. Forks has endured difficult financial times before, and it will certainly survive the end of being "the Vampire Capital of the World." Hallelujah Bill will just have to create a new slogan for his t-shirts.

WORKS CITED

Baron, Christi. "Real Stories of the Quileute Live On." *Peninsula Daily News* 18 August 2009, A7.

Bryman, Alan. *The Disneyization of Society*. London: Sage Publications, 2004.

Buttolph, Lisa, and Jonathon Kussel. *Northwest Economic Adjustment Initiative Assessment*. The Sierra Institute. Web. 12 June 2010 <www.sierrainstitute.us/neai/WA_case_studies/Forks_WA.pdf>.

Clough, Patricia Ticineto, and Jean Halley. *The Affective Turn: Theorizing the Social*. Durham: Duke University Press, 2007.

Dickerson, Paige. "Are Tourists Safe from Vampires? Twilight Takes Over Forks." *Peninsula Daily News* 7–8 August 2009: 1.

_____. "Twenty Called Back for Forks Reality Show." *Peninsula Daily News* 24 December 2009, A5.

_____. "'Twilight'-inspired business owes nearly $40,000, State Department of Revenue Says." *Peninsula Daily News* 4 March 2010, A6.

Erb, George. "How '*Twilight*' Juiced Forks' Economy." *Puget Sound Business Journal* 28 June 2010. Web. 18 July 2010.

Kirshenblatt-Gimblett, Barbara. *Destination Culture: Tourism, Museums, and Heritage*. Berkeley: University of California Press, 1998.

Kosofsky-Segwick, Eve. *Touching Feeling: Affect, Pedagogy, Performativity*. Durham: Duke University Press, 2003.

Stanley, Nick. *Being Ourselves for You: The Global Display of Cultures.* Material Culture Series. London: Middlesex University Press, 1998.
United States Census Bureau. Retrieved February 18, 2010.
Williams, Raymond. *Marxism and Literature.* Oxford: Oxford University Press, 1977.
Willis-Chun, Cynthia. "Touring the Twilight Zone: Cultural Tourism and Commodification on the Olympic Peninsula." *Bitten by Twilight: Youth Culture, Media and the Vampire Franchise.* Ed. Melissa A. Click, Jennifer Stevens Aubry, and Elizabeth Behm-Morawitz. New York: Peter Lang, 2010.

Fanpires
Utilizing Fan Culture in Event Film Adaptations

MAGGIE PARKE

Each product only contains one component. The elements react synergistically, in combination.
— Batman to Vicki Vale in *Batman*

Alone, a film is just a film; but in relation to other media elements, a film and its peripheral elements can become events unto themselves. The event film, similar to the franchise, blockbuster, or cult film, is a new distinction that refers to a film with a massive following, both online and in real-world spaces, whose adaptation and remediation processes become events unto themselves in the form of huge DVD release parties, media-event film releases, or eagerly anticipated game and merchandise production. In this essay I will explore the adaptation of an event film and what can happen when filmmakers — the studio, director, screenwriters, and producers — either incorporate or ignore the fan base of the source novel during the adaptation process. I contend that it is a beneficial practice, as well as simple and inexpensive, to utilize the fan base of an event film. I will discuss the techniques and the benefits that may result from involving the fervent and active community by illustrating various successful and unsuccessful event film adaptations via their box-office earnings.

First, I will examine two event films that did not consider the fan-base in the adaptation process: *Eragon* (2006) and *The Seeker: The Dark is Rising* (2007). Then, I will explore the heavily-considered treatment of fans primarily in *Twilight* (2008), as I was invited onto the set by the filmmakers during the production to conduct research on Hardwicke's adaptation of Meyer's novel. I will also reference a pioneer in the successful utilization of event film fan culture, Peter Jackson's *The Lord of the Rings* trilogy (2001, 2002, 2003). My analysis here is looking solely at the financial returns that may result from fan involvement, and the goodwill imparted to the fandom by doing so. There are copious topics that must still be explored such as artistic impact, critical response, and authorial intent, but they are beyond the scope of this paper.

A Film for the Fans? The Troublesome Path of Adaptation

Catering the film specifically for the fans can be tricky route to negotiate, and it can be artistically limiting as Ian Hunter, Deborah Cartmell, and Imelda Whelehan acknowledge in their discussions regarding the first *Harry Potter* film which was a faithful "photocopy" of the book to film, thus stifling the film as a stand-alone work (Hunter 157). However, incorporating the fan base into the process and making them feel included and acknowledged can provide filmmakers with the freedom to make changes to popular works of literature without incensing the fandom; which could negatively affect box office intakes, as fans could boycott the film, or not see it multiple times.

So what is an event film? It is a relatively new label, with the first major work on the topic to look intensely at one process, *Studying the Event Film: The Lord of the Rings*, published in 2009 (Margolis et. al.). In that work, the term references the adaptation of a film from a text with an active, pre-existing fan-base with a large online presence, and periodic "real world" events to maintain the fervor and energy of the community (Margolis et. al.). When the rights to one of these well-followed books are purchased, the adaptation often departs from being a project for the filmmakers alone, and quickly involves the fan-base whether the filmmakers desire their involvement or not. Jennifer Lamoureux, a moderator on one of the biggest *Twilight* fan sites, *The Twilight Lexicon*, states that "the fans of these popular works often feel a sense of ownership to the original source text"; this is possibly due to the fact that fans first experience the world of the novel as lone, solitary readers, reading the text on their own, and bonding with the characters before they extended their circle of involvement with the text by entering the fan-base online, and finding a community that shares their interest (Lamoureux n.p.).

Once involved in the online fan world, fans' solitary experience is replaced by a community with a shared experience, and in terms of adaptation, their involvement may contribute to a "strength in numbers" mentality as seen in the last fifteen years with the increased use of the Internet for fan interaction and participation. Fandoms are now more able to make themselves known to the filmmakers of the adaptations of event films through letters, petitions, and online movements than they have been in the past due to online, web 2.0 applications such as Facebook, Twitter, and fan sites. Fans can let their ideas be known on all manner of topics relating to the adaptation process from casting choices, locations, and necessary quotes to be retained. I will be careful in the following analysis with the use of words like "culture" and "community" with reference to fan studies as they have both positive and negative connotations in the academic and social spheres (Jenkins 3). Regardless of the perception and legitimacy of the fan, which can be argued at length but is not within the scope of this paper, fans of event films are a financially valuable demographic for filmmakers to consider as they are active, vocal, and may be more likely to see the adapted film more than once; plus their involvement can be secured cheaply and simply with the use of new media applications. This further blurs the line between the filmmaker and the fan, and puts some creative power into the hands of the fans, opening up questions of creative influence and authorial intent, as well as the marketing and business practice for event film adaptors.

Traditionally, book-to-film adaptations are largely in the hands of the filmmakers: the studio, director, screen writer, and producers, and they are often subject to their interpretation only. The author sells the rights to the work, and the adaptation process is out of his or her hands and in the hands of the filmmakers. Occasionally the public hears about an author's involvement in an adaptation, particularly with regard to character development or plot continuation if it is a work in a popular series such as with J.K. Rowling who retained final script approval and creative input in her deal with Warner Brothers for the *Harry Potter* films (2001–2011) (Kirk 94). This is not typical, however, as usually only the director, studio, screenwriter, and producers participate in the development of a novel's adaptation to screen. Historically, the author and the fans were not involved in the script development process. However, with the advent of web 2.0 applications, the fan is now closer to the action and has the potential to affect the box office returns on event film adaptations. Thus fan involvement and its affect on the industry is worth exploring.

Fan Sites and Event Film Adaptations

The fan has had more opportunity in the last fifteen years to become involved in the adaptation process due, in part, to the participatory elements of online interaction with various web 2.0 applications such as Facebook, Twitter, and the hugely active fan sites. Filmmakers have taken notice of this powerful, pre-existing, and organized community, and utilized it. An example of this, and a precursor for *Twilight's* involvement with the fan base, is the production for *The Lord of the Rings* films directed by Peter Jackson (2001, 2002, 2003).[1] One of the owners of TheOneRing.net (TORn), the leading *Lord of the Rings* fan site, was originally "escorted off the set" during its filming in New Zealand, and eventually "graciously invited back" to meet director Peter Jackson during its initial filming in 1999 (TheOneRing.net "About"). This meeting began a partnership for information sharing during the months prior to the films' release. On their website, the owners explain their contact with the filmmakers as a "relationship"; how that relationship and the site "thrived" during the years following the filming and during the films' releases, and how it "enabled TORn to bring its readers some exclusive news and night-of-a-lifetime experiences," such as details of their attendance at Oscar parties and at the films' premieres (TheOneRing.net "About"). The filmmakers offered them exclusive information and breaking news, and in return, the fan site was involved and incorporated into the adaptation process, making them key players in the films' development and marketing. The site provided plentiful positive, free advertising for the film from the site owners who were trusted by the fans to be a reliable source, and who were fans themselves. The site owners projected their good relationship with the filmmakers on their site, which kept the relationships between the filmmakers and the fans positive, and it gave the studio an enthusiastic and well-informed online street team comprised of repeat film-goers to advertise the film.

The filmmakers of *The Lord of the Rings* were among the first to consider and utilize the fans of their film's source novel and to keep them on their side with the help of online applications and participatory interactions during the adaptation process. In an unprecedented move, the filmmakers even invited the fans to submit their name at TheOneRing.net and they would then be included in the credits at the end of the film. At the end of the extended edition of *The Lord of the Rings: Return of the King*, there is a seemingly endless list of fans' names listed, suggesting their contribution to the adaptation as filmmakers; literally incorporating the fans into the film as a members of the creative team by acknowledging them in the film's end credits.

The Lord of the Rings trilogy seems to have set a precedent for managing the fandom of an event film, and comparable methods and actions are evident in subsequent event film adaptations such as with *Twilight's* transition from book to screen. Both groups of filmmakers for *The Lord of the Rings* and *Twilight* pitched themselves as fans themselves, perhaps in an attempt to identify and align themselves with the fan-base. With *The Lord of the Rings*, the actor Christopher Lee who played Saruman in Jackson's film was considered an authority on Tolkien's works, constantly referring to the novels during filming as mentioned in the extras of the extended DVDs. Jackson also hired two Tolkien artists to create concept art for the films: Alan Lee, who illustrated the anniversary editions of *The Hobbit* and *The Lord of the Rings,* with which many of the fans were very familiar, and John Howe, who illustrated the HarperCollins editions of the trilogy, as well as calendars and posters that are now closely and consistently associated with Tolkien's work (Simpson 125). As a result of this, the films had a similar look to the images that fans had been purchasing on books and merchandise, and re-interpreting as fan art themselves, for years. Peter Jackson was even pitched as "a genial, tubby, bare-footed hobbit" (Hunter 157). This level of devotion also spread to the cast as a whole, as it is easy to see how familiar with and passionate about the text the ensemble is through the actors' commentary on the extended DVDs. They are able to recall small details from the appendices of Tolkien's novels such as Pippin's son marrying Sam's daughter, or the history of the elves from Tolkien's creation story, *The Silmarillion.*

All of these elements may not necessarily make a film successful, but it does not seem to harm the film financially, as it made $90.3 million in its opening weekend, and $968.7 million in the worldwide box office earnings, as seen in the table below. From this, one can infer that the audiences that were drawn to the film were large, or perhaps saw the film more than once.

Film	*Budget*	*Opening Weekend*	*Worldwide Box Office*	*U.S. Box Office*
The Fellowhip of the Ring (2001)	$125 million	$90.3 million	$968.7 million	$317.6 million

With *Twilight*, producer Greg Mooradian, who originally secured the rights to Stephenie Meyer's debut novel in 2004 (personal email 2008), said he was hooked on the book ten pages into his first reading; he was "compelled" to pursue it, and has been a fan ever since (personal interview 2008). Similarly, Catherine Hardwicke, the director of *Twilight*, was given her choice of four films to make for Summit Entertainment and she chose *Twilight* because it was her "favorite of all of them by far" (personal interview 2008). In this interview, she said that she was captured by the love story of a mortal girl and a vampire boy, and that she was drawn ino the edgy script about forbidden love. This is not surprising as controversial themes are paramount in her award-winning and controversial film *Thirteen* (2003) which dealt with topics like teen relationships, sex, and drug use. Her enthusiasm and passion for the story is projected in her interviews leading up to the *Twilight*'s release, as well as in the book *Twilight: Director's Notebook,* which illustrates the extent of her work and the personal interest with her own notes, sketches and ideas about the film, now widely available for the fans to devour. By identifying as a fan, Hardwicke aligned herself *with* the fans; she was on their team, and would treat the text reverently, take care of it, and not destroy it because she apparently loved it as the fandom did.

When filmmakers have the reputations as fans and their relationships with the fan site owners are established, they seem to have a certain amount of flexibility to begin adapting the novel to the visual medium of film. They make changes from the text, such as when the color of Edward's car was changed in *Twilight* from bright silver to dark grey, or when one of the supporting characters, Lauren, is deleted in the film and some of her characteristics given to Jessica in order to condense the peripheral players in the story; the filmmakers have far less of the serious backlash from the fans such as that seen in the adaptation of *The Seeker* (2007), which I will go into further details later. *Twilight* avoided the fans' fury due to the filmmakers' positive relationships with them, and also due to how they delivered the news of changes from the book to the film. When the filmmakers made a change, such as in the color of Edward's Volvo or a controversial casting decision, the studio delivered this information to the fans via the fan sites or through Stephenie Meyer's personal website, intimating the apparent approval of the author. Most avid fans know that her brother, Seth, manages her website, and thus anything posted on it would have her approval and she would be aware of the information. These methods provide ample time for the fans to come to terms with the change before they see the film in the cinema, and they are aware that any changes contained in the film have the approval of the author, and are made by filmmaker-fans who seemingly understand and respect the original work.

Adapting an Event Film: The Filmmakers

Film studios are starting to recognize the overwhelming fan involvement that can sometimes accompany a popular adaptation. Summit Entertainment, the studio behind *Twilight,* created two marketing positions to handle the mountains of fan suggestions and comments for the adaptation of *Twilight.* Though the positions were undoubtedly created as a public relations move in the beginning, they seem to have developed into a vital link between the filmmakers and the fans. This has resulted in support from the fandom of the adaptation which means repeat film-goers and free advertising from them via the Internet and word of mouth. I observed these relationships, the cooperation and open conversation that the filmmakers had with the fans on set as well as TwiCon where I could see their ease of communication and interaction via email and telephone. The fan site owners appear friendly with the Summit representatives, as they exchange familiar emails, joke, and discuss their daily lives with each other, and not just their work involving *Twilight*. This camaraderie seems to garner trust and build a relationship, and is also mutually beneficial as it can depict the studio as friendly and cooperative with the fan base, and caring of the story, instead of money-hungry destroyers of beloved texts.

This relationship benefits the fan site owners as well, as they receive invitations to red carpet coverage of the releases, set visits, and they have been consulted for their opinions on information sharing online and ideas for activities at release events. The site staff are certainly experienced with these elements, as they can release a dozen stories a day to a site which receives more than two million hits a week. Also because they have been organizing their own fan events for *Twilight*-themed parties and book releases since 2004, well before the films' later adaptations began; but by adding that step by the studio to consult the leaders of the fan-base, they have secured the relationship, stroked an ego, and gained valuable feedback on an event, usually by just sharing one email, and thus at no cost to themselves.

Not All Adaptations Are Created Equal

Not all filmmakers make these efforts with the fandom in a film's adaptation, however. Two films that are considered to be poor adaptations by fans and critics, and financial disappointments, at least in the domestic box office, are *Eragon* and *The Seeker: The Dark Is Rising*. I will briefly look at both to further illustrate just how well *The Lord of the Rings* began the trend for successful fan involvement and how *Twilight* continued similar practices but has also extended that interaction with digital media elements. This aims to illustrate that ignoring the fans of an event film adaptation can be a factor that can greatly hurt the box office earnings in fan-focused countries, and acknowledges that by incorporating them into the adaptation process, it can add box office success.

Eragon, based on the book by Christopher Paolini, was a highly anticipated film due to its best-seller status and the large, active, online fan base at shurtugal.com, the online epicenter of all things *Eragon*.[2] *Eragon* tells the story of a boy who discovers that he is the last of an ancient, dragon-riding knighthood, who fight for the good of humankind to overcome an evil lord trying to take over the land. Paolini was not a member of the filmmaking team as he, like many authors, sold the rights to the novel and was then no longer involved in the adaptation. Utilizing the author is not necessarily a definitive way to produce a financially and critically successful film, but as fans of these works seem to revere the author as a god-like creator of the universe, dictating what is acceptable within their world and what is not,[3] the authors are a prime influencing factor who can impact their fan bases. As information about *Eragon*'s adaptation such as casting decisions and plot synopses spread online (i.e., that they had wanted to cast someone in his mid-twenties, when Eragon is supposed to be on the young side of his teens), it became evident that large chunks of Paolini's original story had been changed. An emotional discourse ran through the fandom at fan sites like shurtugal.com and dushurtugals.com. Whether due to this unrest or not, the studio brought on veteran producer Wyck Godfrey, also a *Twilight* producer, to see what changes could be made at that point in the production. He informed me that the studio had wanted a "Christmas-spectacular film," but they were aware that fans were unhappy with the way the film was going (Godfrey, personal interview). Godfrey described the minor story changes made such as the casting of the lead character to someone closer to the age of the character in the book, perhaps in an attempt to draw attention to the filmmakers' attempts to honor the text. Godfrey supported the film, despite its negative reviews, and said it was a "challenge, as all beloved adaptations are," but also inferred that Paolini did not show much enthusiasm for a sequel (Godfrey, personal interview).

Despite *Eragon*'s financial success in its first weekend, attributed to its massive world-wide release, it did not maintain its high placement in the box office, and therefore did not garner additional box office returns.[4] The novel and film's main fan base is centered mostly in the United States and the United Kingdom and during the film's sixteen weeks in theatrical release, it earned just $75,030,163 in the United States, and just over £5,154,073 in the United Kingdom. These may seem like respectable numbers in terms of box office earnings, but they are comparatively low when matched against the films that considered the fan base in their adaptations, as well as against its own worldwide box office earnings. Outside of these fan-focused areas, the film had substantial earnings with $245,230,163 in the worldwide box office (pro.IMDB.com).

Film	Budget	Opening Weekend	Worldwide Box Office	U.S. Box Office
Eragon (2006)	$100 million	$23.2 million	$245.2 million	$75 million

This worldwide number is a comparatively large earning, and therefore *Eragon* served its role financially as a spectacular Christmas blockbuster, but these numbers also illustrate that it did not sustain the audience in the countries with the most fans, and therefore the most repeat filmgoers, where additional revenue could have been made.[5] Since the film's release, groups with names such as "*Eragon* was a disgrace to the book" have cropped up on Facebook. This particular group's wall is covered with comments such as, "I hope someday, someone remakes the movie, and that Christopher is actually involved in the making of it!" (Vandersluis, Facebook n.p.), which illustrates a desire for at least the appearance of the author in the adaptation process. Another wrote, "It was actually a decent movie. But it didn't follow the book. AT ALL. Which is why it sucked" (Mortiere, Facebook n.p.), which acknowledges some of the virtues of the film as a story in its own right, but discredits the attempt due to its departure from the original work.[6]

Similar to *Eragon*'s adaptation process is David Cunningham's *The Seeker: The Dark Is Rising* (2007), based on Susan Cooper's Newbery Award–winning *The Dark Is Rising Sequence*. Walden Entertainment obtained the rights to the story in May of 2005 (McNary n.p.), and during the early stages of adaptation, from the casting of a fourteen-year-old American instead of an eleven-year-old Brit, and Cooper's statement that this was not "her film" ("The Role of Fantasy" lecture 2007), it was clear that the studio was making a film "inspired by" and not "based upon" the original books. From these examples it was also clear that honoring the source material was not a primary concern for the filmmakers, nor was involving the author in the process. Cooper, like Paolini, was not involved in the adaptation process, and neither the director, screenwriter, nor producers made attempts to utilize either her knowledge of the intricacies of the text nor to illustrate their interest in involving her to the fans. During preproduction, the filmmakers asked Cooper for her rules for the Old Ones, the mythical heroes in the text, and she gave them an outline of her guidelines, "and they never once looked at them again," according to Cooper ("Unriddling the World" lecture 2007). Cooper's disownment of the film along with the information rapidly spreading on the internet about the changes to the story such as those mentioned above as well as giving Will, the protagonist, a twin brother not in the novel, adding a superfluous love interest for Will, and removing all traces of the core Arthurian material, had the fans protesting on discussion boards, and boycotting the film (Cooper, "The Role of Fantasy...." 2007). Reviews of the film were consistently critical about the translation of the text, stating that this "off-the-shelf teen fantasy [is] not likely to satisfy the post–Potter/LOTR crowd but [is] guaranteed to enrage fans of the source novel" (O'Hara n.p.), and "her fans are appalled by what they see as this dumbed-down version, minus the Arthurian mythology underpinning the original story, and their distress is understandable" (Johnston n.p.). The film spent eleven weeks in theatrical release, earning only $8,791,738 in the United States box office, £788,769 in the United Kingdom, and just $23,591,738 worldwide, including the U.S. and UK markets (Pro.IMDB.com n.p.).

Film	Budget	Opening Weekend	Worldwide Box Office	U.S. Box Office
The Seeker (2007)	$45 million	$3.7 million	$23.6 million	$8.8 million

The Other Option: Filmmakers and Fans

On the other hand, *Twilight*, like *The Lord of the Rings*, has not only considered the fan throughout its adaptation process, but it has extended its interactions with the fandom beyond those of *The Lord of the Rings* and has capitalized on the free advertising and easy access of the internet and popular web 2.0 applications such as Facebook and Twitter, and by working with the fan sites of *Twilight* to maintain a positive relationship with the fans. On these sites, the filmmakers are able to advertise author involvement easily, and bring information about the adaptation directly to the fans thus shortening the divide between the filmmaker and the fan.

In terms of author involvement with *Twilight*, the filmmakers said that they were eager to get and keep Stephenie Meyer working with them, and they advertised that partnership to the fan-base through the fan sites as well as Meyer's own site, StephenieMeyer.com. Meyer was a part of the script development process, with the script circulating from the screenwriter to the director, to the studio, to the producers, and to Meyer herself. She also visited the set of the film eight times during production (Silberman, interview 2008), and has multiple spots on the DVD special features where she discusses the different steps in the writing and adaptation process which portrays her continued involvement; she also gave multiple interviews for MTV.com, who often featured these interviews on their site's popular "*Twilight* Tuesdays," and she has only produced glowing comments on her website about the adaptation process such as, "I am so pleased and amazed and thrilled with what Chris Weitz has done with *New Moon* that I want to talk about it, and to show my support for him" (Meyer, stepheniemeyer.com). Mooradian also pointed out that during the preproduction for *Twilight*, Meyer often spoke up to the filmmakers on behalf of the fans to encourage them to reinsert certain lines from the novels which fans had tattooed on their person or quoted endlessly in fan fiction and online message boards, as the fans would be looking for those lines in the film. These actions solidified Meyer as the fans' champion; the filmmakers ultimately still had control over the book's adaptation to the screen, but they showed their enthusiasm for the adaptation to Meyer and in turn to the fan base as she commented on the process.

Similar to *The Lord of the Rings*, once the filmmakers began establishing their position as fans of the text themselves and as friendly visionaries of Meyer's work, they were able to expand their adaptation liberties and to make alterations to the source text. They would make changes such as adding the supporting character, Waylon, a victim of the nomadic vampires, which is an effective creation for the film as it enhances their threat to the main protagonists in *Twilight*. The filmmakers could release this information to the fan sites with whom they had built relationships so that the fans would have time to digest the changes to the text prior to their first screening. This creates both a defensive and proactive atmosphere, as the filmmakers are creating a system of information release to the fans to minimize the alienation of the fandom, but it also encourages observation of the process which could give the fans an insight into the decisions made in adaptation thus allowing the filmmakers additional freedom within the story.

To further develop the positive relationship with the fan site owners, the studio and producers invited the owners of the biggest fan sites onto the set to meet the cast and crew. Publicist Peter Silberman accompanied them on their visits where they could observe the process and meet the embodiment of the characters that they loved, and the creators of the visualized world of their favorite texts. The fan sites were permitted interviews and photos during these visits, and the information gathered on these one-day visits would sustain the fan base for months, as the fan site owners held onto the information and released it slowly. For example, *The Twilight Lexicon* released a different interview, video, or photo from their one-day set visit to the fans for the months after filming and prior to the theatrical release. This maintained the suspense and heightened the anticipation for more information, and as the fans were receiving the information from valued fan site owners, who received information directly from Summit Entertainment, it added validity to the information; it came "from the source" and not a tabloid.

Event Films and Web 2.0 Applications

In addition to their relationship with the fan sites, Summit also partnered with the largest fan group on Facebook, making it "the official" *Twilight* Facebook page. Lauren Sueno, the originator of the group, describes that their initial "interaction with Summit Entertainment started in January of 2009, with the introduction of the page as a 'partner site' in which Summit would send us media items, notifications, etc. In other words, a 'glorified' media contact send out. These 'partner sites' were known for not posting un-authorized items, gossip, etc." (Personal email, 13 January 2011). Sueno acknowledged that soon, the founders realized that they could do more with Summit Entertainment, and that they might be interested in a partnership to "make the *Twilight* page an Official Summit Outlet. In May 2009, the two sides came together and made our *Twilight* fan page 'The Official *Twilight* Saga Facebook Fan Page.'" This partnership evolved, and they now work with Summit, attending fan events with them or on their behalf, reporting on book, film, or DVD releases, conducting interviews with the cast and filmmakers, and she releases information from the filmmaking team to the Facebook group on behalf of Summit.[7] For example, Bill Condon, the director of *Breaking Dawn*, posted a letter to the fans on the Facebook page where he speaks directly to the fan base and offers "exclusive" information to them. He proceeds to list the people included in his production team from makeup artists to cinematographers and even proclaims his production designer, Richard Sherman, as a "lifelong vampire aficionado." It is a move to inform the fans, and perhaps to calm some of their concerns about the digital depiction of the supernatural Renesmee, the daughter of Edward and Bella, as well as the artistic look and consideration of the shots, or the intentions of the production team. The filmmakers align themselves as fans, thus appealing to the fan base in a familiar way, on the grounds of mutual understanding and appreciation.

This is a symbiotic relationship between Sueno and Summit, as the studio maintains some control over the information that the fans are receiving, but the originator of the group now also has easier access to the film and its peripheral elements due to her connections with Summit, thus raising her profile and status in the fandom as a known blogebrity; the fans also get reputable information from a fellow fan, thus depicting the studio as fan-friendly, and illustrating the seemingly enthusiastic incorporation and consideration of the fans in the filmmaking process.

Twitter has also been a positive realm in which to incorporate the fan base. Numerous *Twilight* actors, Ashley Greene, Billy Burke, Christian Serratos, and Peter Facinelli to name a few, as well as David Slade, the director of the third installment of the *Twilight* Saga, *Eclipse,* are using the popular networking site to promote themselves, and the film, to their fans. They tweet their daily interactions with the film, and Slade even shared teasing photos of the actors on set to bait the fans. He tweeted, "and so to bed dear readers, 6am call tomorrow, back into the fray.... Snow and heartbreak begins in the am (Twitter, Slade 13 October 2009)." He spoke directly to the fans and implied that the tent scene from *Eclipse*, famous amongst fans, was next on the shooting schedule. This provided fans with inside information about the production process and development, and it also created excitement due to the popularity of that scene. He also commented on his work with Meyer early in pre-production: "Reading Stephenie's notes on latest script draft, we are in very good shape" (Twitter, Slade 20 July 2010). This once again illustrated the involvement of the author, and the positive direction of the adaptation process which can instill confidence in the films' progress to his 103,100 Twitter followers.

This early and continued involvement in the fan community may have assisted in the franchise's continued success, as *Twilight* merchandise, book sales, and ticket sales for subsequent film were also high in number. *New Moon* earned $709.8 million worldwide (Pro.IMDB.com n.p.). The fan base has continued to grow online, and additional *Twilight* Events such as Vampire Baseball, TwiCon and Creation Entertainment fan conventions, and *Twilight* themed vacations and workshops currently occur all over the world.[8] At the time of writing, the fervor is not waning, the books are still on various best-seller lists, fan events are growing in number and frequency, and the fan sites are still active places of news, media, and discussion. The next phenomenon is always around the corner, but the *Twilight* fever has not yet ended.

Film	Budget	Opening Weekend	Worldwide Box Office	U.S. Box Office
Twilight (2008)	$37 million	$69.6 million	$351.5 million	$191.5 million

The table below compares the facts and figures of these event films. Although the budgets were vastly different for the films ($37 million for *Twilight* and up to $125 million for *The Lord of the Rings*), it is the box office earnings in comparison to the budgets that is of interest, and the earnings of the event films in the countries with the majority of fans of these popular fantasy adaptations (the United States leading). While *Eragon* made substantial amounts of money in the worldwide box office, it is in the U.S., as well as the UK and other fan-centered countries, where the film did not do as well.

Film	Budget	Opening Weekend	Worldwide Box Office	U.S. Box Office
The Seeker (2007)	$45 million	$3.7 million	$23.6 million	$8.8 million
Eragon (2006)	$100 million	$23.2 million	$245.2 million	$75 million
The Fellowship of the Ring (2001)	$125 million	$90.3 million	$968.7 million	$317.6 million
Twilight (2008)	$37 million	$69.6 million	$351.5 million	$191.5 million

Involving the author, and informing the fan base of an event film about the adaptation process, and utilizing their influence online may positively influence the repeat-going audience of that fandom. These actions are not required for a film to succeed, and they do not necessarily need to limit the filmmakers creative practices, but by extending the inexpensive, interactive methods of web 2.0 applications listed in this essay, and providing at least the appearance of fan acknowledgement, author involvement, and respect for the original work, it incorporates the fan into the process. This can create a more supportive fan base, repeat filmgoers, a free street team to advertise the film, and can allow fans to be supportive of the adaptation rather than disappointed or betrayed by the visual representation of their beloved novel.

NOTES

1. *The Lord of the Rings* trilogy consists of three films, but as they were filmed concurrently, I will refer to them as one work, and discuss their processes during the one long shoot.

2. Description from their website: "Shurtugal.com is the world's largest and most comprehensive website for the Inheritance Cycle books and movie on the internet. The staff work closely the with Paolini family, Random House (publisher), 20th Century–Fox (movie), and Vivendi Universal Games (game developers) to bring the best possible content to site visitors." <http://shurtugal.com/site-stuff/about-shurtugal-com/>.

3. Tolkien Enterprises needs to approve any adaptation or remediation of *The Lord of the Rings*, and removes "unbelievable" aspects within the world, such as the existence of chocolate in *The Lord of the Rings*: Online game which was rejected; similarly they approved Elves' use of money when they are avatars working in society, as elves would not need money in elven worlds (personal interview, LOTRO game designers, 2008).

4. *Eragon* was released in seventy-six markets worldwide and made more than $30 million in its opening weekend of December 13–15, 2006 (Beckett 205).

5. For example, Matthew Vaughn's award-winning *Stardust* adapted from Neil Gaiman's novel made only $134 million worldwide, and Iain Softley's *Inkheart* based off of the novel by Cornelia Funke made only $57.6 million. Both are popular adaptations of a successful original work, and earned less than *Eragon* in the worldwide market.

6. It is unclear when this Facebook group was created, but conversation on it was current up until January 2010 where a discussion of 24 posts listed all of the things that were "wrong" with the film from the book.

7. Sueno stated, "We have daily interaction with a morning email to all of us on the page about what to post, marketing ideas, etc. Heidi and I are also free to post about recent books that we loved, reviews etc." (personal email, 17 January 2011).

8. Vampire Baseball, based off of a baseball scene in the film, was a charity event held at PGE Park in Portland, Oregon, in 2009 where the cast of *Twilight* played baseball with fans, signed autographs, and took photos with them. TwiCon was the first and largest *Twilight* convention held in Dallas in 2009, and Creation Entertainment has taken over organizing conventions associated with *Twilight*. Additionally, bus trips around Forks, Washington, the setting of the novel, are common, and trips such as a *Twilight*-themed cruise and vampire tours are also advertised.

WORKS CITED

Beckett, Sandra L. *Crossover Fiction: Global and Historical Perspectives.* New York: Routledge, 2009.

Bhattacharjee, Nivedita. "Hot Topic March Comps Rise on *Twilight* DVD Sales." Reuters, 8 April 2009. Web. 5 November 2009 <http://www.reuters.com/article/industryNews/id USTRE53792V20090408>.

Bradshaw, Peter. "Eragon Review." *The Guardian*. 15 December 2006. Web. 30 October 2009 <http://www.guardian.co.uk/film/2006/dec/15/sciencefictionandfantasy.family>.

Cartmell, Deborah, and Imelda Whelehan. "Harry Potter and the Fidelity Debate." *Books in Motion: Adaptation, Intertextuality, Authorship*. Ed. Mireia Aragay. Amsterdam: Rodopi, 2005.

Cooper, Susan. "The Role of Fantasy in Children's Lives." Cambridge Forum, Cambridge, MA. 15 November 2007.

Cooper, Susan, and Gregory Maguire. "Unriddling the World." Cambridge Public Library Lecture. MIT Campus, Cambridge, MA. 14 November 2007.

Cristiano, Laura. Personal interview. 7 July 2009.

"Eragon." *IMDB Pro*. Web. 3 November 2009 <http://www.pro.imdb.com/title/tt0449010/box office>.

Floyd, Nigel. "Eragon Review." *2006–12–12 10:40:31Time Out London* 1,895 (2006). 13–20 December. 2 November 2009 <http://www.timeout.com/film/reviews/83511/Eragon.html>.

Godfrey, Wyck. Personal interview. 23 April 2008.

Hardwicke, Catherine. Personal interview. 25 April 2008.

Hunt, Justin. "Don't Make Us Angry...." referencing Rob Andrews, editor of Tiscali. 17 July 2003. Web. 4 November 2009 <http://www.guardian.co.uk/technology/2003/jul/17/new media.film>.

Hunter, I.Q. "Post-Classical Fantasy Cinema: *The Lord of the Rings*." *The Cambridge Companion to Literature on Screen*. Eds. Deborah Cartmell and Imelda Whelehan. Cambridge: Cambridge University Press, 2007.

Jenkins, Henry. *Textual Poachers: Television Fans and Participatory Culture*. New York: Routledge, 1992.

Jenson, Joli. "The Consequences of Characterization." *The Adoring Audience: Fan Culture and Popular Media*. Ed. Lisa A. Lewis. London: Routledge, 1992.

Johnston, Trevor. "*The Seeker: The Dark Is Rising* Review." *Time Out London* 1,939 (2007). 17–23 October. 2 November 2009 <http://www.timeout.com/film/reviews/84797/the-seeker-the-dark-is-rising.html>.

Kirk, Connie Ann. *J.K. Rowling: A Biography*. Westport, CT: Greenwood, 2003.

Lobdell, Jared C. *The Rise of Tolkienian Fantasy*. Peru, IL: Open Court Press, 2005.

MacLeod, Hugh. *Ignore Everybody and 39 Other Keys to Creativity*. New York: Portfolio, 2009.

Margolis, Harriet, Sean Cubitt, Barry King, and Thierry Jutel. *Studying the Event Film: The Lord of the Rings*. Manchester: Manchester University Press, 2009.

McNary, Dave. "A Walk in the 'Dark.'" *Variety Online*. 5 May 2005. Web. 2 November 2009 <http://www.variety.com/article/VR1117922276.html?categoryid=1236&cs=1>.

Meyer, Stephenie. "Good News about New Moon." Web. 7 January 2009 <http://www.stepheniemeyer.com>.

_____. Letter to her fans, 6 November 2009. Web. <http://stepheniemeyer.com>.

Mooradian, Greg. Personal interview. 23 April 2008.

Mortiere, Austin. Comment on Facebook, "The Eragon Movie Was a Disgrace to the Book" fan page. 8 April 2010. Web. <http://www.facebook.com/search/?flt=1&q=eragon&o=65&s=50#!/pages/The-Eragon-movie-was-a-disgrace-to-the-book/281204229531?ref=search>.

O'Hara, Helen. "*The Seeker: The Dark Is Rising* Review." *Empire Online*. 15 October 2007. Web. 4 November 2009 <http://www.empireonline.com/reviews/ReviewComplete.asp?FID=17095>.

_____. "Why Studios Should Ignore the Fans." *Empire Online*. 3 May 2009. Web. 24 October 2009 <http://www.empireonline.com/empireblog/post.asp?id=510>.

"People's Choice Awards Winners." Web. 4 October 2010 <http://www.peopleschoice.com/pca/awards/nominees/index.jsp>.

Rathbone, Jackson. Personal interview. 1 August 2009.

"Scott, Ridley — Introduction." *Contemporary Literary Criticism*. Eds. Tom Burns and Jeffrey W. Hunter. Vol. 183. Gale Cengage, 2004. eNotes.com, 2006. Web. 5 November 2009 <http://www.enotes.com/contemporary-literary-criticism/scott-ridley>.

"The Seeker: The Dark Is Rising." *IMDB Pro*. Web. 3 November 2009 <http://www.pro.imdb.com/title/tt0484562/boxoffice>.

Silberman, Peter. Personal interview. 23 April 2008.

Simpson, Paul, Helen Rodiss, and Michaela Bushell, eds. *The Rough Guide to* The Lord of the Rings. London: Haymarket Customer Press for Rough Guides, 2003.

Slade, David. Twitter. Web. 20 July 2009 <http://twitter.com/DAVID_A_SLADE>.

TheOneRing.net. Web. 4 November 2009 <http://www.theonering.net/torwp/about/>.

"Twilight." *IMDB Pro*. Web. 3 November 2009 <http://pro.imdb.com/title/tt1099212/box office>.

Vandersluis, Joel. Comment on Facebook. Web. 29 March 2010 <http://www.facebook.com/search/?flt=1&q=eragon&o=65&s=50#!/pages/The-Eragon-movie-was-a-disgrace-to-the-book/281204229531?ref=search>.

The Hero and the Id
A Psychoanalytic Inquiry into the Popularity of Twilight

HEATHER ANASTASIU

Why is *Twilight* popular? Why does it resonate with so many people? The statistics at the beginning of this anthology make the wide scope and impact of this phenomenon clear. The question remains, *why*? I use psychoanalytic, archetypal, and reader-response critical principles to examine this pop-culture phenomenon and discover just how *Twilight* manages to captivate readers long after the last page is turned.

Psychoanalytic theory offers a useful lens through which one can examine Edward and Bella's psychological journey and begin to understand why their story so appeals to readers. Freud theorized that a stable conscious identity, or ego, is created through the unconscious forces of id and super-ego. The id is the unconscious part in each of us where our darker passions and instinctual desires — for example, the sex and violence instincts — reside unchecked, always trying to burst out to the surface (*Ego* 20). The super-ego can be considered the unconscious parental or police force that holds back the id desires so they don't get out of control and cause chaos (33). In short, the id is what we *want* to do, but the super-ego is what we *ought* to do. Edward's journey of self-discovery demonstrates this tension; he hungers for Bella's blood, but he isn't sure whether or not he can stop himself from acting on those impulses. In Freudian terms, his id lusts are straining at the bit, but his super-ego restraint works to keep the id in check. Bella likewise experiences transformation. She longs to be near Edward and explore the feelings of romantic and sexual awakening he arouses in her, even when doing so puts her in danger. The formation of identity, or ego, for both characters centers on how they learn to navigate these sometimes destructive unconscious impulses to become stable, whole selves.

Bella and Edward's journey can also be related to the hero narrative described in Joseph Campbell's *Hero With a Thousand Faces.* Campbell argues that myths and fairytales from across time reflect a "universal mythological formula" which he calls the "monomyth" (21, 30). Campbell suggests that the psychological need to work out unconscious problems is what drives humans to tell myth stories in the first place; he says that the unconscious tensions we can't always work through consciously find release through identification with the hero's journey[1] (29). Modern readers similarly need release for psychological tension between id and super-ego, i.e., between desire and responsibility, and *Twilight* provides the platform for this unconscious drama to play out. Normand Holland, a psychoanalytic reader-response critic, further explains how readers experience individual satisfaction by reading about the external drama of fictional characters. Fiction, especially fantasy literature that pushes events and situations beyond the bounds of reality, creates a safe place for exploring the feelings we may be embarrassed or forbidden to think about consciously (818).

As I implement each critical approach, my larger concern is to trace the path of psychological elements from author to text to audience and explore how one woman's personal fantasy, which Freud would suggest bubbled up from her own id impulses, has transformed into a communal myth with individual implications for readers (*Ego* 15–9). The Author-Text-Reader structure provides an overall framework for the essay.

I. Author

Meyer had no professional writing training before she authored *Twilight*, which she began as a means of recording a spectacular dream she had. In an interview, Meyer recalls the dream in detail:

> The dream was vivid, strong, colorful.... It was a conversation between a boy and a girl which took place in a beautiful, sunny meadow in the middle of a dark forest. The boy and the girl were in love with each other, and they were discussing the problems involved with that love, seeing that she was human and he was a vampire. The boy was more beautiful than the meadow, and his skin sparkled like diamonds in the sun. He was so gentle and polite, and yet the potential for violence was very strong, inherent to the scene. I delayed getting out of bed for a while, just thinking through the dream and imagining what might happen next [Morris].

While dream analysis is not the exact science Freud thought it could be, reflecting on dreams can be a means for the conscious mind to explore its unconscious impulses ("Interpretation" 397–414). Of more importance than the fact that the story began as a dream, therefore, is the attention Meyer paid to it. Something about what her unconscious had created captivated her conscious mind, and then she began to explore it intentionally. Meyer says in an interview with Oprah, "I did the dream and then I wanted to see what would happen to them. It was just me spending time with this fantasy world. And when it was finished it was like, 'This is long enough to be a book'" (*Oprah* 6).

Meyer did not self-edit the melodramatic elements of her story, in part because she never thought anyone else would read it, even her husband. She says, "My husband thought I'd gone crazy. I barely spoke to him because I had all these things going on in my head and I wasn't telling him about this weird vampire obsession, because I knew he'd freak out and think I'd lost my mind" (*Oprah* 4).

Here we can infer the subtle play of conscious and unconscious desires. Meyer was embarrassed about the content of her fantasy-life and the fact that she was spending so much time indulging and exploring it. Describing it as an "obsession" further indicates not only the consuming nature of the fantasy, but the unconscious drive to explore it to its fullest. Holland writes, "fantasies that boldly represent the desires of the adult ... will ordinarily arouse guilt and anxiety." He goes on to detail how people "feel a need to transform raw fantasy" into more aesthetically, intellectually, or socially acceptable modes (818). Meyer, believing she was writing only for herself and later, her sister, did not have to exercise as much conscious restraint as she might have if she knew the story would be public, i.e., published, from the start.

Creating an elaborate fiction around the dream also provides a means of abstraction that in and of itself may have shielded Meyer from directly confronting any unconscious issues that drove her to create it. Holland argues that many authors unconsciously write their own fears and desires into fictional characters. By externalizing the conflict, he suggests, they allow the possibility for real internal psychological work to be done. This is not something specifically limited to Meyer. Indeed, Campbell argues that this need to externalize unconscious conflict is the reason behind all myth-making and storytelling.

Holland suggests that the very act of creating the fiction can itself be therapeutic. Readers likewise actively participate in creating texts when they read.[2] Even without one's conscious mind recognizing the conflicts being worked through, the result is nevertheless psychically satisfying. Meyer herself seems to support this idea when she describes the way writing down her fantasy helped her reclaim her own identity after the exhaustive first years of motherhood. Meyer describes herself: "I was really burned out. I really had gotten into that zombie mom way of doing things where *I wasn't Stephenie anymore*

... [Writing *Twilight*] was a release. That was the dam bursting. I'd been bottling up who I was for so long, I needed an expression" (emphasis mine). Speaking of herself as a "zombie" emphasizes the sense of stasis and lack of vitality that often precipitates a metamorphosis.

At a point of personal depletion, Meyer dreams about an adolescent girl on the cusp of transformation. In this case, first love provides the catalyst for that transformation, both for the boy and the girl depicted in the fantasy. By creating a fictional world in which external characters work through trials and conflict toward triumphant renewal, Meyer was able not only to regain the identity she'd lost, but to reshape that identity to express her conscious self at a new stage in life. This echoes the life-renewing possibilities of myth described by Campbell and the therapeutic implications suggested by Holland.

II. Text

Examining Edward and Bella's hero journeys in detail using Campbell's monomyth provides a framework to investigate what about *Twilight* is so captivating and how it connects to other hero narratives that have similarly attracted listeners throughout the ages. While Bella and Edward continue to change throughout the entire four-part series, I focus in this essay on their journey arc within the space of the initial novel, as the foundation of the popular phenomenon.

For Edward, the arrival of Bella into his life forces an awakening from the emotional stasis he subsisted in for almost a hundred years. Edward suddenly faces a heretofore unknown dilemma — he lusts for Bella's blood more than any other, but he is also attracted to her on a personal, human level. Bella similarly has been living a life of stasis, forced into a premature maturity by taking on roles of responsibility where her mother would not. Her move to Forks further dramatizes this; in order to protect her mother's happiness, she moves to a place where she expects her own happiness to be impossible (*T* 7). Her intense sense of responsibility reflects the super-ego's firm grip on her identity, subordinating all other desires. She also feels alienated from those around her and not only those who are her age. She says, "Maybe the truth was, I didn't relate well to people, period" (10). Like Meyer, Bella has fallen into a "zombie" way of life. Yet this too she stoically accepts as inevitable; until she meets Edward.

The moment of crisis upsets the balance of previously accepted behavioral norms. The hero's conscious self, or ego, must navigate through untested waters of vying id and super-ego elements until a new conscious identity can be reborn. Edward makes the decision to pursue the call into the journey toward humanity, no matter the obstacles and dangers to himself or others. Bella likewise begins to abandon her self-imposed roles of responsibility in order to explore the feelings Edward awakens in her.

Both enter a period of trials, simultaneously external and internal. Notably, these trials are also of the violent and sexual variety. This harkens back to Freud's theory that the two driving instincts in humankind are the Eros, or sexual impulse, and the violent destructive impulse (*Ego* 37–47). Freud suggests these two instincts, located in the id, represent the life and death impulses in humans and are often "fused, blended, and alloyed with each other" (38). He explains that the death instinct is merely the id's recognition of the "continuous descent towards death," and that the sexual instinct provides resistant tension by striving for sexual satisfaction and self-preservation (46). The balance between these two intertwined-yet-combative impulses is mediated by the conscious self, but the tension between them is never completely resolved.

The vampire is the perfect symbol for these dual instincts. From Bram Stoker's seminal text, sex and death have been tied inexplicably together in the vampire. This may have been why it was a vampire who starred in Meyer's dream in the first place. Meyer, who by her own admission does not like horror movies or other vampire stories, nevertheless unconsciously chose this dualistic symbol to depict Edward, a symbol Bella is likewise attracted to and eventually wishes to become herself.

In one of Edward's first trials on his journey toward humanity, he rescues Bella with his superhuman speed and strength from a van sliding on ice that would undoubtedly crush Bella to death. Later he comes up with a logical explanation for his having done so — he wouldn't have been able to stop himself from feasting on her blood, had it been spilt. This would have exposed his nature to the humans, a strictly forbidden rule of the vampire world. But, he admits, that wasn't why he did it. He didn't act out of fear of exposure, but because his *human* nature made him want to protect Bella (*T* 272).

Bella, already fascinated by Edward's beauty and dark mysterious nature, is increasingly fixated on him after the car incident. Much of her obsession is couched in terms of sexual awakening. The parts of herself she never before allowed herself to acknowledge come bubbling to the surface. When she thinks of Edward, she feels a "rush of emotion pulsing through [her]" and "flutters through [her] stomach" (*T* 73,192). In the shower, when she acknowledges that Edward is indeed dangerous, but realizes that she wants him anyway, "small shudders trembled through [her]" (195). In a darkened science classroom, an "electric current that seemed to be originating from somewhere in his body" makes her almost hyperventilate (218–9). Later she says, when dreaming of Edward: "It thrilled with the same electricity [...] I tossed and turned restlessly, waking often" (226). These descriptions suggest Bella is experiencing sexual arousal, even in the unconscious realm of sleep. When awake, she feels a "restless craving" to touch his skin (230). The stirrings of her id, her instinctual passions, are straining for release.

Meanwhile, Edward is experiencing sensual id desires of his own, though his are a mingling of sexual longing and bloodlust. Before meeting Bella, Edward had allowed the strict rule of super-ego to determine the entirety of his identity in order to control his vampire nature. The resulting emotional stagnation, however, was just as dehumanizing as the animalistic impulses he so feared. When Bella forces him to lower those defenses and allow his id longings to surface, he faces the danger of swinging to the opposite extreme. He says to Bella, "I got tired of trying to stay away from you. So I'm giving up ... giving up trying to be good. I'm just going to do what I want now, and let the chips fall where they may," and he later remarks, "Hadn't you noticed? I'm breaking *all* the rules now" (88, 199).

Finally, the sexual tensions simmering in the novel boil over. Bella describes their relationship as balancing on the tip of a knife: "We would fall off one edge or the other [...] My decision was made, made before I'd ever *consciously* chosen" (248, emphasis mine). Her unconscious desires have already decided for her. For the first time in her life, Bella's first thought isn't to take care of her mom or dad. All of her determination to take care of others has dissipated in light of the thrilling things Edward has awakened, and she is willing to die for the chance to explore them further. Her super-ego control is completely abandoned, and her potentially self-destructive id longings take center stage.

Edward takes Bella to an Eden-like scene: a meadow in the middle of the forest, far from the rest of the world. Edward is still not sure he can control himself around Bella, and later admits that he had not entirely made up his mind before coming that he even *wanted* to (301). The entire scene provides a lush push and pull between lust and restraint. One moment Bella is tracing the contours of Edward's arm muscles and leaning in open-mouthed to inhale his breath, and the next, Edward has to race to the other edge of the meadow to stop himself from killing her. He comes back, determined to master himself. He lays his cheek against her throat, and then Bella details how "with deliberate slowness, his hands slid down the sides of my neck.... He came to rest with the side of his face pressed tenderly against my chest. Listening to my heart" (276).

He passes the test, suppressing the "deplorable creature" within, and believes it "won't be so hard again" (276). Edward then talks about the "complexity" and "confusion" he feels, because he "is not used to feeling so human" (277–8). He says, "There are other hungers. Hungers I don't even understand, that are foreign to me," i.e., human sexual longings. Before they leave the meadow, he concludes, "I have human instincts — they may be buried deep, but they're there" (278).

Here it is apparent that while the trials that Edward and Bella face are external, they prove instrumental in the formation of their internal identities. Campbell writes, "the incidents [in mythology] are fantastic and 'unreal': they represent psychological, not physical, triumphs [...] fundamentally [the hero's journey] is inward — into depths where obscure resistances are overcome, and long lost, forgotten powers are revivified" (29). In spite of the fact that myth narratives appear to depict external drama, Campbell is suggesting that the true action is internal. Similarly, over and over again, external trials force Bella and Edward to confront internal dilemmas. Will Edward react as vampire or human? Will he unleash his lusts or rein them in so completely he similarly denies his humanity? Will Bella remain a human, or become a vampire? Will Bella's identity be consumed by her desire for Edward, or will she be able to find a middle path to retain an empowered agency over her life? Key to the formation of their identities is their ability to find balance. As a stable person in society, one cannot be entirely ruled by super-ego, which can stifle individual identity. Being ruled by id alone is equally problematic, however, as it would lead to chaos and the destruction of those things held most dear. Only when Edward and Bella begin to maneuver through the murky space between id and super-ego do they realize that they have the power to determine who and what they will be, without denying any aspect of their complex natures.

While Edward manages to control his id desires in the meadow, his journey is far from over. The conflict between lust and restraint is a constant, continuing tension. Bella continues to stretch the limits of Edward's resolve, always wanting to push things further with Edward physically than feels comfortable. This melodramatic tension continues: the push of id, the countering restraint of super-ego, but only until the next longing of id comes bubbling up.

Though the series has sometimes been characterized as chaste and sexually suppressed, *Bitch* contributor Christine Seifert rightly points out that in fact, it is the opposite. Sexual longing is given lush exploration in the novel, a sense which is heightened *because* it is never actually consummated. Seifert terms it "abstinence porn," describing it as "sensational, erotic, and titillating" (23). It is this very tension between longing and suppression, between id and super-ego that drives the book's appeal.[3]

At the end of the novel comes Edward's ultimate test: how will he react when climactic circumstances create a scenario where the exercise of vampiric impulses appears reasonable, even necessary? After James bites Bella in the final chapters, Edward realizes she will transition into a vampire from the venom unless he does something to stop it. The only way to save her from becoming what he considers to be a monster, and potentially losing her soul, is for Edward to suck her blood to get the venom out. Thus, Edward is put in a situation where he has to taste the delicious blood he has been longing for throughout the novel, but at the same time, he must only suck out the venom and stop drinking before he kills her. Can the animal be leashed once it has been given a taste of Bella's blood — blood previously referred to metaphorically as "[his] brand of heroin" (*T* 268)? The answer, of course, is yes. While the id is given a long leash in the novel, at the end of the day, the super-ego is always there to rein it in before it becomes destructive.

While the trials of Edward's journey are more outwardly dramatic, Bella's path to transformation is no less life-changing. Throughout the novel, Bella awakens to aspects of life and desire she had never known or expected to experience for herself. Her sense of lacking connection to other people seems to have found its solution in her relationship with the family of supernatural vampires. Associating with them, however, is soon not enough for Bella. She wants to be one of them, to be a permanent part of their world, the one place she feels she finally *fits*.[4]

Throughout the novel, in spite of her lack of physical prowess, Bella gains agency by actively obtaining the things she wants. While initially her id desires are out of control with the overwhelming excitement of being close to Edward, by the end of the novel, she regains a sense of equilibrium. When Bella believes her mother is in danger, she puts aside her all-encompassing desire for Edward and ignores what she knows he would want her to do. Instead, she goes to face a supernatural being, an action she knows will likely result in her death. Bella's willingness to sacrifice herself to save those she loves is a theme repeated throughout all four novels in the saga.[5] Symbolic sacrifice that brings renewal and redemption is characteristic of heroes in the monomyth (Campbell 16–7).

By the end of *Twilight*, Bella expresses her desire to become a vampire. She doesn't want to be damsel in distress waiting to be saved, the "Lois Lane" to Edward's "Superman." "I want to be Superman, too," she says (*T* 474). This Bella is a far cry from the awkward misfit at the start of the novel. While she will continue to face trials that will require further reassessing of her identity, the paradigm established in book one continues to be repeated in the later novels. Bella continues to navigate her fears, desires, and responsibilities, gaining greater power and agency with each text until by the end of the series she has become a vampire whose unique talents provide the key tactical advantage that diffuses a potentially bloody war.

III. Reader

But just how does the hero reaching a satisfactory conclusion transfer to the reader's own psychical needs? Again, as I am aiming to illustrate, viewing the text as myth can be helpful. As in religious ceremonies, regular, unadventurous people can vicariously partake of the hero's journey of "self-discovery and self-development" through the symbolic aids and ceremonial rites represented in the narrative (Campbell 23). Just as Bella and Edward embark on outer journeys that affect mental and internal psychological transformations, Campbell says "where [participants/readers] had thought to travel outward, we shall come to the center of our own existence" (25).

Holland explains that fiction can work to meet an individual's psychological needs because the abstraction of unconscious desires onto an external figure allows the "express[ion] of his own desires" without "guilt [or] anxiety" (817–8). Holland believes that readers re-create their identity in the text, projecting their "own characteristic patterns of desire and adaptation. [They] interact with the work, making it part of [their] own psychic economy and making [themselves] part of the literary work" (816). Immersing oneself in a fictional work, where external characters experience situations that readers interpret in light of their own unconscious fears and desires, allows the satisfaction of these desires without the conscious acknowledgement of them, resulting in gratification.

The genre of urban fantasy even further facilitates a reader's ability to identify with the characters. Urban fantasy literature creates one less level of abstraction, reeling the fantasy back into reality while still keeping it far enough at bay to remain unthreatening to the reader/participant. Where does Bella discover the god-like Edward? In the mundane setting of a small town high-school science class, seemingly the last place one would expect to find the paranormal or fantastic. A parking lot provides the setting for a display of supernatural power when Edward saves Bella from the van. Anna Silver, of Mercer University, also keys in on the "fantastic realism" in the novel, discussing it as a familiar trope of young adult literature that "allow[s] adolescents to lose themselves in adventurous situations and idealized characters, but it also represents, in dramatic and exaggerated fashion, the conflicts in their own lives" (136).

Campbell proposes that an important aspect of vicariously participating in hero journeys is to help individuals cross the varying thresholds presented at each new stage of life where a metamorphosis is required in order to continue existing as a stable self in a dynamic world. He says, "The purpose and actual effect of [myth] was to conduct people across those difficult thresholds of transformation that demand a change in the patterns not only of conscious but also of unconscious life" (Campbell 10). Freud argues such a "threshold of transformation," to use Campbell's words, only occurs at adolescence, but Jung suggests that similar transitions must take place throughout life (Jung 29–35). By placing the crisis of identity in adolescence for the two main characters, *Twilight* is especially powerful in symbolically depicting the necessary metamorphoses of life.

Adolescent Readers

For adolescents reading the novels, the need for transformation is explicit — society requires them to transition from child to adult roles as they age. Through these novels, adolescents are able to explore their fears and desires in a safe place. Adolescence itself is a liminal space in which individuals are forced to work their way through lingering elements of childhood while also pushing toward adulthood and social responsibility. In the ideal scenario, adolescents will emerge in adulthood with their ego, or conscious self, able to hold unconscious impulses in check.

Identification with Bella can potentially empower girl readers to embrace their emerging sexuality while also navigating the often difficult terrain of claiming agency and voice to express what they want as they transition from adolescence to adulthood. Sex is undeniably a large part of that transition. Reading *Twilight* may provide a non-threatening place for girls to experience vicariously the sexual thrill of romance, freeing their own id desires for the duration of the novel and afterwards, in imaginative spaces of their own creation, exemplified in fan fiction. Danielle McGeough similarly sees this possibility in her essay, "Transformations of the Flesh," wherein she explores representations of the body in *Twilight*. She writes, "Speaking openly about sexual desires and bodily changes is socially risky for teenage girls, and the fantasy world Meyer creates open up the possibility for discussions about the anxieties surrounding adolescent female bodies" (101).

Sociologist Ananya Mukherjea also discovered that much of the fan attraction to Edward focuses on his chivalry and ability to exert self-control. Many girls have expressed their attraction to the vampire Edward because, ironically, they find in him a sense of safety and security (Mukherjea, this volume). This might speak to the way Edward's courteous behavior assuages their own fears about males in their life or provides a sense of stability and certainty in an otherwise unstable, unsafe and chaotic world.

Adult Readers

For adults attracted to the texts, perhaps like Stephenie Meyer, they find themselves depleted by the responsibilities of adulthood, no longer sure of their own identity. Lisa Hansen, founder of the fan site *Twilight*MOMS, explains in an interview posted on the site: "We've found our fountain of youth and everyone should have that in their lives to keep from disappearing into the mundane routines we get into as life settles down." Describing the *Twilight* books as providing a "fountain of youth," to be visited in order to "keep from disappearing" speaks to the thresholds of transformations Campbell mentioned. Hansen openly acknowledges her desire to remain in contact with the vitality associated with youth.[6] The text helps her continually affirm her identity and re-form it when entering new stages of life to avoid losing herself.

At the same time, when Hansen first read the *Twilight* books her daughter was reading, she felt embarrassed that, while she couldn't stop thinking about the book, the only people she could talk to about it were tweens and teens. She started a forum on Myspace that she eventually turned into the *Twilight*MOMS website for women like herself. She writes on her site, "I felt like the only one in the whole world out there my age who was completely obsessed with these books and that there was something severely wrong with me," and she wanted to reach out to other women, if only "to prove to myself that I wasn't going through some midlife crisis!!!" (Hansen). Here we see her embarrassment about enjoying the fantasy presented in the novel, along with the pressing need to find a place to explore the things it made her feel and think.

This echoes the embarrassment Meyer felt as she was writing *Twilight*, when she was too embarrassed to tell her husband and instead talked about it only with her sister. Many adult women who enjoy the book express a sense of guilt or embarrassment at their enthusiastic private reactions. As Jessica Sheffield and Elyse Merlo explore in their essay "Biting Back: *Twilight* Anti-Fandom and the Rhetoric of Superiority," the phenomenon has been popularly characterized in negatively gendered ways, representing *Twilight* "as hyperfeminine: uncontrollable, silly, and irrational" (211). Women or girls who enjoy the series must then negotiate their experience encountering the text with these negative associations.

When I presented this paper at the Southwest/Texas Popular Culture Association Conference in 2010, several women in the audience admitted their surprise and disturbance at being so absorbed when reading the text. Most of the conversation had thus far centered on the negative gender implications the text might have on girls, but when I asked the women in the room if they themselves had found the text engaging, many admitted they had. One woman said sheepishly that she "couldn't put it down." Implicit in her apparent embarrassment was the idea that as an aesthetically mature, intellectual woman, she believed such a low-brow and melodramatic text *should* have no effect on her. Scholars Elizabeth Behm-Morawitz, Melissa Click, and Jennifer Aubrey echo this discomfort when they discuss their "conflicted" relationship to the series; they write:

> Journalists, fans, and scholars alike wonder why the adult series *Twilight* that is oft criticized for its stereotypical portrayals of gender and romance proves so compelling to so many girls and women. We, too, marveled at the appeal *Twilight* had for each of us, given our identities as feminist media scholars [137].

The fact that so many women and girls *have* enjoyed the novel, even sometimes in spite of the fact of their personal feminist identification, suggests that it is meeting needs, conscious or unconscious. Psychologists and mental health professionals repeatedly report that an active fantasy-life can be healthy, but as women, we are often socially reproached for the content of those fantasies. In the safe space of fiction, women can explore emotions and thoughts they are conditioned not to acknowledge as conscious selves in the real world, often because they have been told such fantasies are wrong, stupid, silly, or sinful. Such repression denies women the healthy space to let loose in the realm of fantasy, which can foster unconscious gratification as well as the conscious discovery of fears, desires, and needs.

Men have often had public, culturally acceptable outlets for male fantasies, but women, less so. Men have had *Tarzan*, *Star Wars*, *James Bond*, and even professional wrestling, all stories with similar triumphant symbolic journeys (Barthes 15–25), but ones that are less accessible to women and girls. The popularity of *Twilight* and the output of female dollars for the books, movies, and merchandise can be seen as a political statement for the validity of female fantasy.[7]

Conclusion

While, as Behm-Morawitz, Click, and Aubrey mentioned, everyone from journalists to fans to scholars mention the compelling, immersive quality of the *Twilight* reading experience, few attempt a satisfactory or comprehensive answer explaining *why* this is so.[8] Behm-Morawitz, Click, and Aubrey generically state that "most fans and critics agree that it is the characters in the *Twi-*

light series, as well as the relationships between them, that make the saga so compelling" (138).

What I have proposed in this essay, however, is that the answer can be discovered at a much more interior level; this text dramatically reflects humankind's most basic drives and the need to negotiate between id desires and super-ego responsibilities in order to maintain and reshape our identities in the face of an always-evolving world. Like other enduring myths, *Twilight* provides both the vivid portrayal of unconscious desires and also a platform for vicarious participation in the hero's journey of self-actualization which is psychically satisfying and potentially therapeutic.

Many others have and will continue to point out the problematic elements in *Twilight*, from the lack of quality in writing to the troubling implications of Bella cast in a strictly gendered and heteronormative role. These discussions are valuable and necessary, but the critical community, sometimes too quickly, condemns the entirety of the material, neglecting to observe the possible positive psychological implications of the text alongside the negative. The reality remains that this text and surrounding phenomena is affecting readers, both young and old, and part of the discussion of *Twilight* needs to involve the role it may serve of gratifying individual fantasies through vicarious wish-fulfillment as well as the potentially positive opportunities it provides for self-reflection, self-discovery, and self-renewal.

Notes

1. While Campbell does say that the hero of the monomyth can be either a "man or woman," he notoriously focuses exclusively on male hero journeys, most often speaking of women only in terms of mothers or monsters (19). Nevertheless, I find his framework of the hero narrative still useful as a culturally familiar structure that creates meaning for contemporary readers. *Twilight* can be read as a female version of the hero myth with similar potential for aiding reader participation in symbolic transformations.

2. This is a basic tenet of reader response criticism. For more, see Jane Tompkins' introduction and collection of essays from Stanley Fish, Normand Holland, David Bleich.

3. Many critics take issue with the means of suppression, i.e., Edward's morality, as well as seeing this as a form pro-abstinence didacticism by Meyer (Seifert, Silver, Platt). At the same time, I found Bella's healthy sexual appetite a refreshing reversal of the familiar young adult literature scenario of a male pressuring a female to have sex. While critics see this as a critique of Bella's supposed deficient morality, I think it can also be read as a validation of young women's desire for sexual stimulation/activity.

4. Bella states this explicitly in *Breaking Dawn* after she becomes a vampire (*BD* 524).

5. Silver interprets Bella's self-sacrificial tendency as problematic, citing it as further evidence that "Female power in the series is linked not to aggression [...] but rather to self-sacrifice and the defense of others" (131). Sacrifice in this context, however, may be more a trope of traditional romantic hero literature than a reflection of gender expectations. For example, the resolution of the Harry Potter series also hinges on the main character's willingness to sacrifice himself for the ones he loves in a manner that can be described as passive.

6. This is not to say that the association of vitality with youth isn't problematic, yet youth

remains an undeniably potent cultural symbol for adults to desire and emulate, especially for women.

7. The mixed feminist reaction is explored in several essays in the *Bitten by Twilight* anthology, and a measured, objective discussion is provided by Elana Levine in the "Afterword." Levine discusses the different feminist perspectives and the need for a "multi-perspectival model" that engages women and girls who are "so fully immersed in post-feminist culture that both feminist empowerment and feminine fulfillment have taken on new meanings," without thinking of fans as "the dupes of patriarchy" (283–4). Levine also connects *Twilight* to Janice Radway's research on the romance genre, as have others.

8. Jennifer L. McMahon takes a philosophical approach to understanding the appeal of vampires suggesting "the answer is simple: wish fulfillment," but I found the essay ultimately unsatisfying due to its survey approach and quick conclusion (193).

WORKS CITED

Anastasiu, Heather, Marykate Earnest, and Ananya Mukherjea. "Science Fiction & Fantasy Panel: Nature and the Undead." SWTX PCA/ACA Annual Conference. Albuquerque, NM. 12 February 2010. Address.

Barthes, Roland. "The World of Wrestling." *Mythologies*. 1957. Trans. Annette Lavers. New York: Hill and Wang, 1972.

Behm-Morawitz, Elizabeth, Melissa A. Click, and Jennifer Stevens Aubrey. "Relating to Twilight: Fans' Responses to Love and Romance in the Vampire Franchise." *Bitten by Twilight: Youth Culture, Media, & the Vampire Franchise*. Eds. Melissa A. Click, Jennifer Stevens Aubrey, and Elizabeth Behm-Morawitz. New York: Peter Lang Publishing, 2010. 137–54.

Campbell, Joseph. *The Hero with a Thousand Faces*. Princeton, NJ: Princeton University Press, 1949.

Freud, Sigmund. *The Ego and the Id*. Trans. Joan Riviere. Ed. James Strachey. New York: W.W. Norton & Company, 1960.

______. "Interpretation of Dreams." *Literary Theory: An Anthology*. 2nd ed. Eds. Julie Rivkin and Michael Ryan. Oxford: Blackwell Publishing Ltd., 2004. 397–414.

Hansen, Lisa. "Interview with *Twilight*MOMS Founder." *Twilight*MOMS.com. March 2008. Web. 2 March 2010.

Holland, Norman. "Unity Identity Text Self." *PMLA* 90:5 (1975): 813–22. *JSTOR*. Web. 16 Nov 2009.

Jung, C.G. "The Stages of Life." *Aspects of the Masculine*. Trans. R.F.C. Hull. Ed. John Beebe. New York: MJF Books, 1989.

Levine, Elana. "Afterword." *Bitten by Twilight: Youth Culture, Media, & the Vampire Franchise*. Eds. Melissa A. Click, Jennifer Stevens Aubrey, and Elizabeth Behm-Morawitz. New York: Peter Lang Publishing, 2010. 281–6.

McGeough, Danielle Dick. "Twilight and Transformations of Flesh: Reading the Body in Contemporary Youth Culture." *Bitten by Twilight: Youth Culture, Media, & the Vampire Franchise*. Eds. Melissa A. Click, Jennifer Stevens Aubrey, and Elizabeth Behm-Morawitz. New York: Peter Lang Publishing, 2010. 87–102.

McMahon, Jennifer L. "Twilight of an Idol: Our Fatal Attraction Vampires." *Twilight and Philosophy*. Eds. Rebecca Housel and Jeremy Wisnewski. Hoboken, NJ: John Wiley & Sons, 2009. 193–209.

Morris, William. "Interview: Twilight Author Stephanie Meyer." *Motleyvision.org*. A Motley Vision: Mormon Arts and Culture. 26 October 2005. Web. 2 March 2010.

Mukherjea, Ananya. "Team Bella: Fans Navigating Desire, Security, and Feminism." *Theorizing Twilight*. Eds. Maggie Parke and Natalie Wilson. Jefferson, NC: McFarland, 2011.

The Oprah Winfrey Show. "Twilight Phenom Stephenie Meyer, Karaoke Winner Crowned, Actress Robin Givens." ABC. Harpo Productions, Inc. 13 November 2009. Web. 30 September 2010. Transcript.

Platt, Carrie Anne. "Cullen Family Values: Gender and Sexual Politics in the Twilight Series."

Bitten by Twilight: Youth Culture, Media, & the Vampire Franchise. Eds. Melissa A. Click, Jennifer Stevens Aubrey, and Elizabeth Behm-Morawitz. New York: Peter Lang Publishing, 2010. 71–86.

Seifert, Christine. "bite me! (or don't)." *Bitch* Winter 2009: 23–5.

Sheffield, Jessica, and Elyse Merlo. "Biting Back: Twilight Anti-Fandom and the Rhetoric of Superiority." *Bitten by Twilight: Youth Culture, Media, & the Vampire Franchise*. Eds. Melissa A. Click, Jennifer Stevens Aubrey, and Elizabeth Behm-Morawitz. New York: Peter Lang Publishing, 2010. 207–22.

Silver, Anna. "Twilight Is Not Good for Maidens: Gender, Sexuality, and the Family in Stephenie Meyer's Twilight Series." *Studies in the Novel* 42:1–2 (Spring & Summer 2010): 121–38. *JSTOR*. Web. 28 September 2010.

Tompkins, Jane, ed. *Reader-Response Criticism: From Formalism to Post-Structuralism*. Baltimore, MD: Johns Hopkins University Press, 1980.

Someday My *Vampire* Will Come? Society's (and the Media's) Lovesick Infatuation with Prince-Like Vampires

COLETTE MURPHY

When I was in high school, I remember buying a beautiful yellow ball gown to wear to a school dance. The first time I put it on, I heard Alan Menken's soft piano music in my head, and Angela Lansbury's voice sang in my ear, "Tale as old as time ... song as old as rhyme...."[1] I turned to my friends who were with me and one breathlessly whispered, "You look just like Belle." Fast forward ten years. I'm volunteering at a local high school, helping set up for prom. I overhear two of the girls talking about what they'll be wearing that evening. One excitedly describes her knee-length dark blue tiered gown. Her friend squeals, "You're going to look just like Bella!" It definitely wasn't my first indication that Prince Charming was on the way out; in fact, it put the nail in the coffin (pardon the pun) that for teenage girls today, vampires are the new standard for perfect romance.

In his 2003 self-proclaimed "low-culture manifesto" *Sex, Drugs, and Cocoa Puffs,* Chuck Klosterman critiques Lloyd Dobler, the classic John Cusack character from Cameron Crowe's 1989 film *Say Anything,* and notes that "we all convince ourselves of things like this ... about any fictionalized portrayals of romance that happen to us in the right place, at the right time" (3). In the late 1980s, Lloyd Dobler became the teen girl's ideal of a perfect mate. No longer could a boy just call and ask her to a dance — he needed to stand outside her window all night long blasting Peter Gabriel songs on his boom box. In this way, Lloyd Dobler became the symbol of possibility. Lloyd Dobler was the t-shirt and denim clad equivalent to the prince riding in on a white horse. Dobler was far from "perfect," like Prince Charming is often assumed to be, but to teenage girls, *that* was what love was supposed to look like. Dobler had taken the place of the animated princes who came even before him, made famous by the Walt Disney Company in classics like *Snow White and the Seven Dwarfs, Sleeping Beauty,* and (actually succeeding Dobler) *Beauty and the Beast.* Now, twenty-one years later that search for the "fake love" that was once perpetuated by Disney films in our childhood and romantic comedies in our early adult life is no longer completed by the likes of awkward *humans* like Prince Charming or Lloyd Dobler; instead, vampires are filling the role.[2]

Vampires, in popular consciousness, have usually been associated with horror and fear. Dracula was not someone you wanted to have over for dinner, and no one was going to ask Lestat to the prom.[3] However, by the late 1990s, all of that began to change. As Gary Hendrix of *Slate* pointed out in his review of San Diego's 2009 Comic Con, "bloodsucking is so yesterday ... the modern vampire stalks, seduces, sleeps with, and cries over us. They don't eat us" (np). While vampires have enjoyed literary and pop culture fame since the 1800s, with increasing presence on page and screen beginning in the 1960s, it was perhaps the character Angel in Joss Whedon's television phenomenon *Buffy the Vampire Slayer* that brought this "new vampire" to such popular heights with a teen audience. Vampires were no longer the subjects of horror stories and cult classics; they were teen romance fodder, which led them to become the barometer for measuring the ideal romantic leading male partner for the pre-adult set. Angel, and his recent successor Edward Cullen, have further removed the fear that humans (especially teenage girls) once had of the vampire and have replaced that fear with desire. Angel and Edward are different from the vampires of the past.[4] They are sullen and brooding, sure, but they *care.* They want to listen, they want to talk, they want to slow dance to an unfamiliar alternative-rock song. But they don't want to drink your blood (or, at least, they resist it as best they can) and unlike the previous 1980s party-boy teen vamps, these guys will be your boyfriend. Angel and Edward represent the fantasy of possibility and of self-sacrifice in honor of love. So, these popular vampire stories are not a reinvention of the vampire myth after all; they are a re-costuming of the heterosexual male romantic lead, which is what makes them so overwhelmingly appealing to the predominantly young female audience. Vampires are simply a "modern" Prince Charming with an immortal twist.

The kick-off of the recent onslaught of these new romantic vamps was the relationship between Angel and Buffy Summers. Buffy is "the chosen one";

it is her birthright to slay the vampires. The television series took a bit of a departure from the film, having Buffy move to a new town, Sunnydale, that happens to be on the Hellmouth.[5] Here, Buffy is supposed to stop all forces of evil, especially vampires. However, Buffy's birthright doesn't prevent her from being a typical teenager, and she goes against the plan when she falls in love with her supposed enemy: Angel. As Buffy's title implies, her job is to slay the vampires, not date them. But Angel is different from the other demon bloodsuckers. For one thing, he's been cursed with his soul. So, rather than feeding on helpless humans, Angel patiently waits for blood from butchers' shops or the local blood banks. For the first three seasons, Buffy and Angel continue their on-again, off-again relationship. Eventually, Angel leaves Sunnydale. However, he still returns occasionally when Buffy needs extra help, and she never slays him. He doesn't hunt her, he assists her. In this way, Angel more clearly resembles a Disney version of a fairy tale prince, like Prince Phillip in *Sleeping Beauty*: seemingly distant until he must step up to fight the forces of evil in order to protect the one he loves. This is where the broader pop culture transformation of vampires truly begins to take effect.[6]

While Angel was not the first of this "new vampire" breed, he was the most popular and previously had the longest lifespan in terms of media coverage. After departing Sunnydale on the series *Buffy the Vampire Slayer*, he appeared in Los Angeles on his own series, *Angel*. Angel's popularity, due largely in part to the perception that he was different from most of the other vampires that popular culture had been offering, "launched a sensitive-vampire industry" (Hendrix n.p.). It was Angel's appeal and popularity that laid the necessary groundwork for a full-fledged media event to take place. That frenzy came in the form of the *Twilight* Saga, and the instant love that teenage girls (and adult women) had for the leading vampire Edward Cullen, who mirrors many of Angel's fairytale, prince-like qualities, although he extends them even further. Unlike Angel, he isn't cursed with a soul — he chooses not to eat humans, mostly out of respect and admiration for his father-figure, Carlisle. Edward explains to Bella in *Twilight* that he was "denying [his] thirst for the last, well, too many years" (*T* 269). Edward's denial of his natural self manifests itself in the ways he deals with Bella throughout the novels, as he consistently attempts to sideline Bella in order to protect her. Edward sees Bella as filling the role of the damsel in distress, and he fervently attempts to fill the role of hero and protector because of this perception he maintains of her; even late in the saga Edward shows this when Jasper suggests having Bella present at the fight with the werewolves and Edward, instead, devises the plan with Jacob to hide Bella away (*E* 407–409). Still, it is Edward's chivalry and his attempt to rise above his perceived position in society that casts him in the prince-like role; as he tells Bella in both the novel and film adaptation of *Twilight,* "I don't want to be a monster." Edward is directly pointing out society's perception of vampires (as monsters) and, through his words and actions, encourages us to reject that perception as well.

In terms of being a monster, Edward doesn't have much to worry about in that regard; these modern interpretations of vampires ("new vampires" as they are called here) are hardly monstrous in character or demeanor. In order to fully understand these new vampires, it is important to look at their predecessors, namely the leading male in romance-centered stories such as fairy tales. In an interview with *Entertainment Weekly,* Stephenie Meyer admitted never having read Bram Stoker's *Dracula* or watching any vampire films, including *Lost Boys* and *Interview with the Vampire* (Kirschling n.p.); Meyer's own unfamiliarity with vampire literature and film makes fairy tales a more appropriate historical starting point. Over time, it has been shown that "the fairy tale must be seen as a continuum. At one extreme we find the oral folk tale ... at the other extreme there is the literary tale, written by a specific person at a specific time" (Hallet and Karasek 17). Fairy tales and the types of characters featured within these stories, including vampires, undergo transformations. As noted by Nina Auerbach in *Our Vampires, Ourselves,* "there are many Draculas — and still more vampires who refuse to be Dracula or to play him ... each feeds on his age distinctively because he embodies that age" (1). As such, Angel and Edward aren't simply filling in a pre-cut mold. There is something unique in their transformation and presentation that makes them better situated to be received within their respective contemporary moments, spawning a media phenomenon. The unique trait, ironically, is the departure from the traditional expectations of the vampire and the transformation to include fairytale prince characteristics.

As fairy tale theorist Jack Zipes points out, the popular consciousness relies on a new definition and incarnation of the fairy tale which is a direct result of the fact "that Walt Disney cast a spell on the fairy tale, and he has held it captive ever since" (332). This spell was cast in 1938, when Disney's first animated feature, *Snow White and the Seven Dwarfs,* premiered. Disney's version of the classic Brothers Grimm's fairy tale was the first glimpse at the fairy tale prince that would become the standard for many years. He rode a white horse, was handsome, and swooped in with one kiss at the very end to wake Snow White from her slumber, save the day, and lead the audience to believe they were headed for a happily ever after.[7] Of course, this is just an assumption on the part of the audience. As Bruno Bettelheim points out in *The Uses of Enchantment,* the audience is left with nothing more than the assumption that everything works out for the hero and his beloved once "whatever deed that frees the beautiful princess from her captivity is accomplished" (112). Moving forward from Disney's fairy tales, these roles have continued to perpetuate through other genres marketed specifically toward women, which have the "defining generic feature of ... construction of narratives motivated by female desire and processes of spectator identification governed by female point-of-view" (Kuhn 146). These characteristics are often seen in genres such as the soap opera, melodrama, romance novels, and the like, which "are based on an idea of female fantasy which they themselves anticipate and in some sense construct" (Doane 70).

The relationship between the prince and the lead girl in the story is complicated, yet usually follows the same formula in all of Disney's incarnations of classic fairy tales.[8] Boy and girl meet. Boy and girl fall in love. Something threatens (once or repeatedly) to tear boy and girl apart. Love conquers all and they ride off together into the sunset. One of the reasons that Edward and Bella resonate with a modern audience is because of the ways in which their relationship and their individual character developments mirror the tradition of the fairy tale. While the formula is consistent, the new twist with which we are presented in *Twilight* is the fact that the boy is a vampire. This is a consistent threat, a running undercurrent that is present in the formula even as outside factors simultaneously threaten their relationship. Edward and Bella's relationship highlights one of the purposes of the fairy tale, which is to "take these existential anxieties and dilemmas very seriously and address itself directly to them: the need to be loved and the fear that one is thought worthless; the love of life and the fear of death" (Bettelheim 330). This purpose is actually intensified by the fact that Edward is a vampire. Together, Edward and Bella must overcome even more than their fairytale predecessors did. Edward wants Bella to stay human, to live as much of a normal life as possible, while Bella lives in constant fear of what mortality can bring: not only death, but simply aging. Therefore, the love of life and fear of death operate within every aspect of their relationship, not just climactic battles or conflicts. While the formula is familiar and enticing to the audience, there is an added element of suspense that keeps our attention and prevents it from feeling stale or simply recycled.

The ever-present element of danger and the possibility of death due to Edward's position as a vampire create higher stakes within the relationship between him and Bella, yet Stephenie Meyer's construction of Edward's character includes many of the traditional traits of the fairy tale hero to which we are historically accustomed, such as his ability to follow Carlisle's way of thinking and to be a protector rather than a killer, "as if led by an invisible force and with the confidence of a sleepwalker, [follow] the right course"

(Lüthi 321). Though this is mostly implied through Bella's perspective in the *Twilight* saga, Meyer's intentions to craft Edward as this fairytale prince are more clearly shown in her unfinished manuscript, *Midnight Sun.* The partial manuscript, which was published online via Meyer's official website, retells the first book in the saga, this time from Edward's perspective. After Edward prevents Bella from being crushed by Tyler Crowley's van in the Forks High School parking lot, he discusses his decision to save her once he is at the hospital with Carlisle. During this conversation, Edward realizes "somewhere during that short, thoughtless second when I'd sprinted across the icy lot, I had transformed from killer to protector" (*MS* 66). Edward's acknowledgement of this transformation is the moment he begins to transition into his role as the prince in this modern incarnation of the fairy tale.

Edward's character, especially in the first book of the saga, is also written to include traditionally masculine traits of being "competitive, authoritarian, and power-hungry as well as rational, abstract, and principled" (Zipes 3). While these characteristics are seen throughout the four novels of the saga, the first place in which they all become simultaneously apparent is at the end of *Twilight* when Bella goes to meet James, and after their encounter, Bella is taken to a nearby hospital. In the novel, she and Edward have the following exchange, which is a clear example of Meyer's crafting these two characters to fit within the standard prototype of fairytale prince and love-interest girl. While Bella and Edward are talking, Edward insists that Bella should have waited for him before acting on her own accord.

> "You wouldn't have let me go."
> "No," he agreed in a grim tone, "I wouldn't" [*T* 461].

In this exchange, Edward takes on the authoritarian characteristic, seeking to be Bella's protector. He labels Bella (and she accepts the label) as irrational and implies that he alone should have been the one to handle the situation.

Whereas Edward's characteristics come from both his vampire predecessors, like Angel, as well as the Disney-fied Prince Charmings, like Prince Phillip from *Sleeping Beauty* or the Beast from *Beauty and the Beast,* Bella seems to be cut only from the fairy tale princess cloth. Like the little mermaid (both in Hans Christian Anderson's original tale and in the Disney version), she seeks a life in a world outside of her own, acquiescing to become a part of the supernatural world. Bella slips into the role of most women in fairy tales, as "passive, self-denying, obedient, and self-sacrificial ... as well as nurturing, caring, and responsible in personal situations" (Zipes 3). For Bella, the moment when these characteristics converge with the strongest impact is during the climactic battle scene in *Eclipse.* Bella, having spent time with her friend Jacob Black hearing old legends at the Quileute reservation, places herself in extreme physical danger in an attempt to save both Seth Clearwater and Edward from Victoria. In this moment, Bella asks, "Was I strong enough? Was I brave enough? ... Would he heal fast enough for my sacrifice to do him any good?" (*E* 550). Like Belle from Disney's *Beauty and the Beast*, Bella was willing to trade her own safety — her own life — in order to protect those she considered to be her family.[9] However, as much as Bella fills the traditional roles outlined, as the saga progresses Bella begins to challenge many of the traditional characteristics that are expected of her in terms of the classic fairytale heroine.

As the saga progresses, Bella begins to usurp some of the heroic characteristics that Edward displays earlier on. As Lüthi argues, fairy tales present us with a hero who exemplifies "man's deliverance from an inauthentic existence and his commencement of a true one" (317). By this definition, by the end of the saga, the true hero is Bella. It is important to note here that "hero" and "prince" are not synonymous in fairy tales. Edward maintains the fairytale prince-like qualities throughout the entire saga. Bella, however, transitions from her Edward-appointed perception as damsel in distress to the actual identity of hero. Within the novels, we do see the transition to her true self finalized in *Breaking Dawn* when Bella first sees herself in the sunlight post-transformation from human to vampire. Bella notices how different she appears to everyone else and admits to herself, and to the readers, that she was "born to be a vampire" (*BD* 524). Bella's claim confirms Lüthi's argument; she was never meant to be a human girl, she was meant to be a vampire and, more specifically, a Cullen. Alternate readings of this moment question if Bella was simply supposed to be wife and mother, which is a more passive action as a character. But Bella's most significant actions in the saga that occur in *Breaking Dawn* do not relate to her being a wife and mother; they are a result of her being a vampire.[10] Upon Bella transforming, we learn that Edward's and Aro's inability to read her thoughts and Jane's inability to inflict pain were actually a power she possessed that came into fruition only after she became immortal. Bella's shield ends up being the most significant trait to her character and to her family's survival, and it is only when she begins to take control of the situation and of her destiny that the shield is even able to come into existence.

In the film adaptation of *Eclipse*, Bella previews her ownership of this impending identity transition. She tells Edward that the struggles she faced through the beginning of the saga were about discovering the difference between "who I am and who I should be" (*Eclipse* 2010). Unlike previous heroines who passively sought inclusion into the Prince's reality, Bella recognizes that she is not simply choosing Edward (much to his wry dismay when he quips "So, this isn't just about me?" [*Eclipse* 2010]), she is choosing to begin her true identity. It is interesting to note that though this choice is verbalized in the film, it is not clearly stated in the novel. Many *Twilight* websites, including the *Twilight Lexicon,* have credited this moment in the scene as screenwriter Melissa Rosenberg bringing to life the essence of Bella that was in the book, even if it wasn't explicitly what Meyer wrote. This type of fan interaction with and support of the characters stems from what Douglas Rushkoff defines as a media virus. Media products, acting like biological viruses, infiltrate our public psyche. Consider a regular cold and flu season. Year after year, people fall sick from, essentially, the same virus. The reason that this is possible is because the virus mutates so it appears new and different (and welcomed into) the body, despite the fact that the same cold and flu genetics lurk underneath the protein shell. A similar mutation and reception happens within the media as well. This is why fairy tales "retain a freedom and energy that has survived the transformation" (Hallet and Karasek 20). This is how "vampires blend into the changing cultures they inhabit" (Auerbach 6). *Buffy* and *Twilight* were and are both marketed and widely consumed as teen love stories that happened to include a cast of vampires. These media viruses "spread for one reason ... as long as [their] memes stay shrouded ... the cultural immune apparatus remains unprovoked and the virus is free to run rampant" (Rushkoff 115–116). By promoting the texts in a way that is appealing to teenagers and seemingly superficial to the disengaged consumer, the internal codes of love, passion, desire, and of course, the promise of a prospective "happily ever after" are passed on from generation to generation, from cold and flu season to cold and flu season.

Welcoming and internalizing the media virus is critical to its successful transmission throughout society. As Rushkoff explains, "the attacking virus uses its protective and sticky protein casing to latch onto a healthy cell and then inject its own genetic code inside" (9), which in media terms essentially says, "How do we make this look so interesting and exciting that people will buy it up, even though we're using themes and morals that have been around for centuries?" In the case of both *Buffy the Vampire Slayer* and *Twilight,* the protein shells have been modernized to suit a late 90s/early millennial audience, but the genetic code (morals and ideas) encased within them resonate back to Hans Christian Anderson and the Brothers Grimm. Both *Buffy the Vampire Slayer* and the *Twilight* saga offer an appealing protein shell. *Buffy* aired on both the WB and UPN networks, each known for their programs appealing to a teenage audience. The *Buffy* boxed set of DVDs followed suit by presenting a white box with what appeared to be blood dripping from the top. In comparison, the *Twilight* saga covers are minimalist in their design: black glossy covers with simple red and white photo-graphics that don't really suggest much about the actual plot of the story. More recently, however, the covers of the individual *Buffy* seasons on DVD and the new movie-inspired book covers of the *Twilight* saga resonate more with the previously discussed allusions to the relationship between the beautiful girl, who likely will be the fairytale princess, and the righteous hero, who usually is a prince. On some packages of the individual seasons of *Buffy,* particularly the early seasons, we see Sarah Michelle Gellar (Buffy) in an embrace with David Boreanez (Angel), a position that is mirrored on the new *Twilight* book cover between Kristen Stewart (Bella) and Robert Pattinson (Edward). These images from both *Buffy the Vampire Slayer* and the *Twilight* saga highlight the way in which this relationship between the beautiful girl and the "hero" is the central focus and purpose of the texts, continuing to perpetuate the fictionalized ideas of perfect romance without much sign of alteration.

If the covers of *Buffy* and *Twilight* are the protein shell — a seemingly innocuous structure with unknown materials inside, as Rushkoff suggests — then the actual material of the texts are the genetic code hidden inside the virus. Encased within this protein shell are the memes, which are explained by Rushkoff as the ideas and concepts within the text that have been placed there to have a specific influence on the audience (much like the genetic code within a biological virus), "battling our own genes in an attempt to change the way our cells operate. The only 'intention' of the virus, if it can be said to have one, is to spread its own code as far and wide as possible" (9). The genetic code, in the case of a media virus (as opposed to a regular cold and flu virus — though, again, they operate the same way), is the core moral and social ideas represented within the text. These ideas are both directly stated by the characters and implied through their actions. Initially, the *Twilight* saga was thought simply to be a stereotypical teen love story that happened to feature vampires — not worthy of much attention or concern. However, within the *Twilight* saga, there are potent memes present centering on the consequences of choice and the value of relationships. It is not enough, in this fairy tale, to slay the dragon (or the Volturi) with swords and might. There must be true love ever present, or the "good guys" will lose.

Throughout the four books in the saga, Bella is constantly faced with choices; choices that are motivated by her love for Edward. In fact, it is this love that saves their lives repeatedly. For example, in *New Moon,* Aro senses the appeal that Bella's blood creates for Edward and marvels at the fact that the two of them choose to stand beside each other regardless of the danger and pressures it creates. This tension carries over into *Eclipse* when Bella, adamant in her decision to be changed into a vampire after graduation, is faced with the possibility of choosing Jacob (and therefore remaining human) instead of Edward. Screenwriter Melissa Rosenberg succinctly highlights the memes present in the novels through the graduation speech presented by Anna Kendrick's character Jessica in the film version of *Eclipse.* In Jessica's speech, she states that "this isn't the time to make hard and fast decisions; this is the time to make mistakes" (*Eclipse* 2010). This speech, in light of the choices Bella is facing, indicates the spread of *Twilight's* viral code, which is that the choices we make have permanent consequences. As such, the reasons for making those choices need to be motivated by pure intentions, such as true love. By presenting the memes in two different ways, developed slowly in the novels and presented overtly in the films, their impact on the audience is stronger and more widespread.

The final book in the saga, *Breaking Dawn,* presents the accumulation of the choices Bella makes and the consequences that befall those choices. For example, Bella's transformation from human to vampire is not only a result of her desire; it is a direct consequence of her decision to carry and give birth to her daughter, Renesmee. It is at this point in *Breaking Dawn* that the second most powerful meme — the value of relationships — becomes most apparent. Bella's choices are no longer about her as an individual; they are about her husband, the rest of her family, and now her daughter as well. These actions lead to the final face-off with the Volturi, when Bella must use her shield to protect herself, the other Cullens, and their friends from the Volturi's special powers. One such power is the ability to detect and sever relationships. The way that Stephenie Meyer introduces this power in a significant, climactic moment in the saga is an example of how she is implementing the viral code. If the Volturi (who are the inherent "bad guys") want to break the ties that bind the couples and the families, then the "good guys" (the Cullens and, hopefully, us as readers) need to be in support of staying connected to one another and valuing the strength of relationships, both within the saga itself and, once we have internalized the genetic code of the virus, in our own non-fictional relationships. This is the true power and effect of a media virus. In the same way that Prince Charming, Lloyd Dobler, and Edward Cullen promote interpretations of the perfect man, the complete story lines and character interactions promote desirable behaviors and philosophies that we, the viewers and readers, are expected to take with us outside of the text. If *Twilight* were an actual biological virus rather than the media kind, it might be compared to a mild version of the seasonal flu; it's the kind you hope you catch so you're just sick enough to stay home from work in your pajamas, but not so sick that you can't enjoy whatever bad daytime TV you chose to flip on as you lounge on the couch. Essentially, readers can still be "infected" by the ideas present in the text, but only to a slight degree; just enough to fulfill a temporary desire or fantasy.

In order for the memes to infiltrate society, the virus must continue to spread, and for a substantial amount of time. Since the release of the first book in 2005, popularity has continually surged, and not just among teenage girls. As Rushkoff notes, "the most imaginative of kids' shows appeal to the parents, too" (100); the same is true of books. Though marketed and shelved as a young adult/teen book, the audience for *Twilight* has expanded well beyond that initial classification. In fact, one of the most popular *Twilight*-themed fan sites on the internet is *Twilight*MOMS. As the "About" section of the site notes, it is a forum for "Fans of the *Twilight* series in OUR stage of life ... OUR world of balancing home, work, family, marriage AND our *Twilight* obsession" (*Twilight*MOMS.com). In order to become a member of the site and begin posting to the forums, users must electronically verify through a survey that they are either married, have children, or are at least 25 years of age. The site boasts thousands of members, confirming Rushkoff's assertion that media viruses, like biological viruses, don't discriminate based on age or any other demographic factor; once the virus is unleashed on society, anyone can become infected. *Twilight*MOMS is just one of the hundreds of fan sites that shows how *Twilight* in its many forms, from books to films to merchandise, is "manipulat[ing] adult culture by doing more than one thing with media at the same time" (Rushkoff 125). The spreading infatuation with the *Twilight* saga beyond the perceived intended young adult audience presents an interesting new direction for media initially oriented towards a teenage population. Despite the fact that Meyer has ended the series as told from Bella's perspective, she does claim on her website that "maybe part of me is protecting those secrets because I'm not ready to leave my vampires behind" (n.p.). In the summer of 2010, Meyer did release another novella from the perspective of Bree Tanner, a newborn vampire who initially was only featured in one scene in *Eclipse*. Beyond Bree's story, there is no news of other novels in process. However, Summit Entertainment has begun production of the film adaptation of *Breaking Dawn*, which they have announced will be split into two feature films with the first being released on November 18, 2011, and the second being released on November 16, 2012 (*The Official Website of Stephenie Meyer*). As such, the virus shows no signs of weakening, at least for the foreseeable future. Again, in this way *Twilight* is much like a seasonal flu. There will be people who get vaccinated, the media virus equivalent of which might be not reading the books or seeing the films. There will be people who suffer more severely than others from lack of treatment or medication, or in media terms, a lack of having analytical conversations and being exposed alternative perspectives from other texts. And then there will be the majority of us, who will be affected temporarily to some degree, may retain a pathogen or two, but in general will get up, move on, and wait for the next viral attack to come along.

The *Twilight* saga, and its predecessor *Buffy the Vampire Slayer*, enjoy popularity due to their traditional roots. From Disney's versions of classic fairy tales to Meyer's "new vampire" in Edward Cullen, we are presented continually with the story where "the unlikely hero proves himself ... until eventually he frees the beautiful princess, marries her, and lives happily ever after" (Bettelheim 111). By using marketing techniques that create a strong media virus, Joss Whedon and Stephenie Meyer were able to create and sell this vampire love interest with the same foundational techniques as used to craft fairytale heroes. This has proved to be an enticing formula, as Angel and Edward followed the same patterns and behaviors as Prince Charming and, much to Chuck Klosterman's dismay, even Lloyd Dobler. Society has been bitten by these new vampires, and that is a transformation that cannot be undone. No longer will we wait to hear the coming hoof beats of a white horse in the distance; instead, we're listening for the low engine rumbling of a shiny silver Volvo.

NOTES

1. Referring to the 1991 Walt Disney Company animated feature, *Beauty and the Beast.*
2. For further definition and examples of Klosterman's "fake love," see the chapter titled "This Is Emo" in *Sex, Drugs, and Cocoa Puffs.*
3. Referring to the 1994 film *Interview with the Vampire* starring Tom Cruise and Brad Pitt, based on the first book from Anne Rice's vampire series, *The Vampire Chronicles.*
4. While there have been some literary incarnations of sympathetic vampires, they haven't enjoyed the popular culture awareness awarded to both Angel and Edward. Even if the idea of this type of vampire is not new, *Buffy the Vampire Slayer* and especially the *Twilight* saga do represent the first two texts to have such a severe impact on culture as a whole, rather than just on academic elite or cult-classic audiences.
5. The film *Buffy the Vampire Slayer* shows Buffy as a senior in high school. The movie ends with Buffy riding off on the back of her human boyfriend's motorcycle. The series, however, started with Buffy as a sophomore in high school, briefly explaining in Season 1 that the events of the movie were supposed to have taken place during her freshman year instead.
6. There is an admittedly reasonable argument that this transformation actually began much earlier, with Anne Rice's *Vampire Chronicles.* Specifically, critics point to the character of Louis de Pointe du Lac in *Interview with the Vampire.* However, while Louis does seem cursed with a conscience and admittedly struggles with guilt, he still maintains more of the traditional monster-vampire traits as opposed to prince-vampire traits. Most significantly, he fails to ever carry on a successful vampire/human relationship, which Angel and Edward both do.
7. In Grimm's tale, Snow came back to life when a clumsy dwarf trips and jostles the glass coffin, dislodging the poisoned fruit from her mouth. While the ending is essentially the same (she lives and is able to marry the prince), the Disney version aligns romance and power. He loves her, so he saves her, and in return, she loves him back.

8. "Girl" is the most appropriate term in these stories, since most of the leading females were under the age of 18 (much like our recent "princesses," Buffy and Bella).

9. In Disney's adaptation of *Beauty and the Beast,* Belle's father is captured by the Beast for trespassing in his castle. While imprisoned, Belle's father becomes very ill. In order to save him, Belle offers herself as the Beast's prisoner, so that her father may be freed.

10. Plus, if she wanted to be a wife and mother only, she would have/could have chosen Jacob, or any human character for that matter.

WORKS CITED

Angel: Television Series. Dirs. David Greenwalt and Joss Whedon. Perf. David Boreanez, Alexis Denisof. Twentieth Century–Fox Television, 1999–2004. DVD.

Auerbach, Nina. *Our Vampires, Ourselves.* Chicago: University of Chicago Press, 1995.

Beauty and the Beast. Dirs. Kirk Wise and Gary Trousdale. Perf. Paige O'Hara, Robby Benson. Walt Disney Pictures, 1992. DVD.

Bettleheim, Bruno. "The Struggle for Meaning." *Folk & Fairy Tales.* 4th ed. Eds. Martin Hallett and Barbara Karasek. Toronto, ON: Broadview, 2009. 323–335.

_____. *The Uses of Enchantment: The Meaning and Importance of Fairy Tales.* New York: Vintage Books, 1977.

Buffy the Vampire Slayer: Television Series. Dir. Joss Whedon. Perf. Sarah Michelle Gellar, David Boreanaz. Twentieth Century–Fox Television, 1997–2003. DVD.

Doane, Mary Ann. "'*Caught*' and '*Rebecca*': The Inscription of Femininity as Absence." *Feminist Film Theory: A Reader.* Ed. Sue Thornham. New York: New York University Press, 1999. 146–156.

Eclipse. Dir. David Slade. Perf. Kristen Stewart, Robert Pattinson. Summit Entertainment, 2010.

Hallett, Martin, and Barbara Karasek. "Introduction." *Folk & Fairy Tales.* 4th ed. Eds. Martin Hallett and Barbara Karasek. Toronto, ON: Broadview, 2009. 15–25.

Hendrix, Grady. "Vampires Suck: Actually, They Don't, and That's a Problem." *Slate* 28 July 2009. Web. 23 March 2010.

Interview with the Vampire. Dir. Neil Jordan. Perf. Brad Pitt, Tom Cruise. Warner Brothers Pictures, 1994. Blu-Ray.

Kirschling, Greg. "Stephenie Meyer's 'Twilight' Zone." *Entertainment Weekly* 5 July 2008. Web. 23 March 2010.

Klosterman, Chuck. *Sex, Drugs, and Cocoa Puffs*: A Low Culture Manifesto (Now With a New Middle).* New York: Scribner, 2003.

Kuhn, Anette. "Women's Genres: Melodrama, Soap Opera, and Theory." *Feminist Film Theory: A Reader.* Ed. Sue Thornham. New York: New York University Press, 1999. 146–156.

Lüthi, Max. "The Fairy-Tale Hero: The Image of Man in the Fairy Tales." *Folk & Fairy Tales.* 4th ed. Eds. Martin Hallett and Barbara Karasek. Toronto, ON: Broadview, 2009. 315–323.

Meyer, Stephenie. *Breaking Dawn.* New York: Hachette Book Group, 2008.

_____. *Eclipse.* New York: Hachette Book Group, 2007.

_____. "Midnight Sun." *The Official Stephenie Meyer Website,* StephenieMeyer.com, 28 August 2008. Web. 6 June 2010.

_____. *New Moon.* New York: Hachette Book Group, 2006.

_____. *Twilight.* New York: Hachette Book Group, 2005.

New Moon. Dir. Chris Weitz. Perf. Kristin Stewart, Taylor Lautner. Summit Entertainment, 2009. Blu-Ray.

Rushkoff, Douglas. *Media Virus.* New York: Ballantine Books, 1996.

Say Anything. Dir. Cameron Crowe. Perf. John Cusack, Ione Skye. Twentieth Century–Fox, 1989. DVD.

Sleeping Beauty. Dir. Clyde Gionimi. Perf. Mary Costa, Bill Shirley. Walt Disney Pictures, 1959. Blu-Ray.

Snow White and the Seven Dwarfs. Dir. David Hand. Perf. Adriana Caselotti, Lucille La Verne. Walt Disney Pictures, 1938. DVD.

Tartar, Maria. *The Hard Facts of the Grimms Fairy Tales.* Princeton: Princeton University Press, 1987.

Twilight. Dir. Catherine Hardwick. Perf. Kristin Stewart, Robert Pattinson. Summit Entertainment, 2008. Blu-Ray.

Unknown. "About." *TwilightMOMS.* www.*Twilight*MOMS.com. Web. 28 November 2008.

Zipes, Jack. "Breaking the Disney Spell." *The Classic Fairy Tales.* Ed. Maria Tartar. New York: W.W. Norton & Co., 1999. 332–352.

Team Bella
Fans Navigating Desire, Security, and Feminism

ANANYA MUKHERJEA

In this chapter, I consider some aspects of what motivates and captivates *Twilight* fans and, in particular: (1) how they relate to themes of desire, personal boundaries, and romance; and (2) how the fans negotiate the books' oftentimes contradictory relationship to female agency, sexuality, and feminism. I begin with my own reading of the *Twilight* phenomenon and what I see to be its conservative and anti-feminist underpinnings and then discuss some surveys and interviews with self-described fans of the franchise.

Many of the fans whose words are represented here self-identified as feminist, queer, and/or queer-friendly, and yet they described finding affirming or even emancipatory messages in these books that I found, certainly, to be often enchanting but, also, usually entrenched in gender-conservative, heterosexist, or sexually repressive norms. This apparent contradiction between their readings and my own was intriguing to me, and investigating this discrepancy is the motivation for this chapter. Many girls, women and non-heterosexual boys and men — who do not, as a rule, see their desires driving popular blockbuster franchises — do, in fact, feel that *Twilight* represents and legitimates those desires by identifying them with *Bella's desires* as the driving force of the story (I present data to substantiate this claim). Because these readers identified with Bella's point of view and feelings — hence, Team Bella — this study seeks to treat those desires and perspectives seriously and to inquire into their nature and implications.

The Culture and Politics of Contemporary Abstinence Ideology

First, let me provide some sociopolitical context within which to consider the *Twilight* phenomenon and some of the ways fans engage with it. As is well known to fans and critics, Stephenie Meyer tempers the passionate love story between Bella and Edward with lessons about what constitutes appropriate or inappropriate romantic behavior. In particular, the abstinence message in *Twilight* is clear, with Edward articulating to Bella in *Eclipse* that it is better that they wait, in the interest of her soul and maybe his as well, until after they are married to have sex (*E* 452–454). Edward is an unusual leading man in being so adamant about abstinence until marriage, and he is even more unusual in the fact that he has maintained his own virginity for all of his 108 years. Their marriage obviates the need for such sacrifices, though, so that by the middle of *Breaking Dawn,* the reader is assured that Bella and Edward enjoy an active marital sex life. This commentary on the importance of marriage to sex and romance is a key feature of what initially set *Twilight* apart from many other romances but, as well, of a trend in young adult fiction in contrast to more sexually frank, realist literature of the same genre (see, for example, Judy Blume's *Tiger Eyes* or Laurie Halse Anderson's *Prom*). As *Twilight* fan Marta said about part of the contradictory appeal of *Twilight,* "[It's] all the steaminess without the sex."

In her brilliant history of abstinence culture in the 21st century United States (see, especially, chapter 4), Dagmar Herzog describes how the religious Right's contemporary proscription on all sex and sexual behaviors (including deep kissing and petting) before marriage is frequently justified by the belief that properly marital sex can only stay exciting and intimate if both partners enter their union in a chaste condition. She quotes the website www.Love-Matters.com as stating, "Sex is Awesome! ... But sex before marriage has emotional consequences that can bring lifelong pain" (Herzog 96). Herzog makes the point that premarital chastity is not encouraged on the grounds that all sex is wrong or dirty but, rather, on the grounds that only one kind of sex is right. "Normal" sexual desires are not shoved aside in this rhetoric but placed front and center; only, these desires — especially those of girls and women — are shown to need careful, vigilant control in order to be correctly practiced and likely to be satisfied in the long run. The goal is not to prevent sex from happening but to restrict "morally valid" sexuality to specific circumstances and specific acts between specific people. In addition to increasing pressure to marry young, as Bella does in *Breaking Dawn,* Don Monkerud explains that the abstinence-until-marriage precept denies the right of sexual expression to lesbians and gays, who still are not allowed to marry legally in most U.S. states.

Meyer's series deals with Bella's and Edward's sexuality along these same lines of abstinence ideology, from both characters' virginal status at the beginning of their relationship to Edward's refusal to have sex with Bella until after they are married. Bella learns early on to hold very still and resist the urges of her lust when Edward kisses her, to help him maintain the control necessary to prevent his accidentally killing her. Meyer also explained, in an interview with the website *Twilight Lexicon*, that the venom in Edward's mouth prevents what she called "true snogging" with the human Bella, precluding open-mouthed kisses and other intimacies that might result in the transfer of saliva ("Personal Correspondance [sic] 5"). Each of Meyer's vampires chooses one, true, eternal mate, and there are no gay characters or explicit references to homosexuality at all. Lesser characters might divorce (Charlie and Renee) or conceive children out of wedlock (the mystery surrounding Embry's parentage in *Eclipse*), but these characters produce pain and embarrassment with their actions. Vampire love, in contrast, is presented as perfect, effortlessly monogamous, stable, and endlessly satisfying. Meyer makes it very clear that, after her transformation, vampire Edward and vampire Bella are truly married as equal partners and vigorously enjoy sex as spouses, filling their sleepless nights with their love-making and looking forward to an eternity of more of the same (see *BD*, book 3). Sexuality is not absent in the series. On the contrary, it is ubiquitous, but it is carefully constrained.

Herzog argues that the cultural and political influence of abstinence ideology that grew around the turn of the 21st century revolves around a preoccupation, not only with controlling sexual activity, but also with an anxious need for some way to ensure that sexual relationships can be long-lasting and sexually vibrant in the long term. Further, this culture lionizes purity, virginity, and virgins, encouraging even those who have "made mistakes" before marriage to take new vows of premarital chastity and to choose a "secondary virginity." In *Twilight,* I would read Jasper as representative of someone who lived an indulgent but unsatisfying life before finding true happiness, albeit scarred by regret and cravings, within the secure bounds of his "marriage" to Alice and the "vegetarianism" of the Cullen's. His history of himself, as he recounts it to Bella in the movie version of *Eclipse*, describes how he only learned what real love was from Alice, who introduced him to the Cullens and another way of living from what he had known before. As Herzog writes,

> There are plenty of reasons why young people can find these [abstinence until marriage] messages appealing…. They may not be ready for the potential emotional intensities of a relationship that includes sex — or, on the flip side, they may wish for

romance but are finding only offers of intercourse. The individual's right to say no —anytime, anywhere (a right for which the feminist movement fought long and hard from the 1970s through to the 1990s)— and the moral imperative of consent in sexual relations has been respun into a one-size-fits-all program that says everyone should say no before marriage. It has left no room for people, especially girls, to negotiate practices, to say, "No, not that, but yes, this," making female sexual agency once again seem dirty and suspect. The abstinence movement also succeeds because it is a self-help and self-improvement movement that holds out the promise of perfection [Herzog 99].

The abstinence movement, then, attracts followers because they feel real needs or worries that the movement promises to answer, assuaging anxieties through new vows. I agree with Herzog, however, that the rigidity of the precepts of an abstinence doctrine leave little room for individual preference, exploration, or negotiation and, in particular, disavows all homosexuality and renders female sexuality into a static object to be preserved or given rather than a capacity to be understood and safely developed.

The abstinence movement that can forgive premarital and extramarital heterosexual transgressions as long as new vows are made cannot seem to tolerate homosexuality at all. There have been no calls for chastity until gay marriage (see, for example, Monkerud's critique of the homophobia inherent in abstinence programming, 2009). Instead, as Herzog points out, gays and lesbians and other queers ranged from being portrayed, "as a major source of spiritual and social danger for mainstream America" (71), to, "victims to be pitied" (79), and retrained into heterosexuality by "ex-gay" organizations like Exodus International. That premarital and extramarital chastity has been championed by the same conservative religious and political groups that have found all forms of homosexuality to be intolerable and "unnatural" is hardly news in the post–Bush era, and the fact that Stephenie Meyer's notions of ideal love, romance, and sex are strongly influenced by her Mormon beliefs is not contested either, even by Meyer. Theater scholar Marc E. Shaw, in fact, calls the *Twilight* series a, "textual renewal of Meyer's faith and her commitment, which ties back to the teachings ... in the [LDS] Church" (229). Again, Meyer's perfect, "vegetarian" vampires resist premarital sex and form eternal marital unions, and there seems to be no homosexuality in her world.

What I have offered thus far is my understanding of how Meyer's story abuts and intersects with some of the politics surrounding abstinence ideology in the contemporary U.S. I read the overt message of the *Twilight* saga as very much in line with the defense of the conservative, Christian, heterosexually married family *over and against other ways of living and loving*, and it is this aspect of the abstinence ideology discussed here that I find most problematic. The major religious and political groups that backed George W. Bush's abstinence education policy also strive to censor all other discussion about teenage sexuality, to vilify homosexuality and other religious groups, and to subvert and contain the role of women in society. Contemporary abstinence culture is inextricably enmeshed with these other sociopolitical positions, and the resultant politic is insupportably intolerant and dangerous in its disinformation.

Nevertheless, there are more complicated *latent* messages about gender and sexuality available in *Twilight*, and some of my queer and/or feminist and/or queer-friendly respondents found those messages to be affirming. This contradiction is at the heart of the larger question I ask and explore in the remainder of this chapter. What is the interpretative work that *Twilight* fans do with the text? In particular, how do they come to recognize their own desires and perspectives in Meyer's characters and plot turns and, moreover, how do gay or otherwise queer and/or feminist readers engage with an explicitly traditionalist series?

The Fans

The data from which I draw here are the results of the first stage of a study based on surveying and interviewing self-characterized *Twilight* fans in two major metropolitan areas on the East Coast of the U.S. The participants in this first stage of the study comprise about twenty fans between the ages of eighteen and forty-one, the majority of whom are working class or middle class and of mixed racial and immigration biographies. They come from a variety of religious backgrounds (Muslim; Hindu; Jewish; Christian, specifically Roman Catholic; agnostic). Fourteen respondents self-identified as feminist. All the respondents consider themselves *Twilight* fans, although several also express discomfort with some of the messages or content of the books or movies. All the respondents freely, even enthusiastically, volunteered to participate in this study, fully informed about its goals and methods and eager to talk about their *Twilight* experiences. To maintain full anonymity and confidentiality, however, each participant has been assigned a pseudonym, and specific identifying characteristics have been omitted or blurred. Because this is a sampling of the results of this first stage of the study, the remainder of this essay is not meant to be a definitive explanation of how desire, security, and feminism figure as factors in the *Twilight* fandom. Rather, its goal is to show why it is worthwhile to take the fans, and their work of reading, seriously, and to consider how the above listed factors relate to their experience of the *Twilight* phenomenon.

In her much cited book, *Reading the Romance,* Janice Radway spoke with women who read mass marketed romance novels. As has been the case with much public response to *Twilight* fans, Radway was intrigued and unsettled by the way romance readers were frequently intellectually dismissed. When she spoke with them, though, she learned that they read strategically and selectively. They chose the kinds of romance novels they wanted to read carefully and were articulate about why they chose those kinds of romances over others. They used their reading time actively to decompress and relax, to revive themselves for the child-rearing, housekeeping, and paid labor they had to do, and they read the books critically, often in groups of women with whom they discussed what they read joyfully and intelligently.

Meyer's books are, of course, romances, but what intrigued me was the spectacular surge of popularity of this particular series. Why, I wondered, were so very many readers so very captivated by *these* books? It is important to note that Radway did not suggest that romance novels themselves are necessarily sophisticated in their production. Instead, her study focused on the work that goes into reading them. Similarly, when writing the *Twilight* books, Meyer was a very new author without formal training as a writer. Despite her relatively unpracticed writing and plot production and the pressure of market-driven deadlines for what proved to be an increasingly lucrative series, she did produce something undeniably compelling; one simply need look at the sheer scale of fan reaction and of the profit margin of the franchise to see that. The *Twilight* series does provide ample fantasy and wish fulfillment for the involved reader, but it is not unique in doing so. Much popular fiction and most mass marketed romances provide fantasy, wish fulfillment, and escapism: that is their marketing bread-and-butter. Why, then, does this one, four-part piece of popular romance generate so much and such intense fan devotion?

The data presented here are meant to show that many *Twilight* fans do use the books to produce joy and supportive sociality for themselves and to bolster themselves against the pressures of their lives. As well, the overt abstinence-until-marriage message of the franchise, so disturbing to me, does not necessarily prevent fans from using the story as an outlet for their own desires or, in a couple cases, to better comprehend their own sexuality.

Desiring Men: Scopophilia, Sexuality, and Finding Comfortable Boundaries

Nineteen-year-old Marta, when asked what she found most compelling about the books, answered, without hesitation, that she loved that they offered what she called, "an epic love story," and that she found in Edward, "a kind of perfect man, that you could trust," as much as desire. Twenty-three-year-old Michael, also definitely Team Edward, agreed with Marta, saying, "Edward's a man. He could take care of you and meet all your needs. Jacob's just a kid. He doesn't know what he wants yet." Eighteen-year-old Cecily demurred, preferring Jacob because, "He's ... so gorgeous, but he also just really loves Bella and he just wants whatever's best for her, what *she wants*" (emphasis mine). A majority of respondents, in answering questions about which characters they liked the most and why, dwelt in detail on both the moral fiber and the physical attributes of their favorite male character, frequently overlapping the two. Cecily's twenty-year-old sister Amanda told me, about her favorite secondary character, "I like Jasper. I like how, in the book, he's so tall and protective, all like a lion and, in the movie, he's so little but he's still got the great hair and is totally athletic," following this with a minute narration of his movements and facial expressions in the movie *Twilight* and about his willingness to be wounded in order to shield Alice in the book *Eclipse*.

All these respondents admitted to watching the first movie repeatedly and to rereading favorite scenes in the books over and over, as they tried to visualize exactly how they happened. Forty-year-old Flora said of watching *Twilight* repeatedly in the theater with her teenage daughter, "I loved it. I just focused on a different man each time because they're all so good looking.... That's not how I thought Edward would look like before, but that's how I see him when I read the books now."

Few readers mentioned gazing at the female characters in the same lingering way, even when they liked and identified with them. Gazing upon the men, however, whether in the words on the page or on the screen of the film, was a central feature of the pleasure all the respondents took in *Twilight*. The joys of scopophilia, the love of looking, have historically been the privilege of men — often men gazing appreciatively at other men or boys but usually men looking at women. Angela McRobbie, in *Feminism and Youth Culture: From Jackie to Just Seventeen*, describes how the emergence of magazines aimed at an audience of teenage girls and young women gave them, for good and for bad, images and objects to ogle and desire. They offered instruction, too, in ways to evaluate or communicate what they saw and wanted, using catchwords like, "'scrummy hunk'; 'dishy' ... a language of action, of 'good times,' of enjoyment, and of consumerism" (McRobbie 98).

Building texts around the bodies of desired men might be a relatively new phenomenon. The male leads in Austen and Brontë novels may have been beguiling, but they were seldom perfect. Even as the reader admires Mr. Darcy's height or Mr. Rochester's expressive brow or either man's bank account, s/he is left with relatively little information about what the man looks like *precisely.* Popular romance novels and the newer genre of "chick lit" lavish many words on such description, and Meyer's descriptions of Edward and Jacob are vivid and lovingly detailed. While Shaw argues that the gazing upon in *Twilight* is powerful because it is "bidirectional" and "conversational," he also points out that, "because Meyer fixates on Edward, *Twilight* returns the gaze that is usually reserved for men looking at women ... makes us gaze through Bella's eyes at Edward's beauty, [objectifying him]" (235).

Reveling in this scopophilia can also be a social bonding activity. Another respondent, Anthony, twenty-one, explained that his female cousins had been benignly tolerant of his being gay ever since he came out to his fairly conservative family but that they had never broached the topic with him. When one cousin learned that he was a *Twilight* fan, however, she immediately asked which "team" he was on and then launched into a detailed discussion of Edward *vs.* Jacob. She was eager to discuss the books and, in particular, her love for both Edward and Jacob and, in talking all this over with Anthony, asked him an increasingly personal series of questions about what he found appealing about each male lead character and how Anthony imagined his ideal man. His sexuality suddenly seemed to be a non-issue, taken for granted and secondary in importance to his ability to have opinions on Edward, Jacob, and men as the objects of romance.

Like Bella herself, *Twilight* fans, especially female fans, are caught in a tight spot, and this might be where my reading of the dominant gender message of the books meets that of many fans. They may be desiring subjects, and they may enjoy the looking, but they also often feel the need to constrain that desire, to reign it in within proper bounds. Edward thwarts Bella's efforts to have sex with him in *Eclipse* by telling her that he is worried for her soul. To have "a shot at heaven," he argues, "... the vast majority seem to think that there are some rules that have to be followed ... and I'm going to do my best to keep you out of temptation's way." He tells her that, by postponing sex until after they are married, he means to protect both her virtue and his own (*E* 453–454). Initially hurt and frustrated by Edward's refusal, Bella does relent, eventually to what she perceives as his greater experience and wisdom on this issue but, immediately, to his superior physical strength, which binds and keeps her hands away from his clothes. This is an example of the slippery, contradictory nature of Meyer's narration. When Edward restrains Bella's hands and covers her mouth to silence her during this passionate moment in his bed, it is to *prevent* their having sex. The expected event is carefully set up but is not completed. As Herzog describes the quasi-pornographic quality of some abstinence texts, titillating details are provided in abundance, but they are presented in the name of serving the larger abstinence message (see chapter 2 of Herzog 2008). The film version of *Eclipse* conveyed the central message about waiting until they are married but significantly toned down the physical force Edward uses in this scene.

Flora is an avid *Twilight* fan in her own right, but she maintains to her daughter and husband that she reads the books and watches the movies repeatedly to support her daughter's preoccupation with the franchise. Asked if this was because she was embarrassed by the young adult marketing of the stories, she answered, "No, that's fine. But the youth is, you know, a problem because I'm married, and to a really nice guy, and what would he think about how much I love these romance stories? [I don't want to tell my daughter] it's okay to be married and also to be thinking about some other guy, even if he's not real...." Thirty-nine-year-old Magda told me that her husband tolerates her *Twilight* "obsession" (her word) with equanimity because it "makes [her] happy" and also because he never reads books or magazines and, therefore, has no idea what the series is about. "I would die if he knew that I spend all day dreaming about these high school guys!" Cecily and Amanda's parents do not allow them to date, and both girls said that Edward or Jacob stood in as a sort of surrogate boyfriend in their lives so that the franchise and the time they spent talking about it to each other and their friends took the place of dating, keeping them from feeling its absence as a loss.

Accepting Edward and Jacob as ready objects of desire, then, allowed these fans to be desiring subjects and to indulge some pleasurable actions of desire — the looking and fantasizing and talking about. For Anthony, sharing his desire for these fictional objects allowed him to breach a social boundary that had previously isolated him in his family. For Cecily and Amanda, this same action allowed them to respect a social boundary their family required of them. For Flora and Magda, maintaining expected gender boundaries required a strategic articulation of their desire for *Twilight*'s men.

Security and Protection: Envying Bella and Her Benevolently Paternal Lover

Herzog writes that some of the successes of the abstinence movement are due to the fact that it addresses anxieties that have surfaced in response to the rapidly changing gender roles and sexual standards of the turn of this century. Ariel Levy, in her book *Female Chauvinist Pigs*, argues that what she calls "raunch culture"—a sort of antithesis or reaction to abstinence culture in its emphasis on overt and casual sexuality— now encourages young women to put their bodies and their desirability, if not desires, on display and to constantly push their comfort zones with respect to what they are at ease exposing on a number of levels. This pressure is couched as an opportunity for these women (and, I would argue, young gay men often find themselves in the same position) to assert their individuality and resistance to repression, but raunch culture still prioritizes the dominant male gaze. Whereas abstinence culture cautions young people about the uncontrollability of male desire and the need to reign it in at the beginning, before deep kissing or partial nudity cause it to spiral out of control, raunch culture urges the need to exploit it and use it for power, employing stripper-inspired fashion, for example, to maintain focus, to gain power by becoming the object of desire. The ends are different, but the assumption is the same: that most men are simple, hormone-driven, power-hungry beasts. Therefore, young women, young gay men, and the supposedly rare, ethical man who wants an emotional life beyond his sexual urges, must accept this first fact in order to either suppress it with discipline (abstinence culture) or exploit it for status (raunch culture).

It is a reductive understanding of the complex psychic space where sexuality, emotions, and intellect meet. Regardless, it feels like the truth to many people, and several respondents reported feeling stressed or dissatisfied by their attempts to find their own sexual ideals between the demands of abstinence culture, on the one hand, and raunch culture on the other and using *Twilight* as a vehicle to develop their own ideals. Marta said that she appreciated that, "In the books, the romance is the main thing.... They are really steamy, so I enjoy that, but I appreciate ... all the steaminess without the sex." And Michael described an exhausting date-night out with his boyfriend, during which they had been harassed by homophobic patrons at the restaurant where they ate and then worn down by the loud music and crowd at the gay bar they went to for drinks afterward. "So we just went home and it was so quiet and nice, and I was thinking about how Edward and Bella lie around in her bed, just talking how they want, like in that scene in the movie, and they just feel safe and trust each other [creating their own romantic expectations]." Both Marta and Michael said they identified with Bella's perspective and her strong feelings for the kind of man Edward is and the ways in which they perceive her successfully working to create her own romantic standards and destiny.

Flora and Grace Ann both explained that they approved the books as appropriate reading for their young teenage daughters because it gave them a "safe" outlet for exploring the growing need the girls had for romance and physical relationships. Thirty-seven-year-old Gwen also identified with Bella and said, of taking her boyfriend to see *Twilight* in the theater, "He couldn't identify with it ... I started having sex really young, though, so it's definitely like a guilty pleasure, but it's [also] like a parallel universe from mine, [one] where you get all the whispering and hand-holding you want." As Gwen read the scene from *Eclipse* discussed above, when Bella makes sexual overtures towards Edward, she is neither met with harsh judgment nor with a stronger response from him than she can handle. She does not get what she wants and has her proposals firmly turned down, but Edward's rejection of her advances is framed as benevolent, caring, and respectful.

Susan Faludi, in her book *Stiffed: The Betrayal of the American Man*, comments on the unease that accompanies rapidly changing gender roles, especially for men, as the many opportunities opened up by such change can be obscured by instability and uncertainty. Despite developing new and more flexible ways to engage with fatherhood, sexuality, and emotions, the lack of a clear masculine life-path for many men can affect their self-concept and their relationships with women and with other men, sometimes negatively (see chapters 2 and 3, Faludi 1999). Edward Cullen, with his "old-school" ideas about love and sex, as Bella describes them, and his certainty about exactly what is entailed in his "job description" as a husband, has a strikingly clear — if also rigid, or as he repeatedly describes himself, frozen — vision about exactly what constitutes correct, masculine behavior. As one male respondent put it, "I kind of envy his instincts about what he should do with Bella." Even when he seems to waver, in his early pursuit of Bella in *Twilight* or his offer to have sex with her before their marriage at the end of *Eclipse*, he is ultimately proven right in his inclinations. For many readers, he offers great stability in the clarity of his role and the steadiness of his feelings.

Edward Cullen also represents a more literal sort of security, a level of masculine protectiveness towards his partner that is extreme — and sometimes unsettling — but also extremely alluring for many. Twenty-one-year-old Giulietta was very clear that, while she enjoyed the galloping adventure of the *Twilight* books, she enjoyed it knowing that Edward could not really be harmed himself and that, after the first volume, it became clear that he could not physically harm Bella, nor suffer any physical harm to come to her. This material security was a significant piece of the *Twilight* fantasy for her. In a group discussion with several young female fans, they turned the conversation to a comparison with the Rihanna/Chris Brown intimate violence scandal that was then unfolding in the press. How wonderful would it be, they concurred, to know you could trust your partner entirely to put your safety and well-being first and foremost? They agreed that the safety that Edward offers Bella is a central aspect of why he is an ideal romantic partner in their eyes. Again, this contradicted my primary reading and was not an obvious point to me because it is the very danger that Edward presents to Bella that drives the tension of the first book and much of the second one as well. He quickly and steadfastly emerges as her savior in almost every situation, even when she is too heartbroken over Jacob to drive her own vehicle home. Edward does enter Bella's bedroom and watches her sleep without her knowledge or permission. He dismantles her truck to prevent her visiting La Push against his wishes. Jacob forces Bella to kiss him and hounds her for her attention for hundreds of pages after that. As the adult, feminist professor, these are scenes that stood alarmingly out to me (see Brande 2008 and Housel 2009 for more extensive discussion of these issues). The young fan-readers participating in this conversation did, at times, criticize either Jacob or Edward for these actions, but they also saw the overall message of both men's desire to protect Bella above all as the dominant theme that overshadowed individual flawed attempts towards that end.

A final point about the importance of security for *Twilight* fans was articulated by Anthony. "I was only 13 when September 11th happened, and, definitely ... people from here [South Jersey] died that day ... and I think it would be awesome if I had a boyfriend who could save me from anything and who could live through anything [like Edward]. I want safety. That's what's seductive and hot for me."

I could not have guessed, as I began this project, that it is actually the safety, the benevolently caring paternalism that fans see the major male characters in the books as promising them, that provides a key to *Twilight*'s allure. I was, in fact, worried about the impact of the idea that Edward's deep desire for Bella is the flip side of his deep desire to not just kill her, but to consume her, a tried-and-true metaphor for rape. Shaw, writing as a Mormon of the Mormon influences in *Twilight*, praises Edward's restraint, as did many respondents. He writes, "... [A]lthough [Edward] appears like a high-school homecoming king, he has walked the planet for much longer, making him mature and stable.... He means what he says" (Shaw 231). Edward tells Bella that he does desire her strongly. "'I may not be a human, but I am a man,' [Edward] assured me" (*T* 311). He is not, however, a man whose sexual urges or hunger get the better of him, causing him to make either an object or a meal of the girl he loves. The appeal *of Twilight*, as I have tried to show here, is full of contradictions. While I still find the paternalism of his position to be problematic and possibly at odds with Bella's ability to make and act on her own decisions, many fans view it more generously.

Many seem to feel a real need to imagine that such a man is possible. I see that they identify with Bella's own stated reading of Edward's motivations: that she seeks and needs protection, and he promises it to her, which, in turn, gives her satisfaction and a way to influence him. She repeatedly calls Edward her angel when he comes to her rescue (see, for example, chapter 23 in *Twilight*) and thinks, at one point, "If I had to, I supposed I could purposefully put myself in danger to keep him close" (*T* 211), a strategy she uses very recklessly but, importantly, to great romantic effect and ultimate resolution throughout much of *New Moon*. Bella does, at the end of the series, get what *she wants*, which, to the fans, was crucial.

At the same time, I believe it is imperative to remember that many parts of the book serve double purposes — to arouse longing in readers but, at the same time, to instruct how and why those longings must be contained and controlled. To my mind, the most important aspect of the *Twilight* phenomenon is in its consumption and interpretation, but Meyer's story, however deliciously fantastical, does not occur in a vacuum. It is a product of and it affects our lived social world, with all its politics and its material risks and consequences.

Conclusion

In attending a variety of meetings for scholars of the *Twilight* phenomenon over the past year, I have witnessed a series of debates regarding whether it is legitimate to criticize Meyer for taking the moral positions that she does in her writing. I make no judgment here on her right to compose characters and plots that conform to her ideals for how people should be and act. My discomfort with the anti-feminist and homophobic principles that I see behind those ideals, rather, has made me concerned about the effects her tremendously popular series might have on its many and diverse readers and their notions of what is or is not acceptable behavior. In this chapter, I have tried to explore how some of those fans understand these messages themselves, how they are affected by them, and how they negotiate them in relation to their own convictions, their real lives and their real emotional investments in *Twilight*. In particular, I focussed on issues of sexuality and gender, agency and abstinence.

My questions do remain, as to: (1) how robust or enduring this fandom can be as a vehicle for negotiating or understanding this critical yearning for personal agency or for mutual desire, affection, and security; and (2) what a wider, more varied sample would reveal about how fans engage with these texts. Nonetheless, the *Twilight* fans whose responses structure much of this chapter have persuaded me that, indeed, the series provides a secure outlet for them to begin to indulge and explore important desires and personal boundaries. To return to Herzog once more, "Perhaps they don't want to be pressured, or they're not interested yet — or not anymore. They may not be ready for the potential emotional intensities of a relationship that includes sex — or, on the flip-side; they may wish for romance but are finding only offers of intercourse." This chapter, therefore, presents two facets of analysis. The limitations and political content of the text are important to understand and deserve continued analysis, interrogation, and critique. At the same time, Meyer's series is rich and evocative enough that many of its fans do read actively, joyfully, and creatively, deftly relating *Twilight*, in a host of different ways, to their material worlds and lived experiences.

WORKS CITED

Brande, Robin. "Edward, Heathcliff, and Our Other Secret Boyfriends." *A New Dawn*. Ed. Ellen Hopkins. Dallas, TX: BenBella Books, 2008.

Eclipse. Dir. David Slade. Summit, 2010. Film.

Faludi, Susan. *Stiffed: The Betrayal of the American Man*. New York: Harper Collins, 1999.

Herzog, Dagmar. *Sex in Crisis: The New Sexual Revolution and the Future of American Politics*. New York: Basic Books, 2008.

Housel, Rebecca. "The 'Real' Danger: Fact vs. Fiction for the Girl Audience." *Twilight and Philosophy: Vampires, Vegetarians, and the Pursuit of Immortality*. Eds. Rebecca Housel and J. Jeremy Wisnewski. Hoboken, NJ: John Wiley and Sons, 2009.

Levy, Ariel. *Female Chauvinist Pigs: Women and the Rise of Raunch Culture*. New York: Free Press, 2005.

McRobbie, Angela. *Feminism and Youth Culture: From* Jackie *to* Just Seventeen. Cambridge: Unwin Hyman, 1991.

Meyer, Stephenie. *Breaking Dawn*. New York: Little, Brown, 2008.

_____. *Eclipse*. New York: Little, Brown, 2007.

_____. *New Moon*. New York: Little, Brown, 2006.

_____. *Twilight*. New York: Little, Brown, 2008.

Monkerud, Don. "The Legacy of Bush's Homophobic Prudery." *The Gay and Lesbian Review Worldwide* May-June 2009. Web. 15 June 2010 <http://findarticles.com/p/articles/mi_hb3491/is_3_16/ai_n31914985/>.

"Personal Correspondance 5." *The Twilight Lexicon*. Lori Joffs and Laura Byrne-Cristiano. Web. 11 February 2010 <http://www.twilightlexicon.com/2006/03/11/personal-correspondance-5/>.

Shaw, Marc E. "For the Strength of Bella? Meyer, Vampires, and Mormonism." *Twilight and Philosophy: Vampires, Vegetarians, and the Pursuit of Immortality*. Eds. Rebecca Housel and J. Jeremy Wisnewski. Hoboken, NJ: John Wiley and Sons, 2009.

Twilight. Dir. Catherine Hardwicke. Summit, 2008. Film.

PART II

Once Upon a *Twilight*
Fairy Tales, Byronic (Anti) Heroes, Post-Feminist Romance, and Growing Up in a Twilight World

"How Old Are You?"
Representations of
Age in the Saga

Ashley Benning

It was 8 P.M. on November 21, 2008, and already the line was around the perimeter of the local Mesa, Arizona, movie theater, through the parking lot, and down the other half of the mall. In more populated cities, lines started forming hours, or even days earlier. Women of all ages — and some men — waited respectfully but anxiously for the last shows of the evening to clear out so they could filter into the ten theaters showing the midnight screening. An outsider would have had a difficult time pinpointing exactly what movie this group was waiting to see. A romance, surely, as the estrogen-soaked air would prove. But a teen romance? Possibly. A great number of the ticket-holding crowd was in the teen range. But a great number were much older. To one side, a mini-line formed as women waited for their turn to pose with a larger-than-life cutout of a teenage boy, some women kissing the façade, others draping their bodies seductively over the two-dimensional heartthrob a generation their junior. Then the line jerked forward, like a train out of the station, and started chugging through the front doors. Various squeals of "It's time!" and "Oh, Edward!" and "Team Jacob!" echoed through the parking lot and the sheer volume of the screams made it almost believable that they could travel the few miles north to the home of author Stephenie Meyer, the reason for the evening's frivolity. *Twilight* had hit theaters.

This one instance in the world of *Twilight* fandom illustrates the range in ages of the die-hard fans, and this variance in the ages of the fans is evidence of the universality of the series. How is it that the series attracts both young and old? What age constructs does the series propagate and which constructs does the series reject? How has Summit Entertainment and Little, Brown Books used these constructs for marketing purposes? In a similar vein, what does the popularity of the movies and fan events say about the acceptance of these age representations?

The *Twilight* series is foremost a bildungsroman, or coming-of-age story; thus any exploration of the series through the lens of this genre should include exploration of age in the series as it relates to power, the issues of growth and maturity within the mythological worlds of vampires and the wolves (shapeshifters), the "coming of age" of Bella and her ever-present fear of age and death, and the impotence of parental units (Charlie, Billy, Harry, Renee, and even Carlisle and Esme).

"How long have you been seventeen?"
— Bella (T 185)

In June of 2000, *The New York Times* announced a decision to print a separate Best Seller list for children's books. Prior to this decision, the Best Seller list had been topped by J.K. Rowling's *Harry Potter* series (the three books that had been released) for seventy-nine weeks. Charles McGrath, editor of the *Book Review*, said of the decision, "The sales and popularity of children's books can rival and, in the case of the *Harry Potter* books, even exceed those of adult books.... With a separate children's list we can more fully represent what people are reading, and we can clear more room on the adult list for adult books" (Byam 344). Many advocates of the series voiced outrage at the *Times'* decision to categorize a series that is so clearly enjoyed by children and adults alike as literature for children. Paige Byam, author of the article "Children's Literature or Adult Classic? *Harry Potter* and the Great Tradition," believes that the series should be considered part of F.R. Leavis' "Great Tradition" of English novels which "change the possibilities of the art" and "promote awareness of the possibilities of life" (343) regardless of intended audience. By this definition, *Harry Potter*—and other similar works (like *Twilight*)—would be free of an age label; instead, the series would be appreciated for its literary merit alone. Of the *New York Times'* decision, Byam writes:

> Some regarded this as an attempt to quash adult interest in *Harry Potter* by sending out a message to readers that it is really children's fiction.... Removing *Harry Potter* from the adult Best Seller list was a marketing decision designed to obscure the fact that *Harry Potter* was still outselling top adult fiction and that no other children's book approached it in sales at the time [344].

There was only one other book on the original Best Seller list that was deemed "children's literature," which was Dr. Seuss' *Oh, the Places You'll Go* at number twenty-four. In other words, the success of the *Harry Potter* series was clouded when it was thrust into a category amongst books that, except for the aforementioned Dr. Seuss, would not have made it onto the original adult Best Seller list. Here was the series that had topped the original list for over a year being relegated to stand beside books that couldn't qualify to occupy even the lowest spots on that list.

Whatever the *Times'* motives behind the new list, they have now placed themselves in the difficult position of having to decide which books are for children and which are for adults. Many literary critics — Jack Zipes, perhaps, the most visible — denounce this attempt at categorization as folly, pointing out the absurdity of attempting to pigeonhole books into a genre or field that has never had a clear definition. In fact, the distinction between what is read by adults and what is read by children is a new occurrence, and Zipes points out that the relegation of a book to the children's literature list will result in skewed evaluation of the text. In a section on evaluating literature, from his book *Sticks and Stones: The Troublesome Success of Children's Literature from Slovenly Peter to Harry Potter,* Zipes comments on the impossibility of defining children's literature:

> The problem of evaluating children's literature is, of course, complicated by the accepted notion that there is such a homogenous thing as children's literature: that is, that adults write expressly for children, that their works can have a particular effect on the sensibilities of children, and that we can detect, determine, and alter their values. All of this is nonsense. It is nonsense because children's literature is produced primarily by and for adults, and the evaluative processes established by critics, parents, the press, institutions, authors, and illustrators of what is "good" children's literature exclude, for the most part, the opinions of young people [63].

A decade later, the *Times* has retained this separation of lists, in spite of reader and author outrage. *Twilight* has been categorized as "Young Adult" and, for the purposes of the *New York Times*, "Children's Literature." Meyer has sold almost 50 million copies of the *Twilight* books in the United States alone,[1] causing many critics to bring forward the similarities between the two series. In fact, *Twilight* and *Harry Potter* share common traits with thousands of other coming-of-age stories, perhaps causing the popularity of the respective series: the orphaned protagonist (Don't think Bella is an orphan? Read on.), the sidekick, the revelation of one's unique abilities or birthright, coming to terms with a dangerous world, defeating an evil force. Bella, Arthur, Harry Potter, Luke Skywalker, and hundreds of other popular protagonists have traveled the path mirrored in every adolescent's life, and have come out victorious. Joseph Campbell defines this journey in his work, *The Hero with a*

Thousand Faces, in which he describes the motifs and archetypes associated with the hero's quest; *Harry Potter, Star Wars, Twilight,* and the classic Arthurian legends all follow Campbell's construct of the Hero's Journey to some degree.[2]

No matter what the *Times* may claim, Meyer's series is certainly not confined to a juvenile audience; the series has a large and participatory adult following, as evidenced by conference attendee demographics, fan sites, fan fiction, and film audience demographics. Knowing her wide audience, Meyer had even at one point pursued placing an age warning on *Breaking Dawn.* *USA Today*'s Carol Memmet quoted Meyer: "I was for an age limit of 15 or 16 and a warning ... I think the content is just a little harder to handle, and a little bit more grown-up for really young kids. I have 9-year-old readers, and I think it's too old for them. Some of it's violence, and some of it's just mature themes." Meyer understands her broad audience, but doesn't write to a particular group. Rather, she writes the story as she believes it is meant to be told. (In an interview with the website, *ReadersRead,* she said, "I never think about another audience besides myself while I'm writing.") Interesting that the *Times* has placed her series — so mature in theme that it almost bore a warning label — in the Children's section.

Interplay between age groups is a common theme in the bildungsroman genre as the protagonist must explore the limitations of age in order to grow, and yet age criticism for these literary works is less prevalent than gender or political criticism. Current *Twilight* scholarship is still scant; *Twilight and Philosophy: Vampires, Vegetarians, and the Pursuit of Immortality*, edited by Rebecca Housel and J. Jeremy Wisnewski, was the first notable anthology of criticism, followed by *Twilight and History* (by Nancy Reagin) and *Bitten by Twilight* (edited by Melissa A. Click, Jennifer Stevens Aubrey, and Elizabeth Behm-Morawitz) in 2010. Most critical articles dealing with the series — in the aforementioned anthologies and in broader scholarship — tend to focus on the same few topics: gender/feminism, religion, traditional vampire and werewolf mythology, film adaptations, and fan culture, though there have been forays into the realm of adolescent psychology.

"My mom always says I was born thirty-five years
old and that I get more middle-aged every year."
— Bella (T 106)

While there has been much ado over the age-appropriateness of the series in relation to the targeted readership, few critics have examined the themes of aging, parental authority, maturity, and coming-of-age as components of

Meyer's construct of age in the series.[3] Brendan Shea's article, "To Bite or not To Bite: *Twilight*, Immortality, and the Meaning of Life" (also found in *Twilight and Philosophy*) analyzes Bella's desire for immortality as it relates to her need to love — and be loved — by Edward. Shea writes,

> As Bella understands it, much of her life's purpose is provided by the love she feels for Edward, Jacob Black, and her extended "family." Insofar as her eventual death will prevent her from being there to protect and guide the people she loves, Bella might think that choosing immortality is the best thing for her to do. (Housel 54)

But beyond the fear of being absent from the lives of the people she loves, Bella is also afraid of the aging process.

The prologue to *New Moon* finds Bella standing across from her grandmother on a sunny meadow. The joy of being with her deceased grandmother is short-lived, however, when Bella realizes she is not looking at Gran, but instead at a reflection of her own aged body — the physical changes even starker juxtaposed with the ageless Edward, who stands beside her. This is the reader's first introduction to Bella's age phobia. Prior to this moment, Bella had only voiced concern over her inevitable death and separation from Edward; now, Bella reveals her true concern: aging, and all that it entails. Bella's interpretation of aging includes illness, helplessness, senility, and becoming unattractive to Edward. An interesting note: Gran is the only character in the entire series whose body has biologically matured into old age. The reader (and by association, Bella) only has Gran as an example of the older age bracket. Bella's phobia is grounded in the knowledge that older people die — just as Gran did — and this idea is only solidified as she sees the adults around her deteriorate, Billy Black confined to a wheelchair and Harry Clearwater dying.

In the movie adaptation of *New Moon*, filmmakers took license with Harry Clearwater's age. At fifty-seven years old, Graham Greene is significantly older than the character of Harry Clearwater, who is described as being around Charlie's age (forty-one). Not only is the film version of Harry older, but he also dies under different circumstances. In the novels, Harry dies of a heart attack attributed to high cholesterol and heart disease; in the film, Harry dies of a heart attack after the shock of seeing Victoria on the prowl. The message sent to the audience — albeit subconsciously — is that age makes a person so frail and vulnerable that a shock can cause death.

Contemporary society's paradigm is that aging is a process of decline and that youth is to be idolized and — by whatever means possible — maintained. Society has created and accepted specific age categories: infant, child, adolescent, adult, and elderly. Adults Botox, moisturize, and undergo surgeries to achieve younger looks and treasure the teen years by spending billions of dollars every year catering to the teen market through movies, television, music, and technology. Christine Lagorio of CBS News reported in 2007 that companies spent almost seventeen billion dollars on marketing to kids that year, up 200 percent from what was spent just five years earlier. Lagorio writes, "Marketing firms and advertisers are looking to a younger demographic, increasingly targeting tweens and even younger children. And these kids have a huge control over the flow of parents' spending, statistics show — 8–12-year-olds spend $30 billion of their own money each year and influence another $150 billion of their parents' spending." Based on these numbers, children and teens are given a large amount of spending power in their homes, and according to BrandChannel.com's Vivian Manning-Schaffel, this younger audience will spend money more freely than their parents' generation.[4] She explains that Generation X became caught in a recession just as it reached "purchasing prime," but that Generation Y is "less skeptical and more populous ... Gen Y's approach to life is buy, buy, buy."

Margaret Morganroth Gullette, who has written several books on our culture's views on aging, writes, "Americans are becoming obsessed by age, not because of increasing longevity but because of premature decline. Age is becoming an overriding constructor of difference and an alarmingly ubiquitous focus of subjectivity throughout the life course. Age is the new kind of difference that makes a difference" (35). Thus, it is fascinating when groups that are so different (adults, teens, and even children) become interested in the same thing — for example, the *Twilight* series.

Gullette does not accept the idea that aging is necessarily related solely to the physical. She analyzes cultural ageism and its affect on her own life in *Declining to Decline: Cultural Combat and the Politics of the Midlife*. Of aging, she writes, "The basic idea we need to absorb is that whatever happens in the body, human beings are aged by culture first of all.... Everything we know of as culture in the broadest sense — discourses, feelings, practices, institutions, material conditions — is saturated with concepts of age and aging" (3). It makes sense, then, that marketing firms, the film industry, and the publishing industry would take advantage of this cultural awareness of age in their sales strategies. She later notes, "We think we age by nature; we are insistently and precociously being aged by culture" (6). If what Gullette says is true, that age is a culturally constructed system of meaning and not necessarily tied to the body, then all sorts of new types of age can be found in texts; in the case of *Twilight*, the immortal vampires adopt classic characteristics of aging, but do not biologically age. There are, in fact, several age paradigms within the text: physical age, emotional maturity, intellectual maturity, and various in-betweens, such as the physically mature but emotionally stunted wolves, or the intellectually mature but physically stunted vampires.

The world in the *Twilight* novels is divided into two types of people: immortal and mortal. The wolves straddle both categories as they enter an immortal state while they are actively shifting into wolves, and start aging again once their protective services are no longer needed. There are no old vampires; they all fall somewhere on the spectrum of adolescence to middle-age. This is not to say, however, that mental maturity is stunted. On the contrary, vampires continue to learn and grow over their seemingly endless life spans. Edward, for example, has mastered several languages, piano playing, automobile maintenance, biology and anatomy, literature and art, music history, and countless other hobbies; emotionally, he continues to grow in his understanding of the family unit, selfless love, and sacrifice.[5]

Similarly, the Volturi — though physically young — rule with a wisdom guided by centuries of experience. The Volturi know when to intimidate, when to bribe, and when to wear the façade of innocence. While it is true that they display signs of stagnation — which by definition denotes time and age — their transparent skin and milky eyes do not take away from the fact that their bodies are still frozen in the form of the age at which they were transformed. Conversely, Jasper, the oldest of the Cullen children, struggles daily with his growth as a vegetarian. All vampires can mentally progress; they cannot progress or grow physically.

There are no babies or small children in the vampire world and this is due to two factors. First, it is impossible for a vampire woman to conceive a child, owing to the fact that her body does not go through menstrual cycles.[6] As is seen in *Breaking Dawn*, vampire men can impregnate human women, but those pregnancies rarely end with either mother or child surviving. According to Meyer's mythology, there have been cases of desperate vampire women changing a human baby or small child into a vampire. However, vampire babies cannot mature mentally in the same way that vampire adults can, and these bloodthirsty toddlers usually end up on wild hunting sprees of the local village, killing every human in their sight (*BD*, Book 3).

In fact, children are absent from Meyer's larger world as well. Claire, in *Eclipse*, is the first child to which the reader is introduced, and this only as a minor character in the subplot of Jacob's imprinting dilemma. Renesmee is the only significant child in the series, and she is not exactly a normal child in terms of age observation. Her growth timeline is shortened and she matures so quickly that her parents fret continually over her quality and length of life. After coming to terms with Renesmee's condition, Bella calculates her daughter's lifespan. "She'd ... be an adult in no more than four years. Four years. And an old woman by fifteen. Just fifteen years of life" (*BD* 529). In fact, Renesmee becomes almost a peer to her aunts and uncles as she learns to communicate and understands more about her place in the strange world of immortals.

This presents a small paradox: in a world where some people do not physically age but where the family unit still exists, how is age defined? It is important to define this because, in a traditional setting, elders are considered wise, parents are to be obeyed, and children learn from their parents. In Meyer's world, traditional families are few, parents and elders do not hold to the traditional hierarchies, and Bella must create her own definitions of what it means to age and mature.

Bella's own parents are examples of adults who don't adhere to traditional roles. Renee and Charlie have been divorced since Bella's infancy. Bella's relationship with her mother is reversed as Bella takes on the role of chaperone, protector, and confidant and Renee dates younger men, makes poor life choices, and relies on her daughter's smarts to guide the both of them safely through life.

Though Charlie wears the guardian role in his relationship with Bella — and in his community role as Chief of Police — Bella conversely becomes caretaker for him as well by cooking and doing housework. Charlie requires less mental looking-after than does Renee, but Bella is still concerned over how best to save him from anxiety or stress due to her actions. In *Twilight*, Bella frets over Charlie's safety and hurt feelings when her own life is in danger. She pleads with Edward: "Keep Charlie safe for me. He's not going to like me very much after this, and I want the chance to apologize later" (391). Months later, when Bella falls into a deep depression following Edward's disappearance, she points to the well-being of her parents as her reason for not committing suicide: "I owed too much to Charlie. I felt too responsible for Renee. I had to think of them" (*NM* 110). And even when Bella believes she has died after her cliff diving escapade, she worries about Charlie: "I'm dead, right? I *did* drown. Crap, crap, crap! This is gonna kill Charlie" (502). In instance after instance, Bella puts the feelings and safety of her parents before her own, protecting them from the harsh reality of this new world in which she lives.

In her article "The *Harry Potter* Novels as a Test Case for Adolescent Literature," Roberta Seelinger Trites brings up another significant indicator of a protagonist's growth in a Young Adult (YA) novel: an understanding of the world. She writes, "Growth in adolescent literature is inevitably depicted as a function of what the adolescent has learned about how society curtails the individual's power. The adolescent cannot grow without experiencing gradations between power and powerlessness" (473). In Bella's case, this world-knowledge comes in the form of the famous "How old are you?" scene, where Bella confronts Edward about how old he really is, thus discovering his supernatural characteristics. During this dialogue, Bella learns the truth of the existence of vampires and she has a dramatic paradigm shift. From believing vampires were myths and that Edward disliked her, she has an epiphany: "About three things I was absolutely positive: First, Edward was a vampire. Second, there was a part of him ... that thirsted for my blood. And third, I was unconditionally and irrevocably in love with him" (*T*195). Bella comes to understand her physical powerlessness in the vampire world more fully in *New Moon* when faced with the Volturi — pleading for Edward's life but completely incapable of fighting for it — and in *Eclipse* during the newborn vampire battle (when she must stand aside and watch others protect her), but overcomes this powerlessness in *Breaking Dawn* when she harnesses her unique abilities to shield her family and save them from certain death.

But Bella's new paradigm does more than simply show her a new world; it stretches her knowledge-base beyond that of her parents. The child now knows more about the world than do her parents, and she moves from the realm of student to teacher. It is up to her to either withhold this knowledge or convey it to her parents.

The reader can draw a stark contrast between the Swans and the Cullens: though none of the Cullens age, the vampires have constructed a family with mother, father, and siblings. Even though immortality interferes with the traditional and biological definitions of these familial components, the Cullens have created their own system to mimic that of a mortal family. Carlisle is the oldest vampire, and definitely has the broadest knowledge of the vampire and human worlds, having made a study of them over his centuries-long life. His position as patriarch is fitting. However, Esme's place as matriarch is not as immediately evident (perhaps owing to the gendered implications of the patriarchal family model where Carlisle and Edward — as the "oldest" son — hold the power). She has been a vampire for fewer years than Jasper and Edward, and yet she is the mother figure of the Cullen clan. Her personality is such that she enjoys caring for and loving others and her mothering instinct from her mortal life has carried over into her immortal life. In physical appearance, both Carlisle and Esme are only a few years older than their "children" and yet Edward, Alice, Jasper, Emmett, and Rosalie consider them their parents and defer to them for any major decisions (such as where the family should live and how long they should stay) and Carlisle represents the family in formal situations, as in the battle sequence in *Breaking Dawn* when he speaks to the Volturi on behalf of the Cullens.

However, there is a feeling that the adults in the series, mortal and immortal alike, have limitations: that they are only effective leaders and protectors to a point, and that past that point the children are on their own. Billy Black, for instance, has raised three children on his own. He understands the danger Victoria presents and yet is helpless to protect Jacob from her. The best he can do is keep Charlie — another impotent father — distracted and out of harm's way. Charlie may have power and authority in the human world, but he is no match against a vengeful vampire. Bella protects him by leading James away from Forks. He is similarly powerless to help when Bella faces the Volturi in *New Moon* and when the newborn vampire army comes to Forks in *Eclipse*. And Renee is only ever seen as a mother figure when she nurses Bella back to health after her disastrous run-in with James. She is an otherwise absent parent.

Even Carlisle and Esme have limited power over the safety and well-being of their children. Carlisle provides medical care for Bella in several instances throughout the series, but this seems to be the extent of his ability to protect her. Both parents are completely absent from the major events of *New Moon*; in *Eclipse,* neither parent participates in the battle against Victoria — the most dangerous member of the vampire army — but instead are miles away fighting newborn vampires. In *Breaking Dawn*, Carlisle and Esme try to look after Edward and Bella by facilitating Bella's emergency medical care during her pregnancy, but are absent for the macabre birth of Renesmee. Similarly, these well-meaning parents are present at the final battle in *Breaking Dawn* but the group realizes that they will all die, in spite of their numbers and talents. No amount of parental concern can save the group from the oncoming slaughter.[7]

Catherine Gilbert Murdoch wrote about the absence of mothers in children's literature in her article, "The Adventures of Mommy Buzzkill." She points out that in order for child protagonists to grow, they must leave their mother's side. Authors will often solve this problem by simply having the mother die prior to the story's opening. Murdoch writes,

> Countless fictitious mothers die in childbirth ... or perish in the book's opening pages. Many more stories feature a child away at sea, camp, work, or boarding school, or snatched by magic or kidnappers. An equal volume involve a living, attentive mother who just happens to be absent: the children experience adventure at school, on sidewalks, in the woods — somewhere beyond mother's sphere.

Murdoch used to believe this mother vacuum was caused by society's low opinion of mothers. However, after trying to write a story with a present and capable mother, she realized the truth:

> Mothers in real life are giant, nonstop, buzzkills. "Hold my hand.... Use the safety scissors.... Wear your helmet.... Get a napkin.... Finish your homework first.... Don't let the baby climb the stairs!" ... Mothers in children's fiction, when present, act just as protectively.

How can a protagonist grow into maturity when she (or he) is being shielded by her (or his) mother? Bella's story would be vastly different if Renee was one of Murdoch's capable mothers: Bella might not have ever made it to Forks or, after having met Edward, Renee might have forced her back to Arizona to protect her; Renee might have locked Bella's bedroom window, preventing Edward's access to her daughter, or sacrificed her own life to Victoria, James, or the Volturi to protect Bella. Paradoxically, the figure who is supposed to facilitate healthy emotional growth is actually the figure who stunts growth. Murdoch explains, "The simple act of eliminating mom provides a venue where anything dangerous or magical or gallant can happen. Child heroes are then at liberty to discover, to their shock and satisfaction, that they can survive on their own abilities. In other words, these heroes grow up."[8]

Bella does most certainly grow up. The series is above all the story of a young woman finding her place in the world. With her parents absent from her life (either because of physical or mental distance), she is able to embrace the possibility of a different and dangerous world. Conflicts in her life escalate as she battles against physical enemies (James, Victoria, the newborn vampire army) and emotional ones (insecurity, warring affections, anxiety for the safety of her loved ones, helplessness) until she reaches a climax in *Breaking Dawn*. When she becomes pregnant, she is officially cut off from her parents as they are prohibited from knowing where she is and in what condition. She finds the strength to make the sacrifice of her life to save her unborn child and, later, she finds that she alone has the ability to save her family and friends from certain death at the hands of the Volturi. And, of course, she has made the final physical step toward adulthood for a female: bearing a child. Symbolically, Bella has now passed the mantle of "child" to her daughter and has officially entered the realm of adulthood.

Had Bella's parents been either more involved in her life, married, or simply more observant, Meyer's tale would have ended quite differently (see previous comments regarding Renee). The movie adaptation gives Charlie some "Mommy Buzzkill" qualities as he begs Bella to carry pepper spray and questions Edward's suitability. In both worlds, a little more parental interaction might have ended up with Bella returning to Arizona and Edward running home with some buckshot in his perfectly pressed trousers.

"Am I the only one who has to get old? I get older every stinking day! Damn it! What kind of world is this? Where's the justice?"— Bella (E 119)

In July of 2009, TwiCon Partners, LLC hosted the first major *Twilight* convention. Prior to this event, smaller gatherings had been held in cities throughout the world, but TwiCon was offering one-stop shopping for fans' deepest desires: a forum for academic discussion, a venue for *Twilight*-based activities (Cardio with the Cullens, for example), a vendor hall with everything from movie jewelry replicas to *Twilight* candy, the fantasy of attending a themed ball, and a chance to breathe the same air as some of the stars. My personal experience with TwiCon was as a panelist presenting a paper for one of the academic sessions and discussions, running a seminar on *Twilight* in the classroom, and as assistant to Maggie Parke, the head of Academic Programming. My assumption was that the academic programming would be a side-show, something to keep chaperones occupied while the bulk of attendees — who would surely be under the age of eighteen — visited the temporary tattoo parlor to show their undying love for Edward — or Jacob — in the form of face paints.

Yet a closer look at readership would have changed my perspective right away. While it is true that the *Twilight* books are marketed at a Young Adult audience and, as mentioned before, are categorized as Children's Literature by the *New York Times*, Meyer has gathered a large adult following. The academic programming was well attended and, though TwiCon L.L.C. was not able to provide attendee demographics, my personal experience was that the audiences tended toward the over-eighteen age range. Susan Carpenter of the *Los Angeles Times* recently wrote about the trend of adults snatching up young adult literature:

> It used to be that the only adults who read young adult literature where those who had a vested interest — teachers or librarians or parents.... But increasingly, adults are reading YA books with no ulterior motives. Attracted by well-written, fast-paced and engaging stories that span the gamut of genres and subjects, such readers have mainstreamed a niche long derided as just for kids ["Young Adult Lit Comes of Age"].

Shannon Hale, author of the Newbery Award–winning YA novel *Goosegirl*, called YA lit "the land where Story and Wordsmithery could live hand-in-hand, where ideas sang to me and characters were relatable and flawed but also rich with hope" (*School Library Journal*). For Hale, YA lit is not reserved for readers of a certain age, but is simply literature and — when done well — great literature. This definition applies to the *Twilight* Saga; the success alone of Meyer's novels is enough to prove that the fan base must be multi-generational.

A quick Internet search will prove this point: some of the most popular *Twilight* blogs and fan sites are geared toward adults. *Twilight*MOMS, for example, began as an effort to "bring adult fans of Stephenie Meyer together to discuss anything and everything about the *Twilight* Saga" and there are now almost 30,000 registered members of the forum and over 2 million posts.

*Twilight*MOMS is open to fans of all ages, but requires parental consent for fans under the age of 21 to participate in the forums. The forum rules ask that participants "keep it clean" and "think 'family friendly'" and the focus of the posts are generally the books and movies, the *Twilight*MOMS book club, and other innocuous topics.

Adult *Twilight* Fans is another adult-oriented fan site but visitors to this site will get a very different vibe; the forum guidelines state "We will push the envelope a bit; we don't expect everyone to be saints! This is an adult board after all! We're a solid 'R,' so let's try not to go into the XXX rating." The juicier forum topics are hidden from visitors and can only be accessed by registered forum members over the age of 21 as they contain graphic content.

And, of course, there are many adults who are most decidedly not fans of the series. Book challenges (when a parent requests that a book be removed from a school library) are a regularity with The *Twilight* Saga, book burnings are not unheard of— there are Facebook groups dedicated to *Twilight* book burnings, and YouTube hosts several videos of bonfires in which *Twilight* is the fuel; there are even (unsuccessful) petitions to have the books banned from the entire United States. The American Library Association recently released the Top Ten list of frequently challenged books for 2009; the *Twilight* series was newly added this year and ranked at number five. Reasons offered for its presence on the list are that it is "sexually explicit, religious viewpoint, unsuited to age group" (Morales). One public school district in San Juan Capistrano, California, banned the books from middle school libraries because the district coordinator of literacy programs, Julia Gerfin, "'determined them to contain subject matter which is deemed too mature for our middle school-level students,' an inter-district email said" (*Orange County Register*). The books were later quietly allowed back on the shelves with no explanation given.

"If we had happy endings, we'd all be under gravestones right now."–Rosalie (E 154).

There is still uncharted age theory territory in the *Twilight* world; the future will surely find countless essays dedicated to age representations in the film adaptations, the implications of using actors of different ages than their character counterparts, and the impact of the success of the films on the young actors. The world is still waiting for the film adaptations of *Breaking Dawn*, and Meyer's newest addition to the saga, *The Short Second Life of Bree Tanner*, was released in June of 2010, opening the door to more criticism of age relations within the series. Even without the new and upcoming films and text additions to the *Twilight* canon, there is still much to be said about Renesmee, the mortal adult-child of immortal parents, Edward's role as sometime-parent to Bella, the significance of newborn vampires wielding such power, and the ageless-yet-mortal Quileute characters, who have remained almost untouched in this analysis. Yet even this brief examination of the series reveals the intricate web of age and mortality constructs that Meyer has created and how it has permeated the real world fandom across the globe.

What remains to be seen is if the series has generational staying power. Will today's Generation Y share the book with their children when all the hype has died down? Will the series continue to captivate an audience of young and old alike? Will it find a quaint corner in the young adult section of society, sliding gracefully into the New York Times' label of Children's Literature? Or will it become known as one of the series that broke through the age boundaries and made it possible for readers of all ages to share in a common literary experience?

Only time (and age?) will tell.

NOTES

1. See introduction for current numbers.

2. For more on this line of argument, see Anastasiu's essay in this anthology.

3. See Rebecca Housel's article, "The 'Real' Danger: Fact vs. Fiction for the Girl Audience" from *Twilight and Philosophy,* for an example.

4. For more reading on marketing to teens, see *So Sexy So Soon* by Diane E. Levin and Jean Kilbourne, *Packaging Girlhood* by Sharon Lamb and Lyn Mikel Brown, and *The Lolita Effect* by M. Gigi Durham.

5. Much could be said about the educational progression of the male Cullens in relation to the females, but that's for a different discourse.

6. Meyer provides a detailed explanation of Bella's pregnancy on her website under the FAQs for *Breaking Dawn.* She explains that "female vampires cannot have children because their bodies no longer change in any aspect. There is no changing cycle to begin with, and their bodies couldn't expand to fit a growing child, either." She then offers a small vampire biology lesson in which she explains how it was possible for Edward to impregnate Bella. For more information, see http://www.stepheniemeyer.com/bd_faq.html.

7. Mothers — Renee, Esme, and Jacob's mother — are definitely the more absent/impotent side of the parental unit in this series. For a discussion on gender, please see articles by Shachar and Donnelly in this anthology.

8. "The Ol' Dead Dad Syndrome" by Leila Sales (published September 20, 2010, on the *Publishers Weekly* blog) also touches on the absence of parents in YA literature, though she attributes the Syndrome to author laziness rather than any archetypal cause.

WORKS CITED

Byam, Paige. "Children's Literature or Adult Classic? Harry Potter and the Great Tradition." *Nimbus 2003 Compedium.* Ed. Penny Linsenmayer. Houston: HP Education Fanon, Inc., 2005. 343–348.

Carpenter, Susan. "Young Adult Lit Comes of Age." *Los Angeles Times*. 8 March 2010: Los Angeles Times. Web. 26 November 2010.

Gullette, Margaret Morganroth. *Aged by Culture*. Chicago: University of Chicago Press, 2004.

Hale, Shannon. "How Reader Girl Got Her Groove Back." *School Library Journal* (2008): School Library Journal. Web. 1 November 2010.

Housel, Rebecca, and Jeremy Wisnewski. *Twilight and Philosophy: Vampires, Vegetarians, and the Pursuit of Immortality*. Hoboken, N.J.: John Wiley & Sons, 2009. Print.

"Interview with Stephenie Meyer." *Readers Read*. June 2008 <http://www.readersread.com/features/stepheniemeyer.htm>.

Lagorio, Christine. "Statistics, Reports, and Books About How Companies Target Toddlers to Teens." *CBS Evening News*. 17 May 2007. <http://www.cbsnews.com/stories/2007/05/14/fyi/main2798401.shtml>.

Manning-Schaffel, Vivian. "Has Gen X Fallen Through the Cracks?" BrandChannel.com. 16 December 2002. <http://www.brandchannel.com/features_effect.asp?pf_id=136>.

Martindale, Scott. "School District Briefly Bans Vampire Book from Middle Schools." *Orange County Register* 30 September 2008: *Orange County Register*. Web. 1 November 2010.

Memmott, Carol. "'Twilight' Author Stephenie Meyer Unfazed as Fame Dawns." *USA Today* 30 July 2008. <http://www.usatoday.com/life/books/news/2008-07-30-stephenie-meyer-main_N.htm>.

Meyer, Stephenie. *Breaking Dawn*. New York: Little, Brown, 2008.

_____. *Eclipse*. New York: Little, Brown, 2007.

_____. *New Moon*. New York: Little, Brown, 2006.

_____. *Twilight*. New York: Little, Brown, 2005.

Morales, Macey. "'ttyl' Series Tops ALA's 2009 Top Ten List of Most Frequently Challenged Books." *American Library Association* 14 April 2010. <http://www.ala.org/ala/newspresscenter/news/pressreleases2010/april2010/mostchallenged2009_oif.cfm>.

Murdock, Catherine Gilbert. "The Adventures of Mommy Buzzkill." *The Horn Book Magazine*. Horn Book, Inc., 2009. *AccessMyLibrary*. 26 March 2010 <http://www.accessmylibrary.com>.

Trites, Roberta Seelinger. "The *Harry Potter* Novels as a Test Case for Adolescent Literature." *Style* (Fall 2001): 472–485.

Zipes, Jack. *Sticks and Stones: The Troublesome Success of Children's Literature from Slovenly Peter to Harry Potter*. New York: Routledge, 2001.

Read Only as Directed
Psychology, Intertextuality, and Hyperreality in the Series

ANGELA TENGA

In response to questions about whether Bella Swan is "an anti-feminist heroine," Stephenie Meyer has written, "I never meant for her fictional choices to be a model for anyone else's real life choices. She is a character in a story, nothing more or less" ("FAQ: *Breaking Dawn*"). This surprising denial of readers' deep engagement with fiction—all the more surprising because it comes from a former student of literature—overlooks both the reality of complex reader responses to fiction and the behavior of Meyer's own characters in the *Twilight* saga. Literary figures take on life, meaning, and relevance for many readers, and Meyer's characters demonstrate this through their own active engagement with works of fiction.[1]

The *Twilight* novels trace Bella Swan's journey from awkward adolescence to first love, early marriage, teenage motherhood—and vampirism. Bella's odyssey, however, is less one of horror than one of fantasy fulfilled, and that fantasy is based largely on fictions that she has read. Meyer's series is infused with the flavor of her literary inspirations, which inform not just the imaginary space of the *Twilight* novels, but the very imagination of their protagonist. Fiction is a window into the psyche of the controversial heroine of the *Twilight* series; as a troubled teen who has used fictional models to shape her life, Bella is defined by narrative, while as an avid reader herself, she is a proxy for fans who want to emulate her.

This essay will explore the complex psychological relationship of fiction and reality in Bella's narrative by examining her cultural landscape (presented here in terms of Jean Baudrillard's theory of the hyperreal) and her interior landscape (a psychological profile constructed from textual details). Together, these two forces underpin Bella's constitution of her life as an enactment of fiction. Further, analysis of Bella's reading habits suggests that her life-fiction was strongly influenced by certain fictional sources — including fairy tales and nineteenth-century British novels — and that her autonomous vision of self is limited by women's roles within these fictions. This process, which also can be extended to admirers who take Bella as their own fictional model, is the key to the *Twilight* world.

Bella in the Eye of the Beholder

Meyer has written that she omitted "a detailed description of Bella ... so that the reader could more easily step into her shoes" ("FAQ: *Twilight*"), and the use of first-person narration supports this goal. However, inconsistencies in Bella's account may distance critical readers from her. For example, Bella bypasses a Port Angeles bookshop with "crystals, dream-catchers, and books about spiritual healing" in its windows because she prefers "a normal book-store" (*T* 156). Presenting herself as a practical, reason-driven person, Bella dislikes such signs of a "new-age" orientation, which she seems to dismiss as superstitious — yet "normal" Bella doggedly pursues a romantic relationship with a vampire. Perhaps her most glaring misconception about herself is voiced in *Eclipse*: "I'm not *that girl*, Edward. The one who gets married right out of high school like some small-town hick who got knocked up by her boyfriend!" (275). Ironically, this is a fairly accurate description of precisely which girl Bella is. As feminist scholar Bonnie Mann notes, "Bella turns eighteen, graduates, marries Edward for sex, and gets pregnant, practically all at once" (140). Bella's lack of self-awareness is a red flag for readers who wish to appreciate her status as narrator. She offers a type of limited reliability that is related to "dramatic irony or discrepant awareness" — that is, "a contrast between a narrator's view of the fictional world and the contrary state of affairs which the reader can grasp" (Nünning 58). Although Bella may be honest, she is hardly a reliable source of information about herself. The conspicuous gaps between her personal assessments and observable reality invite careful scrutiny.

Some fear, though, that impressionable readers might view Bella as a role model without examining her critically.[2] Bella and Edward's partnership creates alluring but potentially damaging images of teen romance for adolescent fans, who may overlook the addictive and obsessive aspects of the relationship. There may be genuine danger for Bella's admirers, such as the one who posted this response to an online poll about which *Twilight* character readers would like to be for one day: "I would have to be Bella, being loved by Edward, a best friend in Jacob.... All that drama in my life, sleep or stay awake? Sad or happy? Edward or Jacob? To jump or not to jump? The egg-beater truck or slick car? Bitten or not bitten? ... All worth it in the end, when i'm Mrs. Cullen ... Forever" (Contactqueen). While Bella also has vocal online critics, this comment reveals that some fans identify strongly with her or would like to be in her position.[3]

A serious concern for many of Bella's critics is her low self-confidence. Bonnie Mann's description of Bella as "the locus of exaggerated stereotypically feminine incapacities and self-loathing" (133) highlights a danger for readers who identify with her. While many adolescent girls suffer "substantial drops in self-esteem that far outpace those reported by boys" (Bower 184), Bella's response to such feelings of worthlessness is problematic. She obsesses about Edward, feels defined and validated only by his love, and would "rather die" than be with anyone else (*NM* 45). Moreover, she is willing to sacrifice every aspect of selfhood — from family ties and friendships to autonomy, humanity, and possibly even her soul — to be with him.

Bella's status as a prospective role model for young readers problematizes a central issue in Meyer's work. Bella's self-perception may itself be grounded in literary models that have crossed an unstable boundary between fiction and reality. Readers who emulate Bella are duplicating the core operational process of the *Twilight* series — the substitution of mimesis for genuine experience.

Bella Swan: Heroine of the Hyperreal

Readers who wish to understand Bella can begin by applying Jean Baudrillard's notion of hyperreality. Baudrillard proposes that postmodern society has replaced the "real" world with a "copy" world by "substituting the signs of the real for the real" (2). According to Baudrillard, representations of the real have replaced the things that they represent, claiming priority over them; thus, representation no longer simulates reality, producing a "hyperreal" copy — a copy of a copy. Meyer's novels document the supremacy of this simulated world. As a product of a culture in which representation precedes reality, Bella draws her perceptions and values not from reality, but from the represented reality found in fiction, which she uses as a model for life. In doing so, she shapes a hyperreal world — a reflection of representation — and her relationship with Edward mimics the romances found in fictions that she has consumed.

Baudrillard's theory offers insight about environmental sources of Bella's predisposition to hyperreal experience. However, as the next section will show, Bella's individual background and personality also play important roles in her prioritization of representation. Her emulation of fiction is firmly rooted in her psychological profile—a profile that, as readers can glean from textual evidence, marks her as a troubled teen whose emotional needs have not been met.

Bella Swan: Interior Architecture

Details of Bella's fictive history and her behavior in the fictional present constitute data that can be used to explore her internal construction.[4] This exploration reveals forces that have shaped her relationship with fiction. In their work on psychoanalytic criticism, Morton Kaplan and Robert Kloss have argued that, as "representations of life," fictional characters "can only be understood if we assume they are real," and, further, that "this assumption allows us to find unconscious motivation(s) by the same procedure that the traditional critic uses to assign conscious ones" (4). By connecting Bella's behavior to her background, readers can glimpse the perceptual underpinning of her narrative—i.e., a constitution of self via fictional sources, which become for her a sort of hyperreal template for shaping experience. Three key psychological factors in Bella's formulation of her life are her experience as a parentified child, her dependent personality, and her life-script sources.

Parentification

In the opening pages of *Twilight*, readers learn that Bella has lacked a strong paternal presence and that her relationship with her mother reverses traditional parent-child roles. Bella "exiles" herself to Forks (4), a town that she hates, to release her mother from the burden of parenthood.[5] While her sacrifice may be noble, it also can be viewed as a symptom of a deep-rooted belief in her unworthiness (which Bella frequently voices), which leads her to deny her right to be parented. In placing her mother's real or perceived needs ahead of her own, Bella assumes the role of parent, a pattern that continues when she moves in with Charlie and begins taking care of him. Bella's family situation corresponds to what psychologists call *parentification*—a "role reversal in which the child sacrifices his or her own needs ... to accommodate and care for the logistical and emotional needs of a parent" (Hooper 323).

Though not always damaging, parentification harms some children. According to Gregory Jurkovic, "pathologically parentified children" may face "disruption in identity development" (51). This may account for Bella's persistent complaints that there is nothing special about her, that she is "absolutely ordinary ... except for bad things" (*T* 210). Parentified children may also develop an orientation toward adults and have trouble interacting with peers (Jurkovic 57); Bella comments that she doesn't "relate well to people [her] age" (*T* 10), and the one "boy" to whom she can relate is over a century old. Moreover, Jurkovic notes that "[g]irls may suffer more ill effects from destructive parentification than boys" and that one possible outcome is "a more extreme, traditionally feminine gender role" (51). Thus, Bella may be predisposed toward identification with fictional characters who display the "stereotypically feminine incapacities" cited earlier (Mann 133).

Dependent Personality

Having "parented" her real parents, Bella eventually seeks someone to play the role of the parent that she, in effect, didn't have. This may explain why Bella exhibits behavior that corresponds to symptoms of dependent personality disorder (DPD). People with DPD often lack confidence in themselves (Beck, Freeman, and Davis 268); Bella, forever fixated on her clumsiness and "almost shamefully plain" appearance (*NM* 65), frequently laments that she does not deserve "godlike" Edward (*T* 256). In addition, because people with DPD feel that they need someone to take care of them, they display clinging behavior and submissive tendencies; they also "tend to be preoccupied with fears of being abandoned" (Beck, Freeman, and Davis 268). Bella essentially puts Edward in charge of their relationship and tolerates behavior that could be termed "stalking" even if he weren't a vampire.[6] Moreover, Bella accepts the mortal threat posed by Edward with little or no acknowledgment that her life has, or should have, value. When Edward worries aloud that things between them might "end badly"—a disturbingly casual euphemism for the possibility that he will kill her—she recognizes that she should be scared, yet feels only "an ache for his pain" (*T* 246). Here, Bella elevates Edward's (presumed) emotional distress above her potential death. So great is her need for him that nothing—even the prospect of exsanguination—was "more terrifying ... more excruciating, than the thought of turning away from him" (*T* 248). Obsessed with the fear of losing Edward, Bella would rather be killed by him than rejected by him.

Bella's dependency problems peak in *New Moon*, when Edward leaves to shield her from danger after his vampire "brother" tries to attack her. Patients with DPD "feel devastated ... [by] relationship distance" (Beck, Freeman, and Davis 268), as Bella feels "broken beyond repair" (219) and engages in self-destructive activities, such as cliff-diving into the ocean (359). In Edward's absence, Jacob Black becomes a surrogate caretaker for an infantilized Bella: "He was so big, I felt like I was a child hugging a grown-up" (178). Thus,

Bella finds two "parents" to indulge her dependence. As Bonnie Mann has noted, "Bella's vampire is father and mother" to her, and she is "handed off for safekeeping" to the "well-muscled werewolf ... an equally protective parent" (135). To satisfy her emotional needs, Bella relies on strong males who dominate and, in some respects, baby-sit her.

Life Script

A deeper understanding of Bella's relationship with fiction is gained through the application of Eric Berne's notion of a *life script*— a view of one's life, formed on an unconscious level, that shapes one's ideas about the world and one's role within it. Berne has identified life scripts as "derivatives, or more precisely, adaptations, of infantile reactions and experiences" which constitute "a complex set of transactions" that are enacted over the course of a lifetime (116). In simple terms, life-script composition starts in childhood, when "we take part in stories and believe ourselves to be in them," and ultimately, we formulate a "continuous explanatory narrative that gives meaning to the past, provides a problem-solving blueprint for the present, and predicts the future" (Newton 186). The essence of a life script is an unconscious connection between experience and narrative — the genesis of meaning through storytelling. The script can be influenced by family, friends, and other social contacts (Newton 188) as well as by one's broader cultural context: "Stories — whether they be small children's relating of family events, traditional fairy tales, cultural myths, modern novels, films, or plays — are the way that we map and share our consciousness" (193). Due to her family's early fragmentation and her experience as a parentified child, Bella's family offered no compelling life models, and this lack could have led her to rely more heavily on cultural sources in forming her life script — namely, on fictions consumed in her youth.

Together, these key features of Bella's background suggest why fiction plays such an important role in her life; in composing her life script, she has assimilated fictive models that satisfy the emotional needs of a parentified teen who is dependent on strong males. Readers can see this mechanism at work by examining explicit evidence — what Bella says about her reading preferences — and implicit evidence — how Bella's descriptions of her experience offer clues about her reading background.

Bella's Reading List: A Closer Look

Stephenie Meyer has described Bella as "first and foremost a bookworm" ("Personal Correspondence"), a comment that underscores the prominence of fiction in Bella's world. As a fiction-oriented youth, Bella may have learned too well the lessons taught by the stories that colored her young imagination. Echoes of traditional fairy and folk tales in the *Twilight* series suggest parallels between Bella and fairy tale protagonists, including Red Riding Hood, Sleeping Beauty, the Little Sea Maid, and Cinderella. In addition, Bella enjoys literary classics, such as *Pride and Prejudice* and *Wuthering Heights*. These embedded narratives are models for both Meyer as author and Bella as narrator.

Bella Enchanted?

Fairy tales provide a useful framework for reading the *Twilight* series and offer insight about Bella.[7] Fairy tales often convey veiled warnings on sensitive issues, such as the lesson on the male threat to awakening female sexuality found in the story of the naïve Red Riding Hood. *Twilight* casts Bella in this role; romantically inexperienced, she initially fails to grasp the danger posed by her "wolf" (here, Edward rather than Jacob). Red Riding Hood's wolf uses charm and disguises to stalk her, as Edward beguiles Bella with charm and a perfect disguise of stunning beauty, which make him "the world's best predator" (263). (Ironically, Edward counters Bella's sexual "activation" by enforcing abstinence until marriage — when their honeymoon leaves her battered, bruised, and impregnated with a baby that is about as salutary as the stones that are sewn into the wolf's belly in many traditional versions of the fairy tale.) Red Riding Hood's well-known series of exclamations regarding the size of various parts of the wolf's body exhibits the delicacy required of the fairy tale; all of the body parts that are mentioned serve as proxies for the part that could *not* be mentioned. Meyer, too, maintains deference toward the male anatomy; the traditional phallic associations of the vampire's fangs remain unspoken, and the often sensualized vampire bite is devoid of erotic overtones when Bella is transformed in *Breaking Dawn*, completing the action that *Twilight* begins.

In *New Moon*, Bella takes the role of Sleeping Beauty, a sixteen-year-old maiden who pricks her finger and falls into a deep sleep for one hundred years. Like her fairy tale counterpart, Bella is withdrawn and unresponsive, deeply depressed after Edward's departure. The drops of blood that hint at sexual maturation (at menstruation and first sexual experience) are deferred for Bella, but her arrival at sexual maturity also will be marked by a bloody rite of passage: the vampire's bite, commonly depicted as a mesmeric state followed by the pierce of fangs and a transfer of bodily fluid, has been viewed as a metaphor for sexual activity. To some, it has represented nocturnal emission; "[a] nightly visit from a beautiful or frightful being" that extracts "a vital fluid" from its victim calls up connections from the unconscious, where "blood is commonly an equivalent for semen" (Jones 119). Others have noted the sexualizing force of the vampires' bite, which, for example, transforms *Dracula*'s Lucy Westenra from a "giggly and silly ingénue" to "a highly erotic and captivating woman" (Twitchell 136–37). Of course, the vampire bite was also often used, in older films, as a proxy for physical union, "the explicit sex scene we aren't allowed to view" (Day 22).

In *Breaking Dawn*, Bella becomes the Little Sea Maid (or Little Mermaid), who sacrifices her identity, long life, home, and family for a chance to live as a human and win the love of a prince. Similarly, Bella gives up humanity, life as she knows it, and ties to family and friends to live with Edward forever as a vampire. However, the terms of the bargain are reversed, albeit ambiguously: by marrying the prince, the Little Sea Maid would gain an immortal soul, but Bella might lose hers by becoming a vampire. Bella rejects the idea that Edward is soulless, as legends typically depict vampires; she believes that he has "the most beautiful soul" (*BD* 24). Although Bella's theory is not positively substantiated within the novels, their message strongly echoes that of the fairy tale. Per the terms of her enchantment, the Little Sea Maid would die if she failed to marry the prince, but she is rescued by the daughters of the air, who have no immortal souls but "can make themselves one through good deeds" (Andersen 85); they reward her for refusing to kill the prince in order to regain her mermaid form. The tale suggests that virtue leads to transcendent transformation, just as the Cullens "rise above" their monstrous form "to conquer the boundaries of a destiny that none of [them] wanted" (*T* 307). Meyer suggests that by choosing a "vegetarian" diet, the Cullens have redeemed their souls; in Bella's view, they certainly have done so.

Finally, Cinderella's journey is clearly mirrored in Bella's progression throughout the *Twilight* series. From an initially debased state, Cinderella appears virtually from nowhere to become the belle of the ball and captivate the prince, just as humble Bella becomes the new sensation in Forks and the beloved of a local "prince." As Ruth Bottigheimer notes, the story of Cinderella is a "restoration" tale — one of "social position lost through misfortune and restored by goodness, perseverance, courage, or magic" — but is often perceived as a "rise" tale — one in which a humbly born protagonist advances socially via marriage (*Fairy Godfather* 1). The tale's often overlooked "restorative" features take a backseat in Meyer's reworking; Bella's story is a "rise" tale. Her inability to imagine "godlike" Edward "sitting in [her] father's shabby kitchen chair" (*T* 292) reveals her sensitivity to their social differences, and she greatly elevates her status by marrying into wealth and privilege.

Through its embedded tales, the *Twilight* series encodes messages that fairy tales have long conveyed to young readers. Men are wolfish predators who steal innocence, noble saviors who rescue damsels in distress, wealthy benefactors who provide an avenue to comfort and social advancement, meaning makers with the power to transform women. Implicit in such tales is a message that women are weak and defined in relation to men, while men are powerful, self-defining beings. Meyer's fairy tale, like its models, refuses gender equity. Even in a reading of Bella as a figure of the Little Sea Maid, which seems to infuse light into vampiric darkness by granting Edward a soul, it is Edward's light and Edward's soul that matter, not Bella's light, nor her soul.

While Meyer's embedding of fairy tales within the *Twilight* series is important, even more important here is that Bella herself "reads" her experience in fairy tale terms. Bella's arrival in Forks heralds a new phase of her life in which she will become a fairy tale heroine. Leaving the sunshine of Phoenix for the gloom of Forks signals Bella's entry into her shadow (or "copy") world. While contemplating the incredible notion that Edward might be a vampire, Bella admits that entering the woods — the setting of many fairy tale encounters with the magical or supernatural — makes it "much easier to believe the absurdities that embarrassed [her] indoors" (*T* 137). Readers witness Bella's engagement in this shadowy realm as she invokes fairy tales to tell her own story. For example, she describes her first encounter with Edward's vampire "mother" as "like meeting a fairy tale — Snow White, in the flesh" (*T* 323). Fairy tale connections are especially pronounced in *New Moon*, as Bella is bereaved not just of Edward, but of her fairy tale. Without Edward, Bella feels that she lacks a narrative function: "I wasn't the heroine anymore ... my story was over" (106). Later, reunited with Edward, she comments, "The fairy tale was back on. Prince returned, bad spell broken" (550). Here, she self-consciously interprets her life as a fairy tale, with Edward as her prince and her despair in his absence emotionally processed and transformed into story. When she and Edward are married in *Breaking Dawn*, Bella notes that "Edward had always thought that he belonged to the world of horror stories," but it had always been clear to her "that he belonged *here*. In a fairy tale. And now I was in the story with him" (479). Her immersion in narrative is complete. By the close of the series, she and Edward are installed in a fairy tale cottage in the woods, and, after a dangerous brush with the Volturi, presumably enjoy their happily-ever-after life.

Meyer's adoption of fairy tale models aligns her work with a didactic tradition whose social and psychological functions have been well established. Jack Zipes has examined "fairy tale discourse as a dynamic part of the historical civilizing process, with each symbolic act viewed as an intervention in social-ization" (10), while according to Bruno Bettelheim, fairy tales are integral to childhood development: left "unfed by our common fantasy heritage, the folk fairy tale," a child cannot, he argued, "invent stories on his own which help him cope with life's problems" (121). Bella's invention and coping mechanisms, however, surpass the limits described by Bettelheim; she actually uses fairy tale motifs as building blocks for life. In fairy tales, according to Bettelheim, "internal processes are externalized and become comprehensible" (25).[8] Bella, however, does not just apply fairy tale lessons to her life: she enacts her life as a fairy tale.

Abigail Myers warns readers to "take the *Twilight* saga for what it is: a fairy tale, no more worthy of emulation than *Sleeping Beauty*" (160), but Bella clearly holds a different opinion about fairy tales. To her, the fairy tale is a how-to guide. While young girls who read fairy tales may dream of a prince whose kiss will mark their entry into a world of romance, many eventually learn the difference between fantasy and reality. Bella, it seems, does not, and her construction of her fairy tale life sends a dubious message about the com-plex relationship of fiction and reality.

Pride and Prejudice and Vampires?

In addition to fairy tales, literary classics also figure largely on Bella's reading list. Meyer has cited several nineteenth-century British novels as inspi-rations for the *Twilight* series, but as more thorough discussion of these appears elsewhere in this anthology (see Groper and Shachar), this study offers just a few pertinent observations. The prominence of certain nineteenth-century novels in Bella's world suggests that they were important sources for her life script and that the vision of femininity found in those works heavily influenced her view of herself as a woman.

Meyer has identified Jane Austen's *Pride and Prejudice* as an inspiration for *Twilight*, and readers can easily see Darcy and Elizabeth's journey from alienation to marriage mirrored in Bella and Edward's relationship. What is remarkable, though, is that Bella has options that Austen's women did not have, yet she zealously pursues the same goal that they did: a "good" marriage. To understand Bella's decisions, we must note that Meyer is not the only one who was inspired by Austen: Bella also invokes Austen's name. She identifies her "shabbiest volume" as a collection of Austen's works and names *Pride and Prejudice* as a favorite (*T* 147–48). When Bella laments that the seemingly unattainable Edward shares a name with so many characters from her beloved fictions — "Weren't there any other names available in the late eighteenth century?" (*T* 148)— she hints at a vision of herself as a heroine of a Jane Austen novel, with Edward as leading man. *Pride and Prejudice* is itself a critical puzzle: "An urgent feminism pervades the novel, yet it ends with fantasy weddings to rich and privileged men" (Morrison 4). Readers may detect a similar dichotomy in the *Twilight* series. Bella sometimes professes a superficial feminism — in *Twilight*, for example, she writes an essay that explores "[w]hether Shakespeare's treatment of the female characters [in *Macbeth*] is misogynistic" (143)— yet ultimately, her choices conform to patriarchal norms. Having taken Austen's fiction as a model, though, Bella could hardly be expected to steer her life in a different direction.

Readers also can easily spot connections between *Wuthering Heights* and *Eclipse*.[9] For the purposes of this discussion, the most important connection between the two novels is not the influence of Brontë's work on Meyer, but its influence on Bella. Just after meeting Edward, Bella decides to re-read *Wuthering Heights*— perhaps because in reading, she can explore her attraction to her own personal Heathcliff. In *Eclipse*, Bella comments on the appeal of Heathcliff and Catherine's relationship: "nothing can keep them apart — not her selfishness, or his evil, or even death, in the end" (29), a statement that resonates with her own situation. Moreover, the fixation on fiction is transmitted to Edward in *Eclipse*. He reads *Wuthering Heights* within the novel's fictional time frame and relates Brontë's novel to his life, as Bella relates it to hers. This intertextual relationship heightens the novel's metafictional impact by intensifying and making manifest the connections between two fictional realms. The characters "read" their personal experiences through the lens of fiction as they interpret their lives in terms of Brontë's novel: Edward discovers that he "can sympathize with Heathcliff in ways [he] didn't think possible before" (265), while Bella finally realizes, "I was selfish, I was hurtful ... I was like Cathy, like *Wuthering Heights*" (517). Meyer shows how two fictional characters in her work align themselves with two fictional characters from another literary work. This dramatically underscores the powerful connection between life and fiction that is central in Bella's world — a connection that Meyer also claims to have experienced: "You live a thousand lives when you read a thousand books" ("Q&A BYU").

As Meyer drew on literary classics to craft her fiction, Bella draws on them to build her reality. Her literary models give centrality to men, so Bella does not perceive herself as having value until she gains the attention of a desirable, dominant male, who becomes her center of meaning: "The masculine gaze confers meaning on her otherwise empty existence by giving her a place in the story as the very location through which masculine action instantiates meaning" (Mann 136). The boundaries of Bella's life narrative have been drawn within an imaginary realm that restricts her very ability to imagine a larger vision of herself.

Bella and Edward: A Tale of Two Times?

Some readers view Edward and Bella's sexual abstinence as a model of teen morality. However, their restraint is driven by Edward; Bella tries to indulge her intense passion, but Edward foils her attempts. Meyer's series seems to suggest that "young women are incapable of understanding or controlling their own sexuality; it takes a man to keep them in check" (Siering 51). By granting Edward a virtually proprietary claim to her body, Bella affirms the traditional male ownership paradigm found in her preferred fictions. In the one instance when Bella claims her right to biological autonomy, she insists on carrying to term a half-vampire baby that is tearing her apart from the inside, rejecting every suggestion that the pregnancy be terminated. On one level, Bella appears to show strength and independence by asserting control over her body; however, her insistence also affirms the values of "an old-fashioned world where women were seen as empty conduits of masculine desire and valued for their propensity to self-sacrifice" (Mann 134). Bella's choice demonstrates her belief that her role as a childbearing vessel supersedes her own survival, a belief that is grounded in patriarchal, patrilineal culture.

Bella's ready acceptance of male hegemony sends a strong message about the role of women. To many readers, Bella is a young woman who does not achieve self-actualization. She is "a prize, not a person, someone to whom things happen, not an active participant in the unfolding story" (Siering 51); the *Twilight* series gives to males "active, individuated roles, and passive, objectified roles" to females (Wilson, "Beautiful or Strong?"). To the feminist reader, Bella may indeed serve as an unsatisfactory role model for young women. By the standards of her own fictional models, though, Bella reaches her goals and receives the classic rewards: marriage, motherhood, and upward mobility.

Conclusion

If the *Twilight* series teaches anything, it is that fiction can have a powerful influence on readers. Therefore, we should take seriously the concerns of those like Rebecca Housel, who sees the simulation described by Baudrillard as a potential problem for *Twilight* fans. Her warning to female readers highlights the danger that "members of the younger *Twilight* girl audience are truly buying in to the simulation ... as something attainable, something real" (186–87).

Indeed, the impact of fiction on a young mind can be substantial. Psychological studies have explored how reading fiction may help young readers develop "the capacity to understand and apply emotional experiences" within their own lives (Sklar 491); however, for adolescents, the process of experiencing narratives can be "complicated ... by the volatility of their emotional lives" (493). Furthermore, psychologist Jerome Bruner has argued that "eventually the culturally shaped cognitive and linguistic processes that guide the self-telling of life narratives achieve the power to structure perceptual experience" (694), forming a system of mutual influence between invention/narrative and perception/reality. "In the end," argues Bruner, "we *become* the autobiographical narratives by which we 'tell about' our lives" (694).

Meyer's work documents this process of "becoming" the narrative. Bella recognizes the power of fiction, "how preoccupied [she] could get when surrounded by books" (*T* 156), and the patterning of her behavior after her reading list suggests how fully she has absorbed fictional models. In mundane situations, Bella expresses herself in the melodramatic ways of the heroines of novels that she has read. In *Twilight*, for example, she swoons when Edward's lips touch hers (319); she describes as "horror" her response to a new snow (53), the prospect of a five-mile hike in the woods (254), and going to the prom with Edward (484); she feels "shock" upon learning that Tyler has named her as his prom date (153). However, when she is faced with a truly dire situation, such as being "herded" into a dangerous trap by four men on a deserted street in a strange town (157–61), the dramatic language that she applies to her everyday life vanishes. Taken together, Bella's responses smack of the dangers of reading fiction described by Thomas Jefferson in his 1818 letter to Nathaniel Burwell: "a bloated imagination, sickly judgment, and disgust towards all the real businesses of life" (91).

It is clear that Bella's fictional models lie in a distant past and that her story directly engages that past. Her choices, together with evidence of her inner architecture, suggest that she has not only internalized her fictions, but used them as a blueprint for her reality. As a result, Bella ultimately can assert, "My life was circled by legend on every side. They were all true" (*BD* 137). The narratives that Bella has inscribed into her psyche and used as models for her life now circumscribe her; she is "circled by legend" in a very real and practical sense. She has, in effect, built her very own copy world.

NOTES

1. Meyer's comments about Bella notwithstanding, perhaps not *all* of her characters are mere words on a page. According to *The Twilight Lexicon*, when asked whether Edward was "based on" her husband, Meyer replied "that if her husband were like Edward, she wouldn't have had to create Edward" ("Q&A: BYU").

2. For example, Rebecca Housel's essay on the dangers of *Twilight* argues compellingly that female readers who emulate Bella do so at their own risk.

3. The internet offers abundant evidence of this phenomenon, including a "How to be Like Bella Swan" page at eHow.com.

4. Similarly, Susan Vaught's "A Very Dangerous Boy" compares Edward's behavior with diagnostic criteria for Antisocial Personality Disorder to explore whether he is a sociopath.

5. Please see Benning's essay in this collection for further discussion of this topic.

6. While McClimans and Wisnewski note that in patriarchal cultures, women commonly interpret "controlling and overbearing behavior ... as caring and romantic" (164), Housel warns that real-life Edwards are "stalkers who perpetrate rampant violence against women" (188).

7. This is demonstrated in Murphy's essay in this collection.

8. Ruth Bottigheimer's book-based theory of tale transmission argues that fairy tales are not an "unmediated expression of human beings' emotional need," but a commercially mediated one (*New History* 107). Commercially, Meyer's fairy tale is phenomenally successful: as of March 2010, more than 100 million copies of the *Twilight* novels had been sold (Sellers).

9. These parallels, too, are discussed elsewhere in this volume.

WORKS CITED

Andersen, Hans Christian. *Fairy Tales and Other Stories*. Ed. and trans. W. A. and J. K. Craigie. London: Oxford University Press, 1914.

Baudrillard, Jean. *Simulacra & Simulation*. Trans. Sheila Faria Glaser. Ann Arbor: University of Michigan Press, 1994.

Beck, Aaron T., Arthur Freeman, and Denise D. Davis. *Cognitive Therapy of Personality Disorders*. 2nd ed. New York: Guilford, 2004.

Berne, Eric. *Transactional Analysis in Psychotherapy: A Systematic Individual and Social Psychiatry*. New York: Grove, 1961.

Bettelheim, Bruno. *The Uses of Enchantment: The Meaning and Importance of Fairy Tales*. New York: Vintage, 1989.

Bottigheimer, Ruth B. *Fairy Godfather: Straparola, Venice, and the Fairy Tale Tradition*. Philadelphia: University of Pennsylvania Press, 2002.

_____. *Fairy Tales: A New History*. Albany: State University of New York Press, 2009.

Bower, Bruce. "Teenage Turning Point: Does Adolescence Herald the Twilight of Girls' Self-Esteem?" *Science News* 23 March 1991: 184–186. *JSTOR*. Web. 9 May 2009.

Bruner, Jerome. "Life as Narrative." *Social Research* 71.3 (2004): 691–710. *Gen. OneFile*. Web. 3 May 2009.

Contactqueen. Online posting, 18 August 2008. "If you could be any Twilight character for one day Who would you be? Why? What would you do with your day?" Online poll, 26 July 2008. *The Twilight Forums*. N. p. Web. 19 January 2010.

Day, William Patrick. *Vampire Legends in Contemporary American Culture: What Becomes a Legend Most*. Lexington: University Press of Kentucky, 2002.

Hooper, Lisa M. "Expanding the Discussion Regarding Parentification and Its Varied Outcomes: Implications for Mental Health Research and Practice." *Jour. of Mental Health Counseling* 29.4 (2007): 322–337. *Academic Search Complete*. Web. 10 June 2009.

Housel, Rebecca. "The 'Real' Danger: Fact vs. Fiction for the Girl Audience." *Twilight and Philosophy: Vampires, Vegetarians, and the Pursuit of Immortality*. Eds. Rebecca Housel and J. Jeremy Wisnewski. Hoboken: Wiley, 2009. 177–190.

Jefferson, Thomas. "To Nathaniel Burwell." 14 March 1818. *The Works of Thomas Jefferson*. Ed. Paul Leicester Ford. Vol 12. New York: Putnam, 1905.

Jones, Ernest. *On the Nightmare*. London: Hogarth, 1931. *Scribd*. Web. 29 October 2010.

Jurkovic, Gregory J. *Lost Childhoods: The Plight of the Parentified Child*. New York: Brunner/Mazel, 1997.

Kaplan, Morton, and Robert Kloss. *The Unspoken Motive: A Guide to Psychoanalytic Literary Criticism*. New York: Free Press, 1973.

Mann, Bonnie. "Vampire Love: The Second Sex Negotiates the Twenty-first Century." *Twilight and Philosophy: Vampires, Vegetarians, and the Pursuit of Immortality*. Eds. Rebecca Housel and J. Jeremy Wisnewski. Hoboken: Wiley, 2009. 131–145.

McClimans, Leah, and J. Jeremy Wisnewski. "Undead Patriarchy and the Possibility of Love." *Twilight and Philosophy: Vampires, Vegetarians, and the Pursuit of Immortality*. Eds. Rebecca Housel and J. Jeremy Wisnewski. Hoboken: Wiley, 2009. 163–175.

Meyer, Stephenie. *Breaking Dawn*. New York: Little, Brown, 2008.

_____. *Eclipse*. New York: Little, Brown, 2007.

_____. "Frequently Asked Questions: *Breaking Dawn*." *The Official Website of Stephenie Meyer*. Stephenie Meyer, n.d. Web. 10 June 2009.

_____. "Frequently Asked Questions: *Twilight*." *The Official Website of Stephenie Meyer*. Stephenie Meyer, n.d. Web. 27 February 2010.

_____. *New Moon*. New York: Little, Brown, 2006.

_____. *Twilight*. New York: Little, Brown, 2005.

Morrison, Robert, ed. "Introduction." *Jane Austen's* Pride and Prejudice*: A Sourcebook*. New York: Routledge, 2005.

Myers, Abigail E. "Edward Cullen and Bella Swan: Byronic and Feminist Heroes ... or Not." *Twilight and Philosophy: Vampires, Vegetarians, and the Pursuit of Immortality*. Eds. Rebecca Housel and J. Jeremy Wisnewski. Hoboken: Wiley, 2009. 147–162.

Newton, Trudi. "Script, Psychological Life Plans, and the Learning Cycle." *Transactional Analysis Jour.* 36.3 (2006): 186–195. *ProQuest*. Web. 29 May 2009.

Nünning, Ansgar. "Unreliable, Compared to What? Towards a Cognitive Theory of *Unreliable Narration*: Prolegomena and Hypotheses." *Grenzüberschreitungen: Narratologie im Kontext/Transcending Boundaries: Narratology in Context*. Eds. Walter Grünzweig and Andreas Solbach. Tübingen: Narr, 1999. 53–73. *Google Book Search*. Web. 9 May 2010.

"Personal Correspondence 9." *Twilight Lexicon*. 18 April 2006. Web. 23 May 2010.

"Q&A from the February 2007, BYU Symposium." *Twilight Lexicon*. 9 February 2007. Web. 23 May 2010.

Sellers, John A. "New Stephenie Meyer Novella Arriving in June." *Publishers Weekly*. 30 March 2010. Web. 29 May 2010.

Siering, Carmen D. "Taking a Bite out of *Twilight*." *Ms.* Spring 2009: 50–52. *ProQuest*. Web. 9 June 2009.

Sklar, Howard. "Narrative as Experience: The Pedagogical Implications of Sympathizing with Fictional Characters." *Partial Answers* 6.2 (2008): 481–501. *ProQuest*. Web. 5 May 2009.

Twitchell, James B. *The Living Dead: A Study of the Vampire in Romantic Literature*. Durham: Duke University Press, 1981.

Vaught, Susan. "A Very Dangerous Boy." *A New Dawn: Your Favorite Authors on Stephenie Meyer's Twilight Series*. Eds. Ellen Hopkins and Leah Wilson. Dallas: BenBella, 2008. 1–12. Print.

Wilson, Natalie. "Beautiful or Strong? A Consideration of Female Roles in the *Twilight* Series." Summer School in Forks: A *Twilight* Symposium. Forks High School, Forks, WA. 27 June 2009. Lecture.

Zipes, Jack. *Fairy Tales and the Art of Subversion: The Classical Genre for Children and the Process of Civilization*. 2nd ed. New York: Routledge, 2006.

Torn Between Two Lovers
Twilight *Tames* Wuthering Heights

SARAH WAKEFIELD

"All of the books in the *Twilight* saga have a classical inspiration," Stephenie Meyer confirmed in a June 2008 video released by her publisher ("Stephenie Meyer"). For example, *Twilight* borrows the initial coldness of the lovers in *Pride and Prejudice*, while *New Moon* uses a plot twist from Shakespeare's *Romeo and Juliet*, the hero's mistaken belief that his beloved is dead. In the same video, Meyer noted, "*Eclipse*, for me, was my *Wuthering Heights* homage" ("Stephenie Meyer"). Perhaps motivated by this revelation, Harper Collins issued new editions of *Wuthering Heights* in 2009, complete with *Twilight*-inspired cover art and tags proclaiming it "Bella and Edward's favorite book." By the summer of 2009, *Wuthering Heights* had enjoyed four months at the top of the best-selling classics list at Waterstone's in the U.K. (Adams), and the publisher of the French translation reported that more copies of the novel sold in the first two months of 2009 than typically sell in twelve (Sage). Many Meyer fans, we can presume, sat down with this Victorian novel.

Such popularity did not greet *Wuthering Heights* upon its debut in 1848. Its characters physically attack, threaten, and wish death on each other; plot vengeance against their neighbors and their neighbors' children; and vow to break hearts and coffins open in pursuit of their own desires. Faced with such shockingly un–Victorian attitudes throughout the narrative, Brontë's earliest critics found it hard to articulate redeeming qualities in *Wuthering Heights*. Most chose the word "strange" as a descriptor, if not "a disagreeable story ... eccentric and unpleasant."[1] Now the novel enjoys masterpiece status, and modern critics approach it from dozens of angles to explain its continued appeal; whether examining the heroine, Catherine Earnshaw, as a proto-feminist struggling for identity (Gilbert and Gubar) or exploring Heathcliff's vampire and werewolf traits (McGuire). Three theories in particular inform this analysis: Marxist, with a focus on the capitalist clash between the wealthy residents of Thrushcross Grange and the upwardly-mobile, self-made man Heathcliff; psychoanalytic, emphasizing the neat alignment of Brontë's characters with Freud's three-part psyche; and postcolonial, reading Heathcliff's racial difference in terms of imperialism and master-slave relationships.[2]

Yet Brontë fans don't necessarily approach *Wuthering Heights* from a theoretical angle — instead, as Thomas C. Moser says, "one admires and rereads the novel for the grand passion of Heathcliff and Cathy" (3). This seems to be the primary attraction for our *Twilight* heroine, Bella, who owns a battered copy and who, by page 34 of *Twilight*, is re-reading *Wuthering Heights* for her new English class. When Edward dismisses her favorite book as "a hate story," complaining about the destructive tendencies of its central couple, Bella defends her choice by stressing "the inevitability. How nothing can keep them apart — not her selfishness, or his evil, or even death, in the end.... Their love *is* their only redeeming quality" (*E* 28). Meyer seems to agree with her fictional heroine, creating a four-part saga that echoes the "inevitability" of Cathy and Heathcliff's love (along with impediments to its fulfillment) via its focus on Bella, Edward, and Jacob.

Thematically, the *Twilight* books share with the Victorian novel an insistence on passionate soul mates, the impossibility of living without one's beloved, and the simultaneous impossibility of having one's beloved in a rational world. On the surface, both narratives also engage Marxist and postcolonial conflicts with similar distinctions in social class and race. A rich white boy (Edward / Edgar) competes with a poor brown boy (Jacob / Heathcliff) for the heart of a white girl (Bella / Cathy) who loves them both, in different ways. To mimic the tragedy of *Wuthering Heights* faithfully, Bella ought to marry Edward for the wealth and status afforded by being a Cullen, regret her choice, and keep Jacob as her true soul mate. Instead, if we keep up the comparison, *Twilight*'s revised Cathy marries a newly passionate Edgar and, because her motivation is love rather than money, she's content. Heathcliff, "a fierce, pitiless, wolfish man" (Brontë 83), realizes that Cathy is not his soul mate after all, and happily devotes himself to the daughter of his one-time crush and his rival.

Towards the end of *Eclipse*, when comparing herself to the heroine of *Wuthering Heights*, Bella acknowledges that unlike Cathy Earnshaw, she gets to choose between two truly wonderful men, "neither one evil, neither one weak" (517). Bella herself lacks what many read as Cathy's fatal weakness, the inability to stand by her soul mate, and her options are superior to Cathy's because Edward and Jacob are tamer, hybrid versions of Edgar Linton and Heathcliff. For example, Edward combines Edgar's best qualities — his good looks, wealth, adoring family, and psychological function as the controlled superego to the heroine's ego — with Heathcliff's fierce love.[3] Jacob, the dark, hot-blooded childhood friend, mirrors Heathcliff in everything from his minority roots to his psychological role as the impulsive id, urging the heroine to be more reckless. But unlike Heathcliff, Jacob resists joining his rival's "class," i.e. transforming into a powerful supernatural creature himself, and becomes a wolf against his will.

The mystical rules governing vampires and wolves in the *Twilight* world also eliminate key stumbling blocks from *Wuthering Heights*. Where Cathy Earnshaw dies, vampire venom saves Bella Swan, and Jacob imprints on Renesmee, thereby losing Heathcliff's motivation, grief over losing his soul mate, to spend years methodically destroying two families. In many ways, therefore, we can read the *Twilight* books as a tamer version of the Victorian drama in which becoming a "monster," strangely enough, defuses three crucial conflicts in Brontë's narrative. Supernatural chromosomes displace the desire to move up in social rank, downplay racial tensions, and conveniently unsnarl the lovers' triangle to provide fairy tale endings all around.

What a Girl Wants: Property vs. Passion

The first obstacle in *Wuthering Heights*, social rank, weighs heavily on characters in a classic Marxist scenario of class rivalry. Mr. Earnshaw rescues the orphan Heathcliff and brings him home, but as soon as the patriarch dies, his son Hindley banishes the interloper to the stables. Heathcliff, forced to work as a menial servant, endures constant physical and verbal abuse from his new master. Seeing her true love so reduced, Cathy Earnshaw chooses another, richer husband, whom she loves enough. The social status conferred by marriage in England, as in much of the world, was very clear-cut: the woman took on the class of her spouse, whether she married up or down. Cathy, "queen of the countryside," can only fall to Heathcliff's level, and she complains, "It would degrade me to marry Heathcliff now ... did it never strike you that if Heathcliff and I married, we should be beggars? Whereas, if I married Linton, I can aid Heathcliff to rise" (Brontë 63–64). Cathy resolves to marry into money to rescue Heathcliff from her brother Hindley. She sees no reason to give up her dearest friend just because she has a new husband, either, and tells the servant Nelly Dean, "Who is to separate us, pray? ... Every Linton on the face of the earth might melt into nothing before I could consent to forsake Heathcliff" (64). For his part, Heathcliff runs away and spends the next three years accumulating enough capital, both financial and cultural, to compete with Edgar as a gentleman. Cathy, faced with few other options, marries Edgar anyway.

In a very obvious sense, therefore, class defines the romantic relationships in *Wuthering Heights*. By contrast, social distinctions in the *Twilight* saga figure more subtly in the characters' romantic choices. In Phoenix, Bella Swan lived with her mother in a modest part of town, in sharp contrast to the majority of her privileged classmates. In Forks, she shares a small, one-bathroom house with her working-class, police chief father, and she breathes a sigh of relief to see nothing nicer than a silver Volvo in the high school parking lot. Edward Cullen, the car's owner and adopted son of an accomplished surgeon, lives in a three-story mansion, and, much like Edgar Linton in *Wuthering Heights*, he seems never to have known poverty, judging from his mother's exquisite diamond jewelry and his affluent lifestyle. Bella reacts on a physical level rather than a mercenary one when she first sees Edward's beautiful face, and whereas Cathy admits that Edgar's extensive property motivates her choice of husband, Meyer's heroine is reluctant to say that money plays any role in her attraction. In *Eclipse*, when Jacob accuses her of liking Edward because he's attractive and wealthy, she reacts vehemently: "I'd much rather he weren't either one. It would even out the gap between us just a little bit — because he'd still be the most loving and unselfish and brilliant and *decent* person I've ever met" (*E* 110). Bella even refuses to accept gifts from her boyfriend during her human days because anything besides him makes the gap between them even wider, and she wants to feel that they are as equal as possible. Of course, after she marries Edward, she drives luxury cars, wears designer clothes, lives in a custom-designed cottage, and presumably allows her husband to pay her Dartmouth tuition, all with no complaint.

What Bella seems to want most is not financial security, which motivates Cathy Earnshaw, but the security of being a beautiful, indestructible immortal, worthy of standing beside Edward Cullen for all of eternity. Her sad comments about the physical discrepancies she sees between herself and her soul mate, an angelic, "godlike creature" (*T* 256) with golden eyes and perfect body, easily could apply to a poor girl describing her upper-class lover. One of her most poignant remarks on the subject comes in *Eclipse*, when she reflects that she, like her ramshackle bike, looks pathetic beside a sleek, expensive motorcycle and the boyfriend who purchased it (233). Granted, Bella longs to join the ranks of superior beings because she hopes to look as stunning as the Cullens but primarily because she loves Edward fiercely. This represents a variation on the theme of *Wuthering Heights*, where Cathy chooses Edgar because he represents a good marriage. Raised in the 20th century, where matrimony results from deep affection, Bella wants to marry Edward for less overtly materialistic reasons. She may benefit from the fabulous wealth of his family, but as she reflects while self-consciously driving an armored Mercedes around Forks, "The best parts about being a Cullen were not expensive cars and impressive credit cards" (*BD* 9).

Even though Edward warns her that she is trading her mortality for an inferior, soulless existence governed by bloodlust (in essence that his world is impoverished), Bella stubbornly stands her ground. Rosalie begs her to stay human, offering her own cautionary tale of social climbing and pointing out everything that has been lost; but Bella thinks that she's coming out ahead as long as she has Edward (*E* 168). This conviction epitomizes a crucial difference between the heroines of *Wuthering Heights* and the *Twilight* saga. Cathy Earnshaw lacks the resolve to embrace her true love, poverty and all, and she pays dearly for her weakness, starting from the day that she confesses her plan to marry Edgar Linton. Heathcliff, thinking he is unwanted, disappears, and Cathy's doctor fears she will commit suicide and warns the servants to "take care she did not throw herself downstairs or out of the window" (Brontë 69). She does not see Heathcliff again for three years. Conversely, Bella chooses Edward and the vampire lifestyle he represents. Arguably, since he unites beauty, brains, and wealth (Edgar's traits) in one soul mate (Heathcliff's allure), it hardly seems like a difficult decision, unless we consider the loss of humanity and a potential future with Jacob. Bella will sacrifice both for Edward, and although she, like Cathy, must watch her soul mate disappear in *New Moon*, thanks to her fidelity she only has to endure four months of numbness and nightmares before returning to Edward's arms. Because Meyer does not allow her heroine to betray her heart as Cathy does or to doubt the all-encompassing love she feels for her vampire, Bella avoids a destructive chain of events like that visited on Brontë's characters.

The intensity of the bond between Bella and Edward has led some to complain that the heroine's "ideas about gender roles are decidedly unfeminist" (Sax), particularly that she needs a boy to survive and she quickly embraces marriage and maternity. With this throwback sensibility, she shares even more with Cathy Earnshaw, who, critic Linda Gold argues, has "little outlet for her primal desires; there is a single culturally endorsed position — that of wife.... She must attempt to live through men if she is to live at all" (69). Modern teenager Bella Swan has options. She could move to Florida to stay with her mother, go off to college, or wait a few years to settle down. Her determination to be with Edward and his equal determination to have a conventional relationship do lead her down the aisle, but unlike the case with Cathy, this is not her only option.

Another "unfeminist" plot twist in the *Twilight* saga, Bella's unexpected pregnancy, also seems to draw inspiration from *Wuthering Heights* while highlighting the resolute nature of Meyer's heroine. Fragile after another illness, Cathy Earnshaw appears unaware, or at least unconcerned, about the baby growing inside of her, since she refuses to eat or drink. Susan Rubinow Gorsky goes further, arguing that Cathy "may want Edgar's child to die or she may realize that the baby, controlling her even before birth, will be a living symbol of the loss of freedom and of Heathcliff" (183). Whatever her feelings, she delivers a premature daughter and dies without ever regaining consciousness. By contrast, Bella wants Edward's child desperately and refuses to consider abortion. She gives control of her body to her half-vampire child, who cracks her ribs, causes her to crave blood, and eventually snaps her spine.

The death of the heroine represents one of the key tragedies in *Wuthering Heights*, and supernatural magic helps the characters of the *Twilight* saga avoid such a problematic plot point. Cathy expects to see Heathcliff someday, when he dies, and he spends the next twenty years in agony. Trusting in vampire venom to heal her injuries, Bella resolves to keep her heart beating long enough for the transformation to work. She dies only to be reborn, days later, as an immortal on earth. Therefore, Edward does not have to mourn her or destroy himself; Jacob does not have to seek vengeance for her demise or lose himself in his animalistic side. Without a mutual, devastating loss to feed their animosity, the young men can reconcile. It also helps that the gentlemen in question, especially Edward, no longer embody the absolutes of the male characters in *Wuthering Heights*.

Making a Successful Soul Mate: Edward as Fusion of Brontë's Men

Edward Cullen shares many traits of Edgar Linton, with some Heathcliff thrown in to balance the extremes. Blond and blue-eyed, Edgar Linton is "handsome, and young, and cheerful, and rich" (Brontë 61), the fair-skinned master of Thrushcross Grange. He worships Cathy in an odd predator / prey fashion, able to leave her "as much as a cat possesses the power to leave a mouse half-killed, or a bird half-eaten" (57)—that is to say, not at all. After their marriage, according to Nelly Dean, Edgar "had a deep-rooted fear of ruffling her humour ... and averred that the stab of a knife could not inflict a worse pang than he suffered at seeing his lady vexed" (72). When Cathy becomes ill, Edgar, full of patient, calm devotion, rarely leaves her side. From appearance to financial status to a lion / lamb relationship with Bella, Edward resembles descriptions of Edgar. His indulgences towards the woman he loves include an offer to Jacob, to father Bella's children, if he can convince her to end her pregnancy (*BD* 180). Later, when Jacob hears of Bella's post-vampire plan to stay in touch with Charlie, he disapprovingly thinks Edward is humoring his new bride too much (*BD* 301).

Like Edgar and Heathcliff, most of the time Edward and Jacob resist being forced together, thanks to long-standing enmity and rivalry over Bella. But where Brontë's characters stick to disastrous, extreme positions, Meyer's tamer men can compromise. Edgar remembers Heathcliff as "the gipsy — the plough-boy" (Brontë 74), but, because he loves Cathy, he permits her old friend to visit Thrushcross Grange. Only when he discovers Heathcliff's designs on his sister Isabella does he issue an ultimatum: "Will you give up Heathcliff hereafter, or will you give me up? It is impossible for you to be *my* friend and *his* at the same time; and I absolutely *require* to know which you choose!" (93). Initially, Edward's feelings mirror Edgar's. Right before the first direct reference to *Wuthering Heights* appears in *Eclipse*, the hero informs his girlfriend that socializing on the Quileute reservation isn't going to happen, period. When Bella, showing some of Cathy's rebellious spirit, plans to go to La Push anyway, Edward disables her truck and then arranges a sleepover with Alice as her warden. Edward's concern goes far beyond Edgar's worry over the virtue of his wife and sister; Quileute wolves can kill and maim those they love most, as the scarred Emily, the pack leader's mate proves all too well. Perhaps, then, it is even more remarkable when Edward relents. After Bella escapes to the reservation a second time, he promises to approach the situation sensibly. She can decide whether or not she feels any risk in being around Jacob (*E* 190).

Underneath the cool diplomacy, Edward feels a sentiment much more in line with the antihero of *Wuthering Heights*. One night he comments lightly that the more he tolerates Jacob, the better he understands Heathcliff (*E* 265). The next day, Bella notices her copy of Brontë open to the page where Heathcliff explains that he never would harm Edgar Linton, so long as Cathy liked her husband: "the moment her regard ceased. I would have torn his heart out, and drank his blood!" Edward identifies with characteristics of Heathcliff that complement his amazing self-control, and he refrains from fighting Jacob because it would hurt Bella. If he knows *Wuthering Heights*, he also knows that banishing his beloved's best friend could be catastrophic. When Edgar demands that Cathy choose, permanently, she commits her second, major error, impulsively deciding, "Well, if I cannot keep Heathcliff for my friend, if Edgar will be mean and jealous, I'll try to break their hearts by breaking my own" (Brontë 92). The resulting delirium is one of the primary causes of her death, and Edward avoids the loss of the woman he loves by replacing Edgar's ultimatums with Heathcliff's difficult compromise.

Where Edgar says no, Heathcliff says yes, and Cathy is caught between the two extremes. Psychoanalytic criticism of *Wuthering Heights* argues that with this struggle, the lovers' triangle faithfully replicates the three parts of the Freudian psyche: the superego, id, and ego. Edgar, who "never shirks his duty or tolerates dereliction in others" (Gold 69), acts as the superego, the part of the unconscious mind that dictates appropriate behavior, while Heathcliff embodies passionate, uncivilized instincts associated with the id and Cathy, the conscious mind or ego, tries to reconcile the demands of the other two psychological. I would argue that Edward echoes Edgar's superego function by opposing the id, Jacob, and directing the ego, Bella. Especially when it comes to sex, Edward draws firm lines, admonishing Bella to control herself and preventing her from going too far. When she finds the courage to ask that they try to sleep together before the wedding, Bella sees censure in his eyes, and he scolds her to be realistic (*E* 443). Christine Seifert argues that Bella "is absolutely dependent on Edward's ability to protect her life, her virginity, and her humanity. She is the object of this virtue, the means of his ability to prove his self-control" (25). These descriptions from both *Eclipse* and Seifert place Bella in the role of the ego, receiving rules from Edward. Freud observes that the superego "lays down definite standards for [the ego's] conduct ... [and] if those standards are not obeyed, punishes it with tense feelings of inferiority and of guilt" (97). While somewhat apropos, this also seems too extreme to describe Edward's interactions with Bella. When she wants to move past kissing, his usual retort is a joke about human passions, and while insecure, Bella primarily complains about sexual frustration, with occasional insecurity that he doesn't want her. And of course, it's not just a matter of morality and abstinence, since Edward's venom-coated teeth and iron grip literally can kill Bella if he loses control. Overall, refusing to sleep with Bella outside of wedlock allows Edward to protect his soul mate, preserve his 1917 morals, and flex his superego powers to the maximum.

Reinforcing the connection between Edward and the superego is the natural symbol that Bella associates with him: a perfectly, almost unnaturally circular meadow (*NM* 234). Like the superego, governed by rationality and immune to the demands of the chaotic id, the meadow rests tranquilly in the heart of unchecked wilderness. In a strange coincidence, Edwards's sign matches Cathy's picture of her love for Edgar Linton, since she describes it "like the foliage in the woods: time will change it, I'm well aware, as winter changes the trees" (Brontë 64). By contrast, Jacob gets First Beach in La Push. The rocky beach may put readers of *Wuthering Heights* in mind of Cathy's description of her affection for Heathcliff, which "resembles the eternal rocks beneath: a source of little visible delight, but necessary" (64). But the attached sentiments are reversed for Bella, who wants the foliage, not the rocks. She knows that time will *not* change her feelings for Edward Cullen, because in her eyes, he is her Heathcliff.

Edward identifies with Heathcliff as well and not only for his restraint at not ripping out his rival's throat. The vampire directly quotes only one passage from *Wuthering Heights* to Bella, Heathcliff's anguished exclamation, "I cannot live without my life! I cannot live without my soul!" Arnold Kettle says that this outburst shows "an affinity deeper than sexual attraction, something which it is not enough to describe as romantic love" (163), which is precisely how Edward and Bella feel about their relationship. Yet the statement also can signal a mismatch, argues Dorothy van Ghent, because "one does not 'mate' with oneself, with one's own life, with one's own soul. Cathy and Heathcliff are unthinkable in adult domestication as lovers" (196). The *Twilight* series attempts to correct this problem by making a virtue out of a *Wuthering Heights* stumbling block. Cathy characterizes Linton as decidedly frosty, while she and Heathcliff are kindred spirits: "Whatever our souls are made of, his and mine are the same; and Linton's is as different as a moonbeam from lightning, or frost from fire" (Brontë 63). Later, she complains to her hated husband, "your cold blood cannot be worked into a fever: your veins are full of ice-water; but mine are boiling, and the sight of such chillness makes them dance" (92). *Twilight's* vampires are ice-cold, and Bella often describes her physical reaction to Edward in fiery terms, as happens with their first kiss: "Blood boiled under my skin, burned in my lips" (*T* 282). Where *Wuthering Heights* suggests that unlike elements lead to incompatibility, *Twilight* proposes instead that opposites attract. Bella marvels at the successful first night of her honeymoon, thinking, "Fire and ice, somehow existing together without destroying each other. More proof that I belonged with him" (*BD* 87). Where Cathy and Heathcliff perhaps are too similar, Edward's chilliness makes him more suitable for Bella, complementing her heat.

Running Hot: Heathcliff Gets a Happy Ending

For heat, the *Twilight* saga has Jacob Black. When Bella's classmates see his motorcycle and six foot, seven inch frame, they avoid walking anywhere near him (*E* 77). Just months earlier, Jacob came to the Fork High prom, conspicuous without a tuxedo, but no one noticed him. He has grown into a commanding figure, much like Heathcliff after his three-year absence. As Nelly remembers, "His countenance was much older in expression and decision of feature.... A half-civilised ferocity lurked yet in the depressed brows and eyes full of black fire" (Brontë 75). Similar changes happen for Jacob almost overnight, and he looks not only harder and older but darker: "The open, friendly smile was gone like the hair, the warmth in his eyes altered to a brooding resentment that was instantly disturbing" (*NM* 262). The trigger behind the dramatic alterations is that both men have joined their rival's class. To compete with Linton, Heathcliff methodically "amasses a certain amount of cultural capital in his two years' absence in order to shackle others more effectively" (Eagleton 104) and sets about destroying his enemies. "I have no pity! I have no pity! The more the worms writhe, the more I yearn to crush out their entrails!" (Brontë 119) he tells himself. Rather than gaining property, Jacob becomes a member of Edward's supernatural class, and since he does not choose his transformation, he resents the change. As the descendent of both Ephraim Black and Quil Ateara, he should be chief of the Quileute people by birthright, but Jacob doesn't want these new riches and stubbornly controls what little he can by refusing to lead. Only when Sam decides that Bella and her unborn baby must die, committing the wolves to murder, does Jacob become an Alpha. Because he decides to protect his enemies where Heathcliff refuses to consider mercy, Jacob Black skirts the misery that permeates the second half of *Wuthering Heights*.

Much of Heathcliff's misery stems from his ethnic identity, which postcolonial theory would characterize as subaltern or Other, excluded from mainstream power. Variously described as "a dark-skinned gypsy" (Brontë 5), "as dark almost as if it came from the devil" (29), and "a little Lascar, or an American or Spanish castaway" (40), Heathcliff comes from Liverpool, where Emily's brother, Branwell, visited when the first Irish emigrants, victims of the Great Famine, arrived in 1845. Quite possibly, then, Brontë's brooding hero is Irish. Troubled Anglo-Irish relations go back centuries, from the 1366 Statutes of Kilkenny, which unsuccessfully outlawed English immigrants from taking on Irish customs or spouses, to the 1801 Act of Union, which disbanded the Irish Parliament. As Ivan Kreilkamp insists, however, *Wuthering Heights* often figures Heathcliff as an animal, and therefore "*species* seems as salient as race as a category by which to consider Brontë's depiction of the character" (98). Descended from a species of wolf, Jacob Black has Native American heritage to mark him as an American racial minority, and the Quileute people, like the Irish, intimately know colonization and exploitation. In government treaties in the 1850s, the tribe was forced to surrender all land rights and waited until 1889 for an official reservation, scarcely more than one square mile in size, on the western coast of Washington (Leggatt and Burnett 30). That same year, a disgruntled pioneer who tried to claim the land set fire to every tribal home ("History"), and today, according to Angela R. Riley, over 50 percent of the Quileutes lives below the poverty line.

Strikingly, although the novels skirt such racial information, race (or species) remains a troubling subtext. When Edgar and Edward complain about their rivals, they express concern for their loved ones' safety, citing a generalized danger from "the low ruffian" (89) in *Wuthering Heights* and the ruffian werewolves in Meyer's saga. Because both Heathcliff and Jacob not only have darker skin but different class status than their white adversaries, it can be difficult to determine whether class, race, or both motivate prejudice against them. In fact, citizens in Victorian England often used the same id-based terms — hypersexual, criminal, and superstitious — to describe the working class and non-white races. Postcolonial critic Edward Said further explains that the imperial conquerors see natives as "irrational, depraved (fallen), child-like, 'different'" (40). The *Twilight* saga tries to underplay such racism between its leeches and dogs. For example, Bella refuses to play the species game, informing a disgruntled Jacob that the vampire-werewolf rivalry means nothing to her and she sees everyone as individuals (*E* 130). Furthermore, while one could claim that the vampires control the wolves, since their presence triggers several transformations, one also could argue for the tribe's autonomy. The first Quileute shifter, Taha Aki, became a wolf not in response to "the cold ones" but to fellow tribe member Utlapa, who took over his chief's body and introduced the evils of polygamy and slavery. In fact, any threat in La Push, like the meth dealer whom Sam Uley chases off the reservation, causes the pack to grow (*NM* 173). During the final confrontation in Forks, Aro fantasizes about having guard dogs, but even he sounds a respectful note by announcing to the Volturi that the wolves "are creatures of our supernatural world" (*BD* 705). The characterization paints the shifting Quileutes not only as mythical noble savages, good warriors who share one collective mind and kill only to protect innocent lives, but also as worthy comrades willing to renegotiate treaties.

Nevertheless, because shifting itself seems to be an unintentional, spontaneous act, the Quileute wolves carry shadows of racial stereotypes, particularly the psychological association of non-white races with the id, "the archaic foundation of personality — selfish, asocial, impulsive" (Moser 4). This definition comes from Thomas Moser's apropos description of Heathcliff as the id incarnate, seeking pleasure and flouting social norms. Freud further defines the id as inherited, instinctual energies, which tantalizingly link to the genetic basis for changing into a wolf. Jacob, the cocky boy encouraging others to break rules and unabashedly manipulating Bella into asking for a kiss, often displays id-driven behaviors. While Edward becomes exasperated or coldly furious with Bella, he almost always remains in control. In contrast, Jacob grins, jokes, glares, growls, shakes, hisses, and explodes at her, going through every primal emotion in the book, particularly anger, as Natalie Wilson has noted (67). And, like the id can be a bad influence on the ego, when he's around, Bella sees herself as more immature and prone to reckless behavior (*E* 101). Even Edward admits to Jacob, sounding much like the superego addressing the id, "You connect to her on a level that I don't even understand. You are part of her, and she is part of you" (*BD* 180).

This connection leads Bella to echo Cathy Earnshaw's famous line, "I *am* Heathcliff," after her second kiss with Jacob. Realizing her very real but very different love for Jacob, she reflects, "In this moment, it felt as though we were the same person," sharing the same sorrows and happiness (*E* 528–9). Even after Cathy and Bella marry their husbands, affection for their old friends persists. Cathy finds it hard to hide her ecstasy at seeing Heathcliff after three long years, and later, when she is seven months pregnant and dying, she refuses to let him leave her side. Jacob experiences a similar welcome from a very pregnant Bella, and he's simultaneously outraged and confused by her glowing smiles (*BD* 270).

The excitement springs not so much from Bella as from Renesmee, already sensing a kindred spirit from within the womb. In *Wuthering Heights*, Heathcliff uses and abuses Cathy's daughter as a tool to grind down the Lintons even more. Jacob then diverges again from Brontë's character thanks to the special magic governing Quileute wolves. He *loves* the offspring of his beloved and his enemy because she is his soul mate, and all thoughts of retribution vanish. In both cases, the girl's striking dark eyes, exactly like their mothers,' stop the avengers dead in their tracks. After the second Cathy accuses Heathcliff of stealing her land and money, he furiously vows, "I'll make her repent it forever" and "seemed ready to tear Cathy into pieces" (Brontë 245). Inexplicably, he instead stares at the girl's face and lets her go. Once he thinks Bella is dead, Jacob resolves to crush the whole Cullen family. Then he sees the new baby's eyes are the same shade of chocolate brown as Bella's (*BD* 359), and just like Heathcliff, Jacob pauses. He loses his former identity, including his murderous rage, as he imprints on Renesmee; suddenly nothing matters except cherishing her. Where Heathcliff never gets over the original Cathy, Jacob's whole being shifts, quite involuntarily, to the daughter. The imprinting trait of the pack means they "really had no choice ... like magic" (*E* 418), and Jacob's id energies calm down once he finds Renesmee, just moments after Bella's "death." *Twilight*'s version of Heathcliff fails to win Cathy once again, but instead of unleashing his passions for decades, Jacob finds perfect contentment without his first love; she remains in his life and he receives a happy ending with a vampire-human hybrid.

The introduction of wolves and hybrids to the Forks vampire clan represents one final link to Emily Brontë's masterpiece. Norman Lavers proposes that *Wuthering Height*'s action focuses on one goal: "to rejuvenate" the static and dying Earnshaw family (63). A similar argument can be made for Carlisle Cullen's family, unchanged for decades. His self-denying tribe maintains its distance from the more boisterous Quileute community, similar to the differences between the residents of Thrushcross Grange and Wuthering Heights. Once Bella moves to Forks, the enemies start cooperating to protect her, and the miraculous birth of Renesmee draws more than wolves and the local coven. Vampires come from around the globe to meet the child, reconnect with the Cullens, and cement an extended family ready to oppose the Volturi in the future. For example, the Amazon Zafrina promises to visit Renesmee and be her friend, while Kate and Garrett appear to be falling in love; additionally, everyone learns about four other vampire-human hybrids in South America. Like Brontë's Earnshaws, the Cullens indeed are rejuvenated.

What starts in *Twilight* as two humans and one mythical creature metamorphoses (literally) into a supernatural family unit, providing a fairy tale ending very different from the final pages of *Wuthering Heights*. Feuding classes of vampires and werewolves become a united front determined to protect the small town of Forks from outsiders, a display of solidarity in sharp contrast to the twenty years of persistent distinctions in race and social class that cause Heathcliff to lash out without his beloved. Brontë's Cathy, struggling in vain to have two men, superego and id in her psychological life, chooses death instead. But thanks to her more rational personality, pregnancy, and vampire transformation, Bella Swan gets to keep a whole psyche and both of her suitors because they represent blended versions of the men of the Victorian novel. Her superego husband, a mixture of Edgar Linton and Heathcliff, boasts the charm, wealth, and beauty of the former and the strong physical and spiritual allure of the latter. Jacob provides id-based energies safely moderated by the imprinting process and lavishes Heathcliff's single-minded devotion on her daughter. It may seem paradoxical that transforming Edgar Linton into a vampire and Heathcliff into a werewolf could tame the wild, dark passions of *Wuthering Heights*. Indeed, it's not so simple, for racial and class dynamics persist. Venom and imprinting may work their decisive magic in the *Twilight* saga, but the resulting hybrid characters still echo the fundamental Victorian fault lines between white/dark and rich/poor. Stephenie Meyer pays homage to Emily Brontë by celebrating the Victorian novel's deep love, "something so strong that it could not exist in a rational world" (*E* 599), and also solves Cathy Earnshaw's problem — deciding between two very different yet appealing suitors — by combining the best of their features into two men who can stay in the heroine's life. One ideal husband, still white and firmly upper-class, and one probable future son-in-law, appropriately colonized and domesticated for marriage into the Cullen family, offer a happy ending for Bella Swan.

NOTES

1. Reviews in *Atlas*, *Douglas Jerrold's Weekly Newspaper*, and the *Examiner* all label *Wuthering Heights* "strange." The final observation comes from H.F. Chorley's review in *Athenaeum* 25 December 1847 (Brontë 281–288).

2. For both classic and contemporary examples of Marxist analyses, see Chapter 6 of Terry Eagleton's *Myths of Power: A Marxist Study of the Brontës* and Daniela Garofalo's article "Impossible Love and Commodity Culture in Emily Brontë's Wuthering Heights." For a Freudian psychoanalytic reading, see Thomas Moser's "What Is the Matter with Emily Jane? Conflicting Impulses in *Wuthering Heights*," and for postcolonial studies, see Chapter 2 of Elsie B. Michie's *Outside the Pale: Cultural Exclusion, Gender Difference, and the Victorian Woman Writer*.

WORKS CITED

Adams, Stephen. "Stephenie Meyer's Vampire Pushes *Wuthering Heights* to Top of Waterstone's Classics Chart." *Telegraph* 28 August 2009. Web. 11 March 2010.

Brontë, Emily. *Wuthering Heights*. 4th ed. Ed. Richard J. Dunn. New York: W.W. Norton & Co., 2003.

Eagleton, Terry. *Myths of Power: A Marxist Study of the Brontës*. London: Macmillan, 1975.

Freud, Sigmund. *New Introductory Lectures on Psycho-Analysis*. Ed. James Strachey. New York: W.W. Norton & Co., 1995.

Garofalo, Daniela. "Impossible Love and Commodity Culture in Emily Brontë's *Wuthering Heights*." *ELH* 75.4: 819–840. Project Muse. Web. 11 March 2010.

Gilbert, Sandra, and Susan Gubar. *The Madwoman in the Attic*. New Haven: Yale University Press, 1979.

Gold, Linda. "Cathy Earnshaw: Mother and Daughter." *The English Journal* 74.3 (1985): 68–73. JSTOR. Web. 11 March 2010.

Gorsky, Susan Rubinow. "'I'll Cry Myself Sick': Illness in *Wuthering Heights*." *Literature and Medicine* 18.2 (1999): 173–191. Project Muse. Web. 19 March 2010.

"History." *Quileute Nation*. Quileute Nation, 2009. Web. 26 May 2010.

Kettle, Arnold. "Emily Brontë: *Wuthering Heights* (1847)." *Critical Essays on Emily Brontë*. Ed.Thomas John Winnifrith. New York: G.K. Hall & Co., 1997. 161–179.

Kreilkamp, Ivan. "Petted Things: *Wuthering Heights* and the Animal." *The Yale Journal of Criticism* 18.1 (2005): 98. Project Muse. Web. 25 May 2010.

Lavers, Norman. "The Action of Wuthering Heights." *Readings on Wuthering Heights*. Ed. Hayley R. Mitchell. San Diego: Greenhaven Press, Inc., 1999. 61–68.

Leggatt, Judith, and Kristin Burnett. "Biting Bella: Treaty Negotiation, Quileute History, and Why 'Team Jacob' Is Doomed to Lose." *Twilight and History*. Ed. Nancy Reagin. Hoboken: John Wiley & Sons, 2010. 26–46.

McGuire, Kathryn. "The Incest Taboo in *Wuthering Heights*: A Modern Appraisal." *American Imago* 45.2 (1988): 217–24.

Michie, Elsie B. *Outside the Pale: Cultural Exclusion, Gender Difference, and the Victorian Woman Writer*. Ithaca, NY: Cornell University Press, 1994.

Moser, Thomas. "What Is the Matter with Emily Jane? Conflicting Impulses in *Wuthering Heights*." *Nineteenth-Century Fiction* 17.1 (1962): 1–19.

Riley, Angela R. "Sucking the Quileute Dry." *The New York Times* 7 February 2010. Web. 26 May 2010.

Sage, Adam. "French Teenagers Bitten by the Emily Brontë Bug." *The Times* 16 March 2009. Web. 11 March 2010.

Said, Edward. *Orientalism*. New York: Pantheon, 1978.

Sax, Leonard. "*Twilight* Sinks Its Teeth into Feminism." *Washington Post* 17 August 2008. Web. 23 March 2010.

Seifert, Christine. "Bite Me! (Or Don't)." *Bitch Magazine: Feminist Response to Popular Culture* 42 (Winter 2009): 23–25. EBSCOHost. Web. 23 March 2010.

"Stephenie Meyer Talks about Breaking Dawn." *YouTube*. Little, Brown Books, 11 June 2008. Web. 26 May 2010.

Van Ghent, Dorothy. "The Window Figure and the Two-Children Figure in 'Wuthering Heights.'" *Nineteenth-Century Fiction* 7.3 (1952): 189–197. JSTOR. Web. 26 May 2010.

Wilson, Natalie. "Civilized Vampires Versus Savage Werewolves: Race and Ethnicity in the Twilight Series." *Bitten by Twilight: Youth Culture, Media, and the Vampire Franchise*. Eds. Melissa A. Click, Jennifer Stevens Aubrey, and Elizabeth Behm-Morawitz. New York: Peter Lang, 2010. 55–70.

Rewriting the Byronic Hero
How the Twilight Saga Turned "Mad, Bad, and Dangerous to Know" into a Teen Fiction Phenomenon

JESSICA GROPER

In 1812, Lady Caroline Lamb wrote of her first meeting with the poet Lord Byron. Her famous description of him as "mad, bad, and dangerous to know" has lived on through the centuries for its accuracy in describing Byron and the literary archetype of the Byronic hero. Scholars can easily recognize this character because of his distinctive characteristics; the Byronic hero is attractive, in an unusual, sometimes sinister way. He is dangerous, violent, flouts the laws of society, and lives by his own personal moral code including seeking vengeance if he is wronged. He is exciting in his subversiveness, but to love him is to put oneself and one's soul in mortal danger. Notable Byronic heroes include Heathcliff in *Wuthering Heights*, Mr. Rochester in *Jane Eyre*, and many of Byron's main characters, such as Manfred and the Giaour (both from pieces named after them). Because he is perpetually an outsider who brings death when he enters society, this character is often connected with literary vampires.[1] The linked traditions of vampires and Byronic heroes continue in modern depictions, including *Buffy the Vampire Slayer*, *Interview With The Vampire*, and, of course, *Twilight*.

At first, there seems to be no doubt that Edward Cullen is part of this tradition.[2] His striking good looks, thirst for human blood, superhuman strength, and ability to read minds, all appear to create yet another fictional representation of the vampiric Byronic hero.[3] But I believe that Edward is, in fact, the exact opposite of this representation. Stephenie Meyer's depiction of

Edward is reminiscent of the Byronic hero archetype, but she gives the tradition a different, safer twist to create an anti–Byronic hero. Traditionally, the Byronic hero's tale ends unhappily with death and despair (or with life-altering injury, as with Mr. Rochester's blindness). And this is where Meyer's innovation is evident. She includes all of the danger and forbidden love that excite readers, but she also delivers the happy ending she, and many readers, want.[4] This essay will examine why some readers assume that Edward is Byronic, as well as identify the characteristics and choices Edward makes that truly make him anti–Byronic. Following this analysis, I will address the question of Jacob's role in this anti–Byronic narrative. Like Edward, some of Jacob's actions and choices fall in line with Byronic tradition, however, as will be shown, he is no more Byronic than Edward.

She Was Dreaming of Fictional Characters. So Much for My Conceit.

Not surprisingly, many scholars take it for granted that Edward is a Byronic hero; on the surface, from his good looks to the threat he poses to Bella and all other humans, he easily fits the mold. In "Edward Cullen and Bella Swan: Byronic and Feminist Heroes ... Or Not," Abigail Myers uses *Jane Eyre* to demonstrate how Edward falls into the Byronic archetype. Myers's essay is a side-by-side comparison of *Jane Eyre* and *Twilight*, in which she also explains for her readers the common characteristics of a Byronic hero.[5] However, her analysis is problematic in her choice of Mr. Rochester as a representative of the Byronic hero. In *Jane Eyre*, Mr. Rochester begins as an excellent example of a Byronic hero: he is attractive, secretive, manipulative, and immoral. However, by the end of the novel he becomes the exception rather than the rule, by achieving a happy ending. Myers is not wrong to identify Rochester as a Byronic hero — it is only in the final two chapters of the novel that he becomes a repentant man of faith — but his eventual redemption changes the course of the traditional Byronic plot trajectory, thus making him an imperfect example of the archetype, although an excellent comparison to Edward. Myers also credits Jane Eyre with being the force behind Rochester's redemption. By resisting Rochester and running away from him, Jane remains pure and, thus, deserves to be rewarded with a reformed Rochester for a husband. Myers is unable to make the same link between Bella and Edward, and she fails to expand her analysis to explain why the stories end with similar endings. The fact is, Rochester is a reformed Byronic hero; Edward is not a Byronic hero at all.[6] It is my view that Edward is his own redeemer and that it is the goodness of his character that allows for his happy ending. A close examination of Edward's responses to his Byronic impulses reveals how resistant he is to that role.

Dangerous ... But Not Bad

Without question, Edward is dangerous. In *Midnight Sun*, he estimates that he would only need five seconds to kill nineteen people (12). He demonstrates to Bella numerous times how strong and fast he is. On the other hand, he does not want to be dangerous. He regrets being a vampire and would do anything to be human again. Bella's blood is Edward's biggest challenge; he struggles not to kill her even when he knows he is in love with her. This imminent danger is typical to the Byronic tradition. Customarily, the woman involved with the Byronic hero ends up dead because of the hero's actions. That is not to say that the Byronic hero wants his lover dead; it is just that proximity to him equals danger for her. So, Edward remains in the tradition when he tries to protect Bella from himself and from unforeseen danger. However, his protective role quickly surpasses that of the Byronic tradition.

The Byronic hero may be protective of the woman he loves, but he is also selfish. He takes what he wants and acts as he likes without regard for morality or the safety of others. For example, Heathcliff insists on a meeting with Catherine, even when her maid Nelly explains how sick Catherine is. Too angry with Linton and frustrated by his separation from Catherine, Heathcliff coerces Nelly into sneaking him into the house; only hours later, Catherine is dead. When he is told of the death, one of Heathcliff's first questions is whether Catherine mentioned him before she died. He selfishly caused the final crisis in her illness, yet even in the wake of her death, he can only think of himself and the pain he suffers. The Byronic hero will mourn his lover's death, but he will not change his choices to prevent it.

In contrast, Edward becomes obsessed with trying to protect Bella and to foresee any dangers that might threaten her life, as his tirade to Emmett reveals: "Have you ever thought about how fragile they all are? How many bad things there are that can happen to a mortal? ... Have you *seen* the kinds of things that happen to them?" (*Midnight Sun* 150). As evidenced here, Edward feels the need to protect Bella from any and all potential threats. He would rather let Bella live out a long human life and die naturally than suffer the pain of a vampire transformation, even though it would allow them to live together eternally.

"My virtue is all I have left."

Edward's moral code also separates him from the Byronic tradition. For example, Heathcliff has no problem professing his undying love for a married woman, and his final passionate embrace occurs when Catherine is seven months pregnant. Similarly, in *Jane Eyre*, Mr. Rochester attempts to commit bigamy, and, when that does not work, tries to convince Jane to be his mistress. He couches his request in terms of marriage, insisting that in his heart he is not a married man. Ignoring the laws of God and society, he insists, "You shall be Mrs Rochester — both virtually and nominally." The practical and moral Jane corrects him, "If I lived with you as you desire, I should then be your mistress: to say otherwise is sophistical — is false" (342). Byron's character the Giaour also commits adultery with his host's wife, and the character Manfred indulges in an incestuous relationship. Notably, none of these Byronic heroes perceives his actions as wrong. Heathcliff believes firmly that the love he feels for Catherine is superior to her husband's love. Mr. Rochester was tricked into his marriage by his avaricious father and his wife's family. He sees himself as a victim, and therefore, entitled to pursue his own happiness any way he can. The Giaour regrets that his lover, Leila, has to die as punishment for their affair, but he is not at all surprised. He admits that he would have inflicted the same punishment had he been in Hassan's position: "Yet did he but what I had done / Had she been false to more than one" (ln. 1062–3). Clearly he knew the danger he put Leila in, but his own carnal desires took precedence. Manfred knew that his incestuous love for Astarte (whose exact familial relationship to Manfred is deliberately left obscure) was wrong in the eyes of society and God. However, his repentance throughout the play is for having caused her death. He still loves her and desires her even when she appears as a phantom. His torment comes from her death, not from moral regret for the expression of his unnatural love. For these characters, the sanctity of marriage and societal norms hold little importance, and that is an accepted facet of their Byronic characters. The Byronic hero is not expected to have morals, unlike Edward who is obsessed with making morally correct choices.

In traditional Romantic literature, male characters, like these, who are sexually active outside of marriage, are portrayed as sinful and dangerous, but also exciting. Not so for the female character. She is "The Fallen Woman." In the literary tradition of the fallen woman, a female character enters into a sexual relationship and falls from her high place of virtue to a low position of sin. She is typically led into this relationship by the man who becomes her lover. The male character's ability to seduce, coerce, or force his innocent partner into his bed makes this an ideal role for a Byronic hero. The Byronic hero is handsome and seductive; he has a power over the woman he desires that leads her to make the wrong choices. And, if by some chance she is able to resist him, he is willing to take what he wants against her will. If he chose to, Edward could easily play this role; he knows how easily he could seduce any human female he encounters: "[i]t should be easy enough to lead her in the wrong direction" (*Midnight Sun* 15).

In the novels of the eighteenth and nineteenth centuries, there was no way for the fallen woman to purify herself once she had lost her virtue. The remainder of her story was always full of suffering, punishment, and, quite often, death. The heroines of *Tess of the d'Urbervilles*, *Clarissa*, *The Mill on the Floss*, and *East Lynne*, all of whom die by the conclusions of their narratives, are only some of the many examples of this tradition. Once the heroine's virtue has been compromised, she must be punished. There are specific reasons for this: women were supposed to be the purer sex that did not indulge in base animal passions, and fallen women were capable of bearing illegitimate children who could destroy reputations and complicate inheritances.[7] Most importantly, if the fallen woman sought out or willingly consented to sexual interactions, then she was acting outside of societal norms. Much of the fallen woman story seems old fashioned and sexist to modern readers, as do some aspects of the Byronic hero's story.

Though Byronic heroes and fallen women often go hand in hand, Meyer's texts modernize and rearrange these tropes, making them more palatable to modern readers and changing notions of romance and sexuality. The fallen woman exists within the *Twilight* saga, but the roles are changed and the outcome is transformed, mostly because of Edward's anti–Byronic characteristics.[8] Bella is a modern teenager who sees no problem with having sex with her boyfriend. She is a virgin, but not because of moral qualms. A Byronic hero would happily encourage Bella's sexual desires without any concern for her moral welfare. But Edward will not let their relationship go further than chaste kissing without a wedding. Edward is neither modern like Bella, nor unprincipled like a Byronic hero. While there are the acknowledged dangers of a vampire-human sexual relationship, Edward admits that his main concern is, rather, old-fashioned propriety. Bella and Edward thus trade traditional gender roles; she playing the sexually aggressive and demanding seducer and him the resistant subject of her seduction. Essentially, Edward fills the role of Jane Eyre resisting Mr. Rochester's entreaties. When Mr. Rochester/Bella insists that "It would not be wicked to love me" Jane/Edward replies "It would to obey you" (*Jane Eyre* 355). Bella would happily take on the role of Byronic hero and seduce Edward, but his superhuman strength prevents it. Ironically, Edward can control Bella's body, but he uses that power to keep her pure.

Bella's clearly expressed sexual desires for a vampire render her at least partly fallen. By insisting on marriage, Edward is doing everything he can to keep Bella from becoming that fallen woman. Within the framework of the traditional Byronic story there is a distinct narrative progression from desire to consummation to punishment, to which Bella initially adheres. Bella has chosen a mate who is dangerous and physically other, and she actively and repeatedly tries to seduce him. This further subverts societal standards and leads to Bella's metaphorical punishment, first through the bruises caused by her first sexual encounter on their honeymoon and then through her life-ending pregnancy. By sleeping with a vampire, Bella is participating in an unnatural sexual relationship. Her punishment is a monstrous pregnancy that kills her. Or, this *would* be the punishment if Meyer did not turn this part of the narrative into the ultimate happy ending. In a traditional Byronic tale, the story would end with Bella's death, which would serve as a morality tale about the dangers of being sexually aggressive as well as choosing the wrong mate. Instead, Bella's death is turned into a fantasy story of rebirth as a vampire. This change is possible because Edward's virtuous, anti–Byronic behavior gives him power over the outcome of Bella's story. As the anti–Byronic hero who protected Bella's virginity and tried to conform to more traditional and conservative values, Edward has earned the position of redeemer. While Bella dies for her transgressive sexuality, Edward is able to "save" her by transforming her into a vampire. She is reborn, thanks to Edward, and in her second life she is no longer transgressive. Instead, she takes on the traditional roles of wife and mother. Undoubtedly, Bella sees becoming a vampire as a reward, as do most readers. But Edward is the character who breaks with the Byronic tradition. Bella is not the only one being rewarded, so is Edward.

"I was not Bella's sentence; she was my reward."

The fact that Edward is rewarded instead of punished is another very important difference between him and the Byronic hero. Inevitably, the Byronic hero is punished; he cannot live outside of the law and the moral standards of society and get away with it. While readers may like the excitement of the Byronic lifestyle, they know that it is not "right," and that the hero needs to answer for his behavior. Because of the hero's ability to manipulate power through money and intimidation, his punishment does not come from an official source like the law or a religious institution. Instead, his penalty is usually self-inflicted. At some point in his story, the Byronic hero commits an act whose consequences hurt someone else, usually his lover. While the fate of any woman who loves the Byronic hero is to die, it is the hero's fate to mourn her death and suffer from a guilty conscience. Byronic heroes frequently live long lives, perhaps so they can be tormented for as long as possible. For example, Byron's character, Manfred, is not allowed to die. He is condemned by the spirits around him to live a tortured life: "I call upon thee! and compel / Thyself to be thy proper Hell! ... Nor to slumber, nor to die, / Shall be in thy destiny" (*Manfred* 1.1.250–1, 54–5). His greatest punishment is to continue to outlive the lover he lost.

Edward, however, does not lose Bella. Instead, he marries her, has a child, enjoys a satisfying sex life, and settles into an idyllic existence. His happy domesticity is antithetical to the Byronic narrative. The desire to become human seems to dissipate once Bella becomes a vampire, and even his rivalry with Jacob is resolved through Jacob imprinting on Renesmee and becoming Edward's "son." Further, the fact that Bella's transition into vampiric life is so smooth and natural lessens Edward's culpability. It is not a tragic ending, but a joyful beginning. By a set of rules specific to this story (rules established by an author more interested in fairy tale endings than in gothic or Byronic tradition) Edward has earned the happy ending his predecessors, both Byronic and vampire, have not been allowed.

"I was thinking about right and wrong, actually."

One of the fundamental differences between *Twilight* and the Byronic tales, ironically considering Meyer's religious upbringing, is the absence of God. While there is a great deal of religious subtext, there are very few references to God, and the majority of the characters are not religious. The Byronic hero may not believe in God or in society's organized religion,[9] but the other characters and the readers of Byronic tales believe that God exists. The Byronic hero acts outside of what is right, and the punishments he inevitably suffers are brought down on him by an angry God. In *Jane Eyre*, Mr. Rochester makes the decision to risk his soul and Jane's by entering into a bigamist marriage. He hopes his deep love for Jane and her innocence will justify his decision in God's eyes. As he takes Jane in his arms, he prays that these reasons are enough to protect him from God's punishment: "It will atone — it will atone.... It will expiate at God's tribunal. I know my Maker sanctions what I do" (287). He asks God's pardon, even though he knows that it will not be granted. Within moments a storm comes and the tree under which Mr. Rochester proposed is struck by lightning and split in two. There can be no clearer indication of God's disapproval.

Edward makes a declaration similar to Mr. Rochester's when he tells Bella he is tired of avoiding her. He says, "I decided as long as I was going to hell, I might as well do it thoroughly" (*Twilight* 87). As with Mr. Rochester, Edward's statement indicates a knowledge of right and wrong and a potential for punishment. However, unlike in *Jane Eyre*, there is no lightning strike from an angry deity. If God exists, he does not appear to disapprove of Edward's actions. And, if there is no God, there are no consequences.[10]

Yet, Edward continues to fear divine punishment. In the Byronic story, the dangerous hero stands out because he lacks faith in the religious values followed by the majority of the other characters, and the reading audience. Many readers of *Twilight* see religious symbolism throughout the text, including readings which identify the Cullens as representatives of the Holy Trinity or as Mormon ideals.[11] However, within the text, most of the characters are detached from organized religion and do not seem worried about divine judgment, which makes Edward's nagging moral concerns seem as antiquated as his insistence on abstinence. This raises the question, how can the only character who fears God be bad? No one in Bella's family goes to church regularly. In *Breaking Dawn* we learn that Angela Weber's father is a minister when he performs Edward and Bella's marriage ceremony (48). In *Eclipse*, Charlie makes a comment about Jacob "taking the Lord's name in vain" (586), after he is injured. There is implied disapproval; strange, considering, as Bella points out, "Charlie considered himself a Lutheran, because that's what his parents had been, but Sundays he worshipped by the river with a fishing pole in his hand" (*New Moon* 36). Besides those brief allusions, all references to God and religion come from the Cullen house. It is Carlisle Cullen who owns the ancient crucifix from his father's church, and it is Carlisle with whom Bella discusses heaven, hell, and damnation. Carlisle believes implicitly in the existence of God and hopes that his family's "vegetarian" lifestyle will earn them redemption. Edward doubts the possibility of redemption. To him, "God and heaven exist ... and so does hell. But he doesn't believe there is an afterlife for our kind ... he thinks we've lost our souls" (*New Moon* 37).

Edward believes in a very specific divine authority, and it is not one that sanctions his existence. Briefly, in *Midnight Sun*, he allows himself to imagine that Bella was created specifically for him by a guardian angel:

> [T]he angel formed Bella in such a fashion that there was no way that I could possibly overlook her. A ridiculously potent scent to demand my attention, a silent mind to enflame my curiosity, a quiet beauty to hold my eyes, a selfless soul to earn my awe. Leave out the natural sense of self-preservation — so that Bella could bear to be near me — and, finally, add a wide streak of appallingly bad luck [217].

It is a tempting fantasy, but almost immediately Edward rejects it. His reason is based in ideology: "I could not think well of a higher power that would behave in such a dangerous and stupid manner" (217). Because Edward is determined to believe in God, and because he is convinced that vampires are evil, he cannot believe in a God that would allow him to be happy. Nor could he possibly be a chosen protector for an innocent human.

But his concern seems unfounded. There are no divine signs warning him, and given the near-indestructible nature of vampires, he may never have to answer for his choices, if there *is* anyone to answer to. The Cullens do not live in a world where there is a Van Helsing or a Buffy Summers on the hunt for them and capable of killing them. The only dangers they face come from their own kind, a threat that is only a problem when it comes to Bella, or from the werewolves, from whom they could easily flee. In a traditional Byronic tale, the hero would take advantage of his indestructible state to live outside the rules and do whatever he wanted. Edward instead seems to be most concerned with following the rules and fitting in. By giving her characters consciences, Meyer reassures her readers that Edward and Carlisle are, in fact, good and worthy of trust. Even if Edward is uncertain of his own redemption, the reader, like Bella, knows that he will go to heaven, if he ever dies.

Humans Need Bathroom Breaks

Typically the Byronic hero flouts institutional authority and even tries to overthrow it. Edward and his family, however, neither resist social authority, nor try to undermine or destroy it, even though they could. If anything, they actively participate in it, submitting to mind-numbing high school educations over and over again so as to remain part of human society. It would be potentially easier for the entire Cullen family if they withdrew from human society, thus removing the daily temptations and the need for pretense. And yet that seems to be a sacrifice they are not willing to make. They are drawn to communal living and human interaction. Their lives center around their ability to maintain the charade of normalcy that will allow them to stay in one community as long as possible.

In *Our Vampires, Ourselves*, Nina Auerbach notes that over the course of vampire literature, the vampire has emerged as a participant in human society. The monster is allowed to blend in more with society, but because of that, vampires must develop weaknesses, such as sensitivity to sunlight, that keep them apart: "For as twentieth-century vampires became more material and thus more human, they acquired an allergy that forbade them to live human lives. They exchanged crypts for stylish homes, but they could not leave those homes at will" (Auerbach 123). Meyer takes away these "allergies." Her vampires are free to roam wherever and whenever they like. They need only protect their secret by staying out of direct sunlight and resisting the urge to commit murder and they can be part of human society. Theoretically, this should make them more dangerous; they look different from humans, but they can move among them freely. But in *Twilight* this social freedom allows the Cullens to interact with humans in a non-predatory manner. Indeed, their entire coven mourns their loss of humanity, and they do their best to mimic it, even in their vampire states. When Bella first observes James and his coven, she is aware of the difference between them and the more civilized vampires she is used to. She describes their movements as "catlike" and notes the unkempt state of their clothes and Victoria's hair "filled with leaves and debris from the woods" (*Twilight* 375). It is only when they observe the Cullens' "more polished urbane stance" (376) that they stand more erect and try to look less wild. Being part of human society makes the Cullens less animal-like. They are therefore less ruthless, less savage, and less frightening, all characteristics that are necessary for Meyer to convince her readers that Bella is safe with them.

Atara Stein, author of *The Byronic Hero in Film, Fiction, and Television*, argues that the Byronic hero does not fit into society, even when he tries to. He may attempt to do good deeds and help people, but even with good intentions, he "cannot be reintegrated into society, even if he has benefited that society with his heroic actions; he must be re-humanized, then exiled or destroyed" (Stein 2). It is true that no matter how carefully they play their parts, the Cullens never actually fit into society. They are isolated by the discomfort and fear they instinctively provoke in humans. However, that changes once Bella enters their lives. In *Midnight Sun* we see Edward become more human as he attempts to make himself less frightening to Bella. He realizes that the people around him react less fearfully and the women show more attraction. As he tries to learn about Bella, Edward becomes more involved in the lives of their classmates. All of this serves to re-humanize him. According to Stein's theory, just at the point when Edward is beginning to find his place in society, he should be rejected and sent back into isolation. Instead, Edward breaks the Byronic tradition by being accepted. With Bella as his means of entry, Edward participates in human society throughout the course of the series. He sits with Bella's friends in the school cafeteria, his family throws a graduation party, and he participates in the human ritual of a wedding. The further complications of the werewolves and Charlie knowing about Bella's transformation actually allow Edward and his family to remain part of the Forks society for much longer than they had intended. The self-imposed isolation the Cullen family has lived with for generations is no longer required; they create a community for themselves.

"She thinks you're very unselfish ... are you really?"

The inherent difference between Edward and the Byronic hero is that Edward is not selfish enough. He is not the completely benevolent creature Bella sees; but really, Edward is no more or less selfish than the average person. He wants Bella. He knows that he should stay away from her and let her live a normal human life with a normal life span. He fights with his physical needs and emotional desires, but eventually they overpower his logic. He is in love, and so he acts in his own self-interest. But then, so does Bella. She is just as demanding and manipulative when it comes to being with Edward and protecting their relationship. And, at the same time, they are both altruistic in their desires to bring happiness and safety to each other.

The Byronic hero is not like this. He acts selfishly, trying to gain whatever he wants, and running over anyone who gets in his way. It may be that what he wants is his lover, but he does not consider what is best for her or how to protect her from any danger he may create. At the end of *Jane Eyre*, Mr. Rochester admits that he acted wrongly when he tried to seduce Jane. "I did wrong: I would have sullied my innocent flower — breathed guilt on its purity" (495). It is because Mr. Rochester acknowledges his mistakes that he is redeemed and allowed to eventually reunite with Jane, but he only comes to this realization because Jane escapes from him before his seduction succeeds. Most of the time, the Byronic hero does not give his lover the option of escape, as Edward does. Therefore, she almost always gets caught up in the battles he starts and she suffers for this.

The Byronic hero may claim to be selfless. In the *Wuthering Heights* passage quoted in *Eclipse*, Heathcliff claims that he loves Catherine the most because he would never deny her a friendship with Edgar Linton, no matter how much Heathcliff hates him. Heathcliff plays the role of the devoted lover who would have given Catherine anything. But the reader knows this is a false portrayal. At this point in the novel Heathcliff is in the middle of tearing Catherine's family apart as an act of revenge. This is far from unselfish. Heathcliff declares, "The moment her regard ceased, I would have torn his heart out, and drank his blood! But, till then — if you don't believe me, you don't know me — till then, I would have died by inches before I touched a single hair of his head!" (146). All that Heathcliff professes in this passage is his willingness to refrain from committing violence or murder until Catherine gives him permission. Edward is the one who draws the comparison between himself and Heathcliff, but he significantly understates the sacrifices he makes to keep Bella happy. He does not just tolerate Bella and Jacob's friendship while secretly looking forward to the day when he can kill Jacob. He accepts and encourages the friendship, and even willingly shares his role of protector with Jacob, putting Bella's safety and happiness before his own prejudices. And, unlike Heathcliff, Edward understands Bella's love for Jacob. He acknowledges that Bella is capable of loving two men and does not chastise her for having those divided feelings. Meyer takes the love triangle from *Wuthering Heights*, but instead of punishing Bella for her fragmented affections, she is rewarded with a superior boyfriend who deserves her devotion.

With all this attention to Edward as the anti–Byronic hero, the natural progression is to question Jacob's role. Often in the Byronic narrative there is another male character who is a more suitable lover for the heroine, but his suitability also makes him less exciting, and the reader cannot help sharing the heroine's preference for her Byronic lover. It is hard to imagine any reader wishing Jane Eyre had married St. John Rivers and moved to India, and while Edgar Linton is a sympathetic character, readers can see that Catherine should have married Heathcliff, for everyone's well being. Given the passionate "team Edward" versus "team Jacob" debates, this is definitely not the case in *Twilight*. But Edward's anti–Byronic status does not require Jacob to be his opposite. Sometimes Jacob verges on becoming a Byronic hero, as evidenced in his angry verbal and physical outbursts, his lack of judgment regarding Bella's safety, and his shunning of society after Bella's final rejection.[12] Further, in some ways Jacob takes on Heathcliff's antagonistic role in the love triangle with Bella and Edward. He is manipulative in his interactions with Bella and is not above using guilt and deception to win her. However, characteristics such as recklessness and temper tantrums do not equal a Byronic hero. Jacob is far too caring; he has an emotional connection to his pack and many other people around him, and a dream of happy domesticity with Bella, both of which are completely counterintuitive to a Byronic hero.[13] And, since Edward resists the Byronic role, Jacob does not have to play the Edgar Linton or St. John Rivers role. This complicates the reader's response to the love triangle in *Twilight*, but in a way that is romantically exciting and familiar: we have all been emotionally conflicted at some time. Meyer challenges her readers to understand Bella's internal conflict, and does not offer an easy answer.

"*I was like Cathy, like* Wuthering Heights, *only my options were so much better than hers*"

Meyer has said that *Twilight*, the novel, was loosely based on *Pride and Prejudice*. Early in the novel, Bella spends some time reading Jane Austen, but after that, Austen's novels are never mentioned again. Yet, a closer look reveals Austen hovering just under the surface. In the world of *Twilight*, love is a life or death situation. What you love most may kill you, and living without love is impossible. Meyer learned about passion from novels like *Wuthering Heights*, in which love and hatred are intertwined, and plays like *Romeo and Juliet*, in which death is welcomed when love is lost. No one could imagine Elizabeth Bennet imitating Juliet and committing suicide over the loss of Mr. Darcy; Austen's characters are far too logical to behave the way Shakespeare and Brontë's characters do.

And yet, it is Austen's characters who marry and live happy lives with their loves. This is because Austen's romantically successful characters are grounded in reality; they consider the consequences of their actions before making decisions. While his delivery is pompous, Mr. Darcy makes a legitimate point about the class differences between Elizabeth Bennet's family and his own: "Could you expect me to rejoice in the inferiority of your connections? To congratulate myself on the hope of relations, whose condition in life is so decidedly beneath my own?" (Austen 127). As Bella points out, "a man and a woman have to be somewhat equal…. They have to save each other equally" (*Twilight* 474). Like Mr. Darcy, Edward sees the significant differences between himself and Bella. He deliberates over the likelihood that their relationship will succeed and tries to foresee difficulties before they arrive. In both of these novels love conquers pragmatism, but according to Austen, it is through this care and deliberation that characters achieve their happy ending. Characters who take unnecessary risks or jump into action without planning, end up with unhappy lives and relationships. Romeo and Juliet die, as do Catherine and Heathcliff. The lovers are not allowed to unite in life. This is where we can see Meyer's writing inspiration. She takes the excitement and danger from novels like *Wuthering Heights* and gives them the happy endings of the quieter Austen novels. Readers are given the pathos of love, yearning, and separation, but also the joy of union and fulfillment. While there may be much more danger and excitement in *Twilight*, Meyer was still following the Austen formula all along with Edward as a modern day Mr. Darcy. By doing this, Meyer gives herself, and her readers, the satisfying ending that Byronic stories could not offer.

Recreating a literary tradition involves many pitfalls. The story and characters must be modernized to appeal to readers without losing the magic of narrative traditions. Nineteenth century readers were accustomed to novels with disappointing conclusions that taught a moral lesson, while modern readers, especially adolescents, demand happy endings.[14] Meyer's *Twilight* series answers this demand, transforming a literary tradition for a new generation of readers. Meyer takes the Byronic hero archetype and instead of warning her readers away from him, she reforms him into someone safe and dependable. The reader of *Twilight* is meant to see Bella's eventual death as romantic and satisfying. The vampire story is no longer a cautionary tale against seduction and evil; instead it is another romance with a few more obstacles to overcome. What effect that will have on future vampire fiction remains to be seen, but there is now a generation that views vampire characters not as terrifying and evil, but as romantic and compassionate. Meyer's readers learn that having a vampire boyfriend who wants to kill you is not as dangerous as it seems.[15] In the *Twilight* series, Meyer teaches the reader that sometimes "mad, bad, and dangerous to know" is not what it appears. Perhaps it has just become exciting, sexy, and mostly harmless to know.

NOTES

1. In fact, Lord Byron was the model for Lord Ruthven, the vampire protagonist of John Polidori's *The Vampyre*, the first extended English language vampire story.

2. Many *Twilight* scholars explicitly describe Edward as a Byronic hero. See, for example, Kate Cochran's "'An Old-Fashioned Gentleman'? Edward's Imaginary History" and Abigail Myers' "Edward Cullen and Bella Swan: Byronic and Feminist Heroes ... Or Not."

3. Deborah Lutz, in her discussion of "the dangerous lover," also points out brooding facial expressions, dark expressive eyes, pale skin, and secret nocturnal habits as common features among Byronic heroes.

4. Given that it involves Bella's death, there are readers who do not see the saga's conclusion as a happy ending. Meyer, however, obviously intended it to be seen that way and there are millions of readers who rejoice in Bella's rebirth as a vampire and eternal life with Edward.

5. It should also be noted that Myers is writing for a significantly younger readership.

6. Like Abigail Myers' work, my essay references Mr. Rochester a great deal, but it is with a focus on his early behavior, before he is punished for his Byronic sins and eventually reformed.

7. For an introduction to the complex English common law and its relationship to novels of the eighteenth century see Eleanor F. Shevlin's "'Imaginary Productions' and 'Minute Contrivances': and Property in Eighteenth-Century England." Shevlin references many primary sources as well as scholarship, thus providing an excellent reading guide on the subject.

8. See John Granger's description of Bella as a "vampire-goddess shorn of her fallen (and falling down) humanity" (Granger 90).

9. The Byronic heroes' relationships with God differ. Some believe in his existence but ignore his laws, some pray to pagan deities, some renounce belief completely. They generally share a disdain for organized religion, however, and are eager to expose hypocrisy in characters that condemn the Byronic hero's words and actions while claiming to be devout.

10. Interestingly, Edward can repeat Mr. Rochester's words "I know my Maker sanctions what I do," and mean them if he takes "Maker" to mean, not God, but Carlisle, who was responsible for Edward's vampire transformation.

11. See John Granger for excellent discussions of both of these readings.

12. And, like Heathcliff, he also has a significantly darker complexion than his competition.

13. Likewise, being a vampire is not enough to qualify a character as a Byronic hero. Carlisle, Jasper, and Emmett are handsome and threatening like Edward, but their loving, committed marriages to other vampires disqualify them; the Byronic hero must be part of the romantic plot.

14. Readers of Young Adult fiction know that the vast majority of that genre's novels have happy endings. Sometimes there is tragedy in the form of the death of a friend or the failure of an important plan, but the protagonist learns and grows from these experiences and finds a satisfying conclusion to his or her story.

15. To a lesser extent this also happens in Charlaine Harris' Sookie Stackhouse novels (the inspiration for *True Blood*) and in L. J. Smith's *Vampire Diaries* novels (also recreated for television). Both of these series show human women in romantic relationships with vampires, however, they also include significantly more violence. The romantic lead vampires are more threatening than Edward because they sometimes do drink human blood, and their ties to the human world are much more tenuous.

Works Cited

Auerbach, Nina. *Our Vampires, Ourselves*. Chicago: University of Chicago Press, 1995.

Austen, Jane. *Pride and Prejudice*. 1813. Ed. Donald Gray. New York: Norton, 2001.

Brontë, Charlotte. *Jane Eyre*. 1847. Ed. Michael Mason. London: Penguin Books, 1996.

Brontë, Emily. *Wuthering Heights*. 1847. New York: Signet Classic, 1993.

Byron, Lord George Gordon. "The Giaour." *Lord Byron Selected Poems*. Eds. Susan J. Wolfson and Peter J. Manning. London: Penguin Books, 1996. 167–208.

_____. "Manfred." *Lord Byron Selected Poems*. Eds. Susan J. Wolfson and Peter J. Manning. London: Penguin Books, 1996. 463–506.

Granger, John. *Spotlight: A Close-Up Look at the Artistry and Meaning of Stephenie Meyer's Twilight Saga*. Allentown, PA: Zossima Press, 2010.

Lutz, Deborah. *The Dangerous Lover: Gothic Villains, Byronism, and the Nineteenth-Century Seduction Narrative*. Columbus: Ohio State University Press, 2006.

Meyer, Stephenie. *Breaking Dawn*. London: Atom, 2008.

_____. *Eclipse*. London: Atom, 2008.

_____. *Midnight Sun*. StephenieMeyer.com. 28 August 2008. Web.

_____. *New Moon*. London: Atom, 2007.

_____. *Twilight*. New York: Hachette, 2006.

Myers, Abigail E. "Edward Cullen and Bella Swan: Byronic and Feminist Heroes ... Or Not." *Twilight and Philosophy*. Eds. Rebecca Housel and J. Jeremy Wisnewski. Hoboken, NJ: John Wiley & Sons, 2009. 147–62.

Stein, Atara. *The Byronic Hero in Film, Fiction, and Television*. Carbondale: Southern Illinois University Press, 2004.

A Post-Feminist Romance
Love, Gender and Intertextuality
in Stephenie Meyer's Saga

HILA SHACHAR

In this essay, I wish to discuss the manner in which Stephenie Meyer's *Twilight* saga draws from the historical mode of romance, including its more recent variations in the form of popular Harlequin and Mills and Boon romance novels. I am here referring to romance as a mode rather than as a genre, for as Barbara Fuchs points out, romance "appears within a variety of genres" (2). Indeed, well-known novels such as Emily Brontë's *Wuthering Heights* and Charlotte Brontë's *Jane Eyre*, which are considered iconic love stories in Western culture, cannot be entirely defined as "romance" novels. But these novels nevertheless draw from the themes, conventions and characters of the romance mode.

The same could be said about Meyer's *Twilight* books, which draw from numerous literary influences including the paranormal, fantasy, young adult and of course, romance. By focusing on the romance aspects of the *Twilight* saga, I am not suggesting that such aspects are ultimately more dominant or important in the novels. Rather, this focus highlights issues that add to the way we can approach the texts more critically and bypass the often dismissive attitudes that the books have attracted by considering how they are part of a "dialogue" with other narratives marketed toward women. In particular, I wish to analyze the books in relation to the narratives that they explicitly draw from, such as *Wuthering Heights*, and others which are not explicitly stated, such as *Jane Eyre* and romantic novels of the Mills and Boon variety.[1]

It is important to point out that I am not working under a critical strategy of authorial intent, but rather under the assumption that texts, as cultural productions, display the concerns of their contemporary times in ways that often bypass authorial intent. While Meyer's *Twilight* saga is the product of an individual author, no text comes to fruition in a social or cultural vacuum wherein the meaning of a book can be reduced to the author's intent alone. As the writer Angela Carter notes, "[i]f you read the tale carefully, the tale tells you more than the writer knows, often much more than they wanted to give away" (*Expletives Deleted* 3). As a product of a contemporary Western society, Meyer's *Twilight* saga displays the preoccupations and ideologies of such a society, particularly those concerning our ideas of love, gender, and the social legacies of feminism.

But more than simply displaying current cultural trends, the *Twilight* saga also speaks to contemporary readers' desires, particularly female readers. Indeed, I believe that part of the enormous popularity of the novels lies in their simplicity. This evidences what feminist critic, Imelda Whelehan, has termed a post-feminist rhetoric of "uncomplicated" gender ideologies "in which women" (and I would add, men) "perform far simpler roles" than the kind of complex negotiations required in modern life (22). As Janice Radway has demonstrated in her seminal work *Reading the Romance*, this "uncomplicated" appeal has always been associated with popular romance novels (189). Radway writes that romance novels are "dominated by cliché, simple vocabulary," "standard syntax" and a process of reading in which their female readers "rely on standard cultural codes ... that they accept as definitive. It has simply never occurred to them that those codes might be historically or culturally relative" (189, 190).

It is precisely as historically and culturally relative that I wish to engage with gender ideologies, the romance mode and Meyer's *Twilight* saga. By focusing on the manner in which the saga draws from inherited romance narratives and conventions in its characterizations of Bella and Edward, this essay argues that the *Twilight* novels ultimately participate in a post-feminist backlash that recycles traditional notions of love, masculinity and femininity for the contemporary age, rather than re-evaluating them and offering a more complex version of gender relations for modern readers.

But in order to analyze the books in relation to romance in a contemporary context, we must first consider what romance *is* in more detail. Romance is notoriously difficult to define, and I do not seek to provide a comprehensive or conclusive definition of it here. Fuchs has termed romance a "slippery category," writing that critics disagree "about its origins and history, even about what it encompasses. Yet, paradoxically, readers are often able to identify romance almost tacitly: they know it when they see it. My students call it 'that fairy tale feeling'" (1–2). Although rather vague, this description of romance highlights key aspects of the romance mode: the mixture of a love story, an idealized narrative, the improbable and a happy ending. Romance most commonly deals with an imaginative love story that revolves around either an extraordinary hero/heroine, or an extraordinary pair of lovers.[2]

Yet despite its utilization of idealized narratives, it is also about love in the real world. Romance narratives teach us how a man and woman *should* behave, what desire and love actually are, and how to attain such a love. They are also most commonly told from a female perspective and marketed toward women. Radway's analysis of contemporary romance fiction and its female readers has revealed how romance narratives often function "as a set of instructions" for their readers, compelling them to adopt certain behavior, identities and gender ideologies (188). Her study demonstrates the extent to which romance narratives are not de-politicized love stories that deal with individual and personal feelings alone. Indeed, romance is often one of the key aspects that highlights the social and cultural contexts of such novels, and that demonstrates our notions of what it means to be a man or a woman; and also what it means to be in love, as defined by our specific history, culture and society.

Another important aspect to note is that romance is not simply concerned with narratives of love, but historically, has also been aligned with the themes of self-discovery and adventure. As Fuchs writes, romance narratives "are often organized around a quest, whether for love or adventure, and involve a variety of marvellous elements" (4). It is not surprising that romance narratives have been aligned with the supernatural when we consider that traditional romance narrative conventions began to develop in the twelfth century when chivalric tales were popular. These tales often revolved around knights who went on quests, battling otherworldly beings and seeking both the love of the ladies they have left behind and adventure.[3] The themes of the quest and self-discovery have evolved over time so that when we reach the nineteenth century in Charlotte Brontë's *Jane Eyre* for example, such a quest is told from a female perspective and is more psychologically complex. Jane's quest, which forms part of her love story with Edward Rochester, is a quest for self-realization, economic independence and most importantly, an identity.

What her quest also highlights is that the romance mode became increasingly aligned with women's social and cultural position. Jean-Michel Ganteau writes that "romance is concerned with things foreign, foreign in more than just the obvious sense of the term. The foreign (from the Latin *fors, foris*) is what is outside the walls of the city, what escapes common experience. It is the realm of the other" (226–227). In other words, romance deals with what is unfamiliar and apart from the everyday, with aspects in society that are rarely considered within the "realistic" and rational language of patriarchal societies. Such aspects are, more often than not, characterized as "feminine," including emotions, feelings, the irrationality of love and issues of private experience. Indeed, part of the appeal of Meyer's *Twilight* books lies in their overt voyeuristic tone, almost as if we are reading a young woman's private diary. This alignment of romance with the feminine is important. This is because it allows for narratives that explore female experiences and concerns that are often marginalized, or not considered, in a primarily patriarchal and masculine-orientated society. Sometimes, aspects of the supernatural, such as vampires, werewolves, dragons, or fairies, which are linked with romance, are often another way that such experiences and concerns are explored on an imaginative level.[4]

Bella's Quest: Feminine "Self-lessness" and Belonging

A primary aspect which Meyer's *Twilight* saga shares with the novel that it continually references, *Wuthering Heights,* is its adaptation of the romance theme of the quest. Both Meyer's books and Brontë's novel rewrite the traditional medieval quest of chivalric romances from a knight who rides off into battle in order to attain love, into a young woman who is entered into a love-quest that involves a complex process of self-alienation. Such a quest is immediately evident in *Twilight*:

> Facing my pallid reflection in the mirror, I was forced to admit that I was lying to myself. It wasn't just physically that I'd never fit in. And if I couldn't find a niche in a school with three thousand people, what were my chances here?
>
> I didn't relate well to people my age. Maybe the truth was that I didn't relate well to people, period.... Sometimes I wondered if I was seeing the same things through my eyes that the rest of the world was seeing through theirs [*T* 9–10].

It would be easy to dismiss this passage as simply another example of a common theme in young adult fiction: the experience of dislocation as one is growing up. However, I believe that there are other layers of meaning at work here, most importantly, through the literal and metaphorical similarities that can be drawn between Brontë's Catherine and Meyer's Bella.

Significantly, Catherine's expression of alienation from her world and herself comes at a similar moment when she has caught her own reflection in the mirror and does not recognize her own image. This occurs when she enters into the following dialogue with her maid, Nelly, who narrates the incident:

> "Don't *you* see that face?" she enquired, gazing earnestly at the mirror.
>
> And say what I could, I was incapable of making her comprehend it to be her own; so I rose and covered it with a shawl. "It's behind there still!" she pursued, anxiously. "And it stirred. Who is it? I hope it will not come out when you are gone! Oh! Nelly, the room is haunted! I'm afraid of being alone!" [Brontë 109].

This incident occurs as Catherine lies dying, pregnant and ill in her marriage bed. It is the culmination of her increasing self-alienation throughout the novel, which she often expresses through her deep attachment to Heathcliff as one who shares her lack of belonging in the world.

Heathcliff and Catherine's relationship has been romanticized as an example of star-crossed lovers who are at war with the confines of their social world. Yet, a careful reading of the text reveals that Catherine's attachment to Heathcliff is primarily based on her desire to locate a sense of belonging and a type of subversive rebellion against the norms of femininity which she is expected to enact as a middle-class, nineteenth-century woman. Heathcliff offers her a form of escape from herself and the limitations of her social position and gender. Her love for him is inescapably tied to the state of childhood itself as a time in her life in which she was not expected to curtail her sense of self to fit societal dictates of femininity. Indeed, at the very same time when she experiences this self-alienation, she also declares her wish that she were "a girl again, half savage and hardy, and free" (Brontë 111).

What I find striking is the fact that both the *Twilight* saga and *Wuthering Heights* locate their female protagonists' desire for a sense of belonging through the narrative of a deep attachment to a man. Furthermore, such an attachment is based on a process of self-alienation. The similarity between these two passages also extends to their imagery. Both young women look into the mirror, expressing a lack of belonging and identity. The significance of the symbolism of the mirror in relation to female identity cannot be underestimated. The symbol of the mirror has a long history of aligning femininity with notions of beauty and objectification wherein women are taught to view themselves as objects for a desiring masculine gaze, rather than as subjects.

Indeed, in many of the *Twilight* saga novels, Bella is obsessed with her (false) sense of unattractiveness, often resulting in careful scrutiny of her appearance in the mirror. For example, in the beginning of *New Moon*, Bella examines her face in the mirror for signs of "impending wrinkles" as she recovers from a haunting dream in which her aging body is a sign of horror, rather than of personal development (*NM* 7). In such instances, Bella's scrutiny of her physical appearance assumes the work of Edward's own desiring gaze throughout the novels, in which she considers herself as a physical object for an external gaze. This demonstrates how Bella has internalized such a gaze as a form of self-criticism, highlighting a gender politics in which young women create their sense of worth through self-destructive definitions of their identity as dependent upon the masculine gaze, and their pleasing appearance for such a gaze. This ultimately results in a sense of alienation from themselves as objects, rather than subjects. It is telling that both Bella and Catherine look in the mirror and not only see someone who does not belong, but also someone who resembles a "pallid" ghost. That is, they see a "self-less" being, "with all the moral and psychological implications that word suggests," to use Sandra Gilbert and Susan Gubar's apt words (21).[5]

The difference between Bella and Catherine, however, is that Bella does secure a sense of belonging, whereas Catherine does not. In *Breaking Dawn*, there is a particularly memorable passage which details Bella's newfound power as a vampire. As her daughter and husband watch her, Bella reflects on how she has changed since becoming a vampire:

> As a human, I'd never been best at anything.... After eighteen years of mediocrity, I was pretty used to being average. I realized now that I'd long ago given up any aspirations of shining at anything. I just did the best with what I had, never quite fitting into my world. So this was really different, I was amazing now — to them and myself. It was like I had been born to be a vampire. The idea made me want to laugh, but it also made me want to sing. I had found my true place in the world, the place I fit, the place I shined [*BD* 523–524].

Both Catherine and Bella die during childbirth, yet Bella emerges from this death seemingly victorious. It can therefore be argued that she has rewritten Catherine's politics of lack of belonging as a woman. The argument would then be that as a nineteenth-century woman facing more limitations upon her freedom, Catherine cannot emerge victorious from the other side of the "self-less" mirror, while Bella, a modern woman, can. And yet, I am reluctant to propose such a victorious argument on behalf of Bella and modern women. This is primarily because Bella's final "victory" must be viewed in relation to the nature of her quest throughout the saga.

The book that I believe highlights Bella's quest most potently is *New Moon*. Significantly, it is not what is said in this book, but rather what remains unsaid. When Edward abandons Bella, there are several blank pages that follow, with only the names of months written on them, highlighting her sense of extreme loss (*NM* 85–92). I find these pages telling in their blankness for they almost stand as literal examples of the metaphorical meanings that are conveyed through them and throughout the novel. Namely, that upon Edward's departure Bella has not only lost her "true love" but also his world; the world that she anticipated joining and in which she saw herself developing a sense of belonging. Without him and his world, Bella retreats back to her "pallid" and ghostly reflection, continuously refers to herself as a "zombie," and loses her connection with the world of everyday experience in a hazy mist of trauma (*NM* 106, 115, 124, 152, 159). This "blankness" highlights that she has no concept of self-identity or belonging without Edward and the world he can create for her. Throughout *New Moon* Bella is a primary example of Gilbert and Gubar's description of traditional passive femininity as a "selfless" being who cannot attain an identity or a place within the world of experience without being defined in relation to the masculine (21, 3–44).

We have to ask ourselves whether Bella's "success" in fulfilling her quest of belonging in *Breaking Dawn* is actually a victory at all given that it reads as the natural culmination of the politics of "self-lessness" that is detailed in *New Moon*. It is significant that Bella can only attain her place in the world, can only "shine," once she has literally laid down her life in the service of motherhood. That is, she has had to selflessly sacrifice herself in order to meaningfully belong anywhere. This sends confusing messages to the presumed audience of young girls and women who read the novels. While Bella is "victorious" from one perspective, from another, this is false victory that simply elevates her often morbid and suicidal willingness to destroy herself in the service of others throughout the novels into a mystical veneration of feminine self-sacrifice. Ultimately, what this suggests is that "true love" is only attainable for women once they give up something, most commonly, themselves.

In fact, Bella's "victory" in *Breaking Dawn* resonates with the criticism that has been placed upon many Harlequin and Mills and Boon romance novels. Such criticism displays the manner in which Meyer's *Twilight* saga employs a similar ideological framework to popular romance novels. Tania Modleski writes that a

> television commercial for Harlequin Romances shows a middle-aged woman lying on her bed holding a Harlequin novel and preparing to begin what she calls her "disappearing act." I can't think of a better phrase to describe ... what is deplorable in the appeal of such fiction ... [f]or this world, very like the real one, insists upon and rewards feminine selflessness. Indeed ... the heroine of the novels can achieve happiness only by undergoing a complex process of self-subversion, during which she sacrifices her aggressive instincts, her "pride" and — nearly — her life [36–37].

There is no "nearly" in *Breaking Dawn*; Bella does indeed sacrifice her life, in the most violent manner, to attain happiness. Her reward is, of course, power, but what type of power is she actually given? The answer to this question is quite revealing for it is essentially the power to "extend" herself as a shield to protect her family.

What I found highly ironic when reading *Breaking Dawn* is the extent to which Bella's unique type of "power" is almost like a direct example of the traditional ideology of femininity that was dominant in Brontë's nineteenth-century England. In 1864 the well-known nineteenth-century author and critic, John Ruskin, delivered a lecture called "Of Queens' Gardens" in Manchester, which was subsequently published in 1865. In this lecture, he both summarizes and participates in the construction of the dominant ideological model of nineteenth-century femininity. Ruskin writes that a woman must be:

enduringly, incorruptibly good; instinctively, infallibly wise — wise, not for self-development, but for self-renunciation: wise, not that she may set herself above her husband, but that she may never fail from his side: wise, not with the narrowness of insolent and loveless pride, but with the passionate gentleness of an infinitely variable, because infinitely applicable, modesty of service [99–100].

"Service" is the keyword here — women exist to service others and must sacrifice a sense of self in order to perform such a service. One of the most important legacies of such ideas of femininity is of course that to this day, women are still defined in relation to, and in the service of, others; most commonly, their children and husbands. From this perspective, Bella is not simply a manifestation of traditional nineteenth-century ideologies of femininity, but also, a typical heroine of romance. As Radway has demonstrated, the romance heroine is usually defined by her ability and willingness to care for others, rather than more individual qualities relating to herself alone (209).

It is still difficult to conceptualize female identity without defining women in relation to somebody else as a mother, wife, or daughter; that is, as an attachment of a man or a family. This is, in a sense, a sacrificing of female individual identity. Upon entering adulthood young girls are continually reminded through magazines, television, films, music and books that their primary function is now to construct themselves as desirable entities for men. They are taught to view themselves in an alienating fashion as objects which can only attain meaning and a place in the world in relation to others, rather than in relation to themselves. It is this process of self-alienation that Catherine rebels against. While *Wuthering Heights* presents a woman who is dissatisfied with the image of herself that is formed through the subsuming of her identity into motherhood and patriarchal femininity, the *Twilight* saga presents a young woman who willingly sacrifices herself in the service of such an image of femininity.

Furthermore, Bella's "power" highlights that her new immortal body's eternal function is to be useful to others: to protect them, to nurture them, to hide them. The passages describing Bella using her body and mind to create a shield for others are particularly striking, because they summarize an argument that many feminist critics have made: that women's bodies and minds are not their own within a patriarchal society, but rather are the ideological property of those who require their service, making it difficult to conceptualize of a truly individual female identity (*BD* 690–691, 726–729).[6] Bella has effectively swapped one form of feminine passivity and self-lessnness for another, which is presented in the attractive guise of "true love" and happiness.

One of the ways in which the culmination of Bella's quest highlights the contemporary concerns of modern Western societies is precisely through this veneration of feminine self-sacrifice and the similarities which can be drawn between nineteenth-century ideologies of femininity and Bella's characterization. Such veneration and such similarities highlight what Whelehan has termed a form of "retro-sexism" evident in contemporary British and American societies (11). This "retro-sexism" has, at its core, a definable thread of backlash against the legacies of feminism, arising out of deep anxieties about the roles of men and women in the face of increasing divorce rates, family breakdown and the encroachment of women upon traditionally "masculine" arenas of power.[7] Whelehan's analysis of backlash against feminism draws from Susan Faludi's landmark examination of contemporary backlash discourse in America. The central argument of Faludi's work is that an undeclared ideological war is being waged in contemporary American culture against the gains of feminism, in which traditional notions of passive and domestic femininity prevail.[8]

Susan Douglas explores these same issues in her more recent work, *Enlightened Sexism*, which traces the complex forms of contemporary gender politics and responses to feminist legacies within popular culture. Both Douglas and Whelehan agree that backlash against feminist interrogations of traditional femininity, which questioned the idea that women are inherently and biologically passive, domestic, and defined in relation to men and the family home, are not simply exemplified by explicit and overt criticism, but can also appear in nostalgic and romantic re-creations of past ideals of gender (Douglas 211; Whelehan 11). As Douglas rightly points out, despite the fact that we are inundated with a barrage of images of "assertive" femininity, contemporary popular culture continues to slide back to old-fashioned judgments upon women based on their "looks, 'niceness,' and domestic skills, especially child rearing," in which women are presented as the passive attachments of men, masculine desires, children and the home (211).

Adding to these arguments, I believe that the continuing formula of many Mills and Boon novels which display a romance plot dependent upon a passive and "self-less" ideal of femininity as the path to true love and happiness often provide the most compelling form of backlash against feminism. Meyer's *Twilight* saga ultimately participates in this naturalizing of past ideals of femininity as a formula for true love. As such, it evidences a distinct "post-feminist" approach which utilizes the rhetoric of women "having it all" (happiness, true love, a loving partner, fulfillment, belonging, money, security, "power,") with a deeply conservative politics that suggests "having it all" actually means retreating back to traditional notions of femininity.[9] However, post-feminism is not simply concerned with women but also with men, as is Meyer's *Twilight* saga.

Edward's Masculinity: Violence, Money and Love

Douglas has noted that part of what "feeds" the emergence of a new form of contemporary "assault" on feminism is a "sense of threat to male dominance" (57). This is an issue that is also explored in great detail by Whelehan who argues that a new post-feminist focus on the role of men is evident in contemporary Western societies, with increasing concern about the encroachment of feminist ideals upon traditional definitions of masculinity (113–134). As Whelehan writes, "feminism and female empowerment" are becoming "associated with male decline — even at times responsible for it — in a failure to envisage a state of affairs where women can further their own achievements without damaging those of men. But there are two separate issues at stake here, and it is unhelpful to find them constantly expressed as one idea" (113–114). Yet, they are often presented as one idea, especially in romance novels which continue to reinstate traditional ideas of what it means to be a man through a romance plot that presents the man as powerful and the woman as a passive innocent.

Modleski notes that the romance formula of Mills and Boon and Harlequin novels rarely varies: a young, inexperienced, poor to moderately well-to-do woman encounters and becomes involved with a handsome, strong, experienced, wealthy man, older than herself by ten to fifteen years. The heroine is confused by the hero's behavior since, though he is obviously interested in her, he is mocking, cynical, contemptuous, often hostile, and even somewhat brutal. By the end, however, all misunderstandings are cleared away, and the hero reveals his love for the heroine, who reciprocates. (36)

Part of the function of such a "formula" is not simply to define women's identities in relation to innocence and passivity, but also to link masculinity with economic and worldly status and a physical superiority which is often displayed through a romanticized brutality and violence. The actual "happy ending" is not as ideologically important as the elaboration of the courtship described in these novels, for it is during the courtship that dominant ideas about femininity and masculinity are defined.

Writing in 1979, Angela Carter argues that "[t]oday, most women work before, during and after marriage. Nevertheless, the economic dependence of women [upon men] remains a believed fiction and is assumed to imply an emotional dependence that is taken for granted as a condition inherent in the natural order of things" (*The Sadeian Woman* 7). Sadly, the same could be said today, and I believe that part of the consequences of popular romance novels such as the Mills and Boon variety or Meyer's *Twilight* saga is the perpetuation of such a "fiction" as "the natural order of things." Furthermore, these books also naturalize the use of masculine physical power and masculine brutality in various ways, such as the supernatural (it's not his fault he hurts me, he's just supernaturally strong), or the romance plot (he really loves me, I just can't see it, so he has to prove it physically).[10]

What is striking to me is how similar the romance "formula" is to the plot and characterizations of Bella and Edward in the *Twilight* saga. Most importantly for my discussion here, it seems to me that Edward is like a combination of two archetypal romance heroes that have contributed enormously to the development of contemporary romance heroes: Heathcliff from *Wuthering Heights* and Edward Rochester from *Jane Eyre*.[11] Meyer's Edward combines Rochester's elevated economic and social status with Heathcliff's brutality and sheer physical prowess. An examination of Edward's characterization in relation to both Rochester and Heathcliff reveals the *Twilight* saga's use of past ideals of gender. I believe that such a use not only participates in recent backlash against feminism, but also signifies a dominant aspect of the romance mode that has been explored from its inception: the idea that love is inherently linked to economic status and security (Cranny-Francis 177–192).

Some of the most violent and shocking passages of *Wuthering Heights* involve Heathcliff's brutality to those who are physically weaker than himself, including dogs and women (Brontë 133, 239, 248). The novel does not downplay or romanticize his violence, indeed, Catherine herself refers to him as "a fierce, pitiless, wolfish man" (Brontë 90). It is therefore ironic that Heathcliff has become an archetypal romantic hero. Ironic, but not surprising, because those aspects of his masculinity that are abhorrent in the novel have become naturalized as defining characteristics of masculine identity. Rochester does not share Heathcliff's overt brutality but displays another important characteristic that is a defining aspect of masculinity in popular romance novels: wealth and social status.[12] The combination of these two aspects provides us with a stereotypical view of men as physically strong, economic providers who define the social status of their wives through their own.

It is quite evident that Meyer's Edward is created from such past heroes.[13] Kate Cochran argues a similar point in her own analysis of Edward's characterization, noting that he embodies the "Byronic heroes from Bella's favorite romantic novels," including "*Pride and Prejudice*'s Darcy, *Jane Eyre*'s Rochester, and *Wuthering Heights*'s Heathcliff" (8). His enormous physical strength not only signifies the supernatural, but also an ideology of hyper-masculinity. Bella is always in direct threat from his physical power, teetering on the edge of annihilation. Indeed, their very first meeting is motivated by his desire to kill her (*T* 20). Furthermore, one of the aspects which Bella describes as catching her attention when she first meets Edward is not simply his beauty, but also, his wealth. His expensive clothing and car set him apart from the other boys who vie for her attention and highlight his uniqueness and "superior" masculinity.[14] Bella later defensively tells Jacob that Edward's money does not interest her when he questions the motivation behind her love (*E* 110). However, it is quite clear from her initial attraction to Edward that her fascination with him is tied, at least in part, to his wealth.

The *Twilight* novels are punctuated by descriptions of Edward's strength, Bella's danger while being near him and his desirable wealth, to the extent that trying to list these instances here would be tantamount to quoting the novels in their entirety. But there is one particular passage that has remained in my mind as encapsulating Edward's masculinity and these themes. This is Bella's description of the morning after the consummation of their marriage:

> Under the dusting of feathers, large purplish bruises were beginning to blossom across the pale skin of my arm. My eyes followed the trail they made up to my shoulder, and then down across my ribs. I pulled my hand free to poke at a discoloration on my left forearm, watching it fade where I touched and then reappear. It throbbed a little.... Edward placed his hand against the bruises on my arm, one at a time, matching his long fingers to the patterns [*BD* 89].

This passage is one of the most violent "deflowering" or "morning after" passages I have read in contemporary romance novels. It almost reads like a rape-fantasy with the rapist literally "imprinting" himself upon his victim's flesh, as if she were an object.

Even more disturbing is the moral context in which this description is given, which echo the kind of excuses men and women make in response to rape and domestic violence.[15] It is Bella who initiates this consummation (she asked for it) and in turn tries to convince Edward that she is not hurt despite evidence to the contrary, whilst Edward apologizes profusely (he didn't mean to hurt me, he loves me) (*BD* 87–96). We have to ask ourselves how much of this is actually "romantic" and how much of it is simply confusing and demeaning in the messages that it sends across about love and violence. Just as importantly, the wider setting for this act of violent consummation is a luxurious and remote fairy tale island that can only be bought with Edward's family wealth, inescapably linking wealth and economic security with both love and violence as determining aspects of the hero's masculinity.

We have to remember that the *Twilight* saga is written in a context that has seen considerable re-evaluation of what it means to be a man that does not necessarily rely on a man's ability to provide economically or to use his physical strength. It is not simply that Meyer is perpetuating old stereotypes and utilizing past and present romance heroes. More significantly, as a member of a contemporary Western society that has seen legal, social and economic changes regarding the roles of men and women, Meyer is not coming from an uninformed social and cultural position when it comes to these issues. She therefore has other ideological paths to explore, which she chooses not to.

This is why I believe that the *Twilight* novels participate in a post-feminist politics of feminist backlash. The novels display what Whelehan calls the "circular logic" of backlash rhetoric which "works by reassuring people that 'old' values hold sway because they are undeniably true," rather than seeking to re-evaluate gender ideologies in a contemporary age that is vastly different from the historical contexts that created the "old values" in the first place (18). In *The Aftermath of Feminism*, Angela McRobbie provides the social and cultural background for such a "circular logic" (75). She notes that the "old values" continue to emerge as a form of "truth" that has been obscured by feminist discourse because of a perceived threat to "young men" who are characterized as the "losers" of feminist legacies (75). McRobbie writes that "one form the backlash against feminism takes is to argue that it has gone too far" and has "contributed to male under-performance" (75).

McRobbie and Whelehan argue that part of the logic of returning to past ideals of masculinity is based on the desire to "strengthen" men who have been "weakened" by feminist re-evaluations of gender and the real changes that have occurred in contemporary societies as a result (McRobbie 75; Whelehan 113–134). However, I believe that when it comes to the specific case of romance novels, part of the logic is also to locate the hero within a traditional romance plot that has always been part of the romance mode. This is the concept of linking love with economic security. When the knight of twelfth-century chivalric tales rode off to faraway lands, it was often part of an adventure that tested his manhood and allowed to him to acquire wealth, making him a suitable partner for his beloved lady. From the beginning, romance narratives were not simply idealized tales of love and adventure, but they displayed the manner in which our concept of love is defined by our real material conditions and economic concerns. Indeed, Anne Cranny-Francis calls popular romance novels "economic stories displaced into love story terms" (183). What this highlights is that despite the fact that romance narratives incorporate unrealistic and idealized elements and have often been termed "escapist," they are, in fact, significant engagements with the everyday world.

The *Twilight* saga's fairy tale ending comes complete with a cottage hidden in the woods, displaced from the "real" world and populated by supernatural beings and an everlasting "true love" (*BD* 752). There could seemingly not be a more unrealistic imagery or more fantastical way to end a novel. And yet, what I want to suggest is that the *Twilight* saga engages with, on an imaginative level, the concerns and issues that face many men and women when it comes to their most intimate relationships and the development of their identities. For Naomi Zack, who examines such gender politics in *Twilight and Philosophy*, Meyer's novels suggest the limits of feminist inquiry. She argues that "serious scholarly feminist seem not to be aware" that the types of qualities which the books endorse, such as "practicing heterosexuality in the form of fulfilled romantic love and fertility," "looking good according to prevailing beauty norms," and "attaining power in the world as it is, rather than the world as it should be," are "very important to a majority of young American women" (Zack 125). I would conversely argue that "serious" feminist scholars such as Whelehan, Faludi, McRobbie and Douglas are acutely aware such aspects are desired by many women. However, rather than assuming such aspects are therefore naturally desirable, they instead question how and why women and indeed, men, are taught to desire them.

For me, the *Twilight* saga does not demonstrate Zack's proposed cultural "gap" between feminist thinkers and "the masses" (125). Rather, it ultimately reminds me that popular romance novels have a role to play in the reaction to and construction of everyday reality. Meyer's *Twilight* saga compels us to consider the fact that as members of modern societies, we have a choice to either accept inherited modes of love and gender, formed in vastly different historical contexts to our own, or to question them, forming our own ideas of masculinity, femininity and love. While I admit I find Meyer's hidden cottage appealing, I would like to see it populated by different types of heroes and heroines in the future.

NOTES

1. See also Groper's essay in this anthology.

2. For a more detailed discussion of the common elements and history of romance, see Fuchs 1–11.

3. See Fuchs 4–9 and 37–65 for more detailed discussions of medieval chivalric tales in relation to the development of romance.

4. For more detailed discussions of supernatural themes and fiction see Cooper; Le Guin; Cavaliero; and Belsey 150–183.

5. It is important to point out that Gilbert and Gubar's *Madwoman in the Attic* is a seminal and groundbreaking feminist work in the study of nineteenth-century and women's literature.

6. For example, see Gilbert and Gubar 3–44; de Beauvoir 395–396, 450–451; and Carter, *The Sadeian Woman* 3–10.

7. These issues are continually discussed in Whelehan's *Overloaded*, which should be referred to for a more detailed analysis.

8. This is an issue that is continually discussed throughout Faludi's well-known work, *Backlash*, which should be referred to for further analysis of the topic.

9. For a more detailed discussion of "post-feminism" and the various meanings attached to this term, see Whelehan 90–93.

10. See, for example, the arguments put forth by Torkelson in this anthology.

11. See also Groper's essay in this anthology.

12. See Cranny-Francis's *Feminist Fiction* for a more detailed discussion of this theme in romance narratives.

13. Further evidence of Meyer's use of previous novels such as *Wuthering Heights* in her characterizations lies in the continual references to *Wuthering Heights* in the *Twilight* saga. For example, see *Eclipse* 9, 19, 28, 265, 517.

14. See also Wilson's article in *Bitten by Twilight*.

15. See also the arguments put forth by Torkelson in this anthology.

Works Cited

Belsey, Catherine. *Desire: Love Stories in Western Culture*. Oxford: Blackwell, 1994.

Brontë, Emily. *Wuthering Heights*. Ed. Ian Jack. Oxford: Oxford University Press, 1998.

Carter, Angela. *Expletives Deleted: Selected Writings*. London: Vintage, 1993.

_____. *The Sadeian Woman: An Exercise in Cultural History* (1979). London: Virago, 2000.

Cavaliero, Glen. *The Supernatural and English Fiction*. Oxford: Oxford University Press, 1995.

Cochran, Kate. "'An Old-Fashioned Gentleman'? Edward's Imaginary History." *Twilight and History*. Ed. Nancy R. Reagin. Hoboken, NJ: John Wiley & Sons, 2010. 7–25.

Cooper, Susan. *Dreams and Wishes: Essays on Writing for Children*. New York: Margaret K. McElderry Books, 1996.

Cranny-Francis, Anne. *Feminist Fiction: Feminist Uses of Generic Fiction*. Cambridge: Polity Press, 1990.

De Beauvoir, Simone. *The Second Sex*. 1949. Trans. and ed. H. M. Parshley. London: Vintage, 1997.

Douglas, Susan J. *Enlightened Sexism: The Seductive Message that Feminism's Work Is Done*. New York: Henry Holt, 2010.

Faludi, Susan. *Backlash: The Undeclared War Against Women*. London: Chatto & Windus, 1992.

Fuchs, Barbara. *Romance*. New York; London: Routledge, 2004.

Ganteau, Jean-Michel. "Fantastic, but Truthful: The Ethics of Romance." *The Cambridge Quarterly* 32.3 (2003): 225–238.

Gilbert, Sandra M., and Susan Gubar. *The Madwoman in the Attic: The Woman Writer and the Nineteenth-Century Literary Imagination*. 1979. New Haven: Yale University Press, 1984.

Le Guin, Ursula K. *Language of the Night*. New York: Putnam Adult, 1979.

McRobbie, Angela. *The Aftermath of Feminism: Gender, Culture and Social Change*. London: Sage, 2009.

Meyer, Stephenie. *Breaking Dawn*. London: Atom, 2008.

_____. *Eclipse*. London: Atom, 2007.

_____. *New Moon*. London: Atom, 2006.

_____. *Twilight*. London: Atom, 2005.

Modleski, Tania. *Loving With a Vengeance: Mass-Produced Fantasies for Women*. New York: Methuen, 1982.

Radway, Janice A. *Reading the Romance: Women, Patriarchy and Popular Literature*. Chapel Hill: University of North Carolina Press, 1984.

Ruskin, John. "Of Queens' Gardens." 1865. *Sesame and Lilies: Two Lectures by John Ruskin*. Ed. G. G. Whiskard. London: Henry Frowde, 1912. 84–123.

Whelehan, Imelda. *Overloaded: Popular Culture and the Future of Feminism*. London: The Women's Press, 2000.

Wilson, Natalie. "Civilized Vampires Versus Savage Werewolves: Race and Ethnicity in the *Twilight* Series." *Bitten by Twilight: Youth, Culture, Media, and the Vampire Franchise*. Eds. Melissa A. Click, Jennifer Stevens Aubrey, and Elizabeth Behm-Morawitz. New York: Peter Lang, 2010. 51–70.

Zack, Naomi. "Bella Swan and Sarah Palin: All the Old Myths Are *Not* True." *Twilight and Philosophy: Vampires, Vegetarians, and the Pursuit of Immortality*. Eds. William Irwin, Rebecca Housel and J. Jeremy Wisnewski. Hoboken, NJ: John Wiley & Sons, 2009. 121–130.

PART III

Twilight Through an Intersectional Lens

Patriarchy, White Privilege, Heteronormativity, Rape Culture, Religion

Maybe Edward Is the Most Dangerous Thing Out There
The Role of Patriarchy

MELISSA MILLER

In *Twilight*, Edward implores Bella to stay out of the woods near her house by telling her, "I'm not always the most dangerous thing out there" (192). The passage serves the narrative functions of cluing the reader in to the conflict that is about to come while also cementing Edward's role as the "good-guy." While Edward might pose no physical threat to Bella, to assume that he poses no danger would be ill-advised. This essay's primary claim is that the *Twilight* narrative — as seen through the lens of the Bella/Edward relationship since it is the one that is framed as the most desirable and the one with which readers most identify (Behm-Morawitz, Click, and Aubrey; Clasen) — promotes a dangerous and damaging ideology of patriarchy that normalizes and rationalizes the control of women by men. This claim is grounded in an understanding that popular culture artifacts in general, and romance stories in particular, do much more than entertain us, they reflect and illuminate our lived realities. The claim is supported by a comparative analysis between the *Twilight* saga novels and common signs of an abusive partner to demonstrate one way in which oppressive patriarchal themes of male social dominance are presented in *Twilight* before discussing the potential implications of those themes.[1]

The Twilight *Saga Is Just Entertainment, Right? Why Should We Care?*

Before entering into a proper analysis about the impact of patriarchal themes in *Twilight*, it is important to understand why one would analyze an artifact of popular culture at all. One view situates popular texts like the *Twilight* saga as "low" art, or mass produced schlock meant to dupe unsophisticated audiences, like us, into passivity (Horkheimer and Adorno; Benjamin). Cultural studies scholars, however, see popular culture as an aspect of mass culture (Storey, *Cultural Theory*), or the values and ideas that members of a society form from common exposure to the same cultural activities, communications media, music and art, etc. Thus, examining popular culture texts exposes how they are used to assert social values upon others (Barthes). Female-targeted popular culture artifacts — like the *Twilight* saga — are sites that are especially worthy of examination since they place the female/feminine experience at the forefront of media critique (McRobbie and McCabe; Modleski; Radway; Ang; Mellencamp). One of the central concerns of feminist media analyses, then, is to examine patriarchal ideology as it relates to power and agency in society (Baumgardner and Richards; Durham; Storey, *An Introduction*; van Zoonen). Analyzing texts through a feminist lens can serve as a means of exposing and critiquing patriarchy in popular media and, in the process, help to liberate audiences from traditional, stereotypical representations (Durham). It is also a way to understand the concept of gender as a social construction, and posits media texts as critical sites for the negotiation of gender roles.

A cursory examination of the gender roles in the *Twilight* saga reveals what Cynthia Enloe calls a "Culture of Imminent Danger," which she defines as a culture "sustained by the classical patriarchal caveat that women are in the sort of danger from which only rational men can protect them" (234). One way in which the *Twilight* saga reinforces a "Culture of Imminent Danger" is seen in the roles of the adult male and female characters. For example, male characters have roles or occupations that establish and support their strength, rationality, and protector status (i.e., police chief, town doctor, or tribal elder). Meanwhile, female characters in *Twilight* are symbolically annihilated; they are largely trivialized and either "symbolized as child-like adornments who need to be protected or they are dismissed to the protective confines of the home" (Tuchman 8). Renee, for example, is muted throughout the story — we know only that she has decided to follow her new husband to spring training camp in Florida and that she is "childlike" and "harebrained" (*T* 4). Before Renee remarried, Bella saw herself as her mother's caretaker. Esme is also superficially presented. As the matriarch of the Cullen clan, she is characterized only by "her ability to love passionately" and her strong "mothering instincts" (*T* 307, 368). Bella, too, has been seen as falling victim to symbolic annihilation. In the discussion topic "Bella, is she a bad influence for teens?" on the *Twilight*MOMS.com fan site, for example, fans express concern that Bella is a "weak" character because she sees herself as less beautiful than Edward, less intelligent, and clumsier than everyone else. Bella, because she is the weak and vulnerable one, is in constant need of care and protection; she is dependent upon Edward for survival.

Indeed, we see what happens to Bella when she is abandoned by the protective influence of Edward — she becomes a "lost moon" (*NM* 201). Later, in *Eclipse,* Renee observes that Bella is like a "satellite, or something" in relationship to Edward (*E* 68). A satellite can be understood as any object that moves around a larger object. Comparing Bella to a moon or other satellite is significant since each symbolically places Edward at the center and Bella in the periphery. This scenario illustrates Edward's role as the actor and Bella's role as the reactor in the *Twilight* saga. When Edward moves, so does Bella. When Edward leaves, Bella, too, checks out. Likewise, it implies that the orbiter is the least valuable one in the relationship. Take, for example, the Earth's relationship to the Sun. The Earth — as a support system for human life — is important in its own right, but the Sun has far more importance. Without the Sun, the Earth is annihilated. Without Edward, Bella is annihilated.

Because the symbolic annihilation of women in media fails to address the full range of women's real-life goals and potential, it plays an important role in establishing and normalizing ideology that helps those in power stay in power. But, Bella exists in a world much different than ours. How much potential can we expect Bella to posses in a situation where she is forced to battle super-human forces? *Twilight* author Stephenie Meyer acknowledges this when responding to critics. She says:

> There are those who think my stories are misogynistic — the damsel in distress must be rescued by strong hero.... When a human being is totally surrounded by creatures with supernatural strength, speed, senses, and various other uncanny powers, he or she is not going to be able to hold his or her own. Sorry. That's just the way it is [Meyer, *The Story*].

Meyer's explanation makes sense — to an extent. But, because the *Twilight* saga narrative is set against the backdrop of fantasy does not mean its capabilities for reinforcing the oppressive ideology that exists in our real-world go unrealized. For example, Bella only finds her inner-strength by conforming to the masculine standard put forth by Edward — in this case, by becoming a vampire. Though Edward cannot reverse himself to his human form, symbolically, when Bella changes for Edward it legitimizes a longstanding cultural norm of women adjusting their desires to accommodate those of male partners.

The counter to this claim might sound something like this: "Edward doesn't want Bella to change! People may not agree with Bella's choices, but isn't their strength in the fact that *she* made them?"[2] While we are given the illusion that Bella is a free agent making a free choice between a mortal life with Jacob and an immortal life with Edward, Bella's decisions were already predetermined for her by the time she made them and made in the absence of any real option. Bella's reaction to Edward's absence in *New Moon* establishes their relationship as destiny; if she is to survive, they must be together. While her disposition improves when she is with Jacob, Jacob is removed as a viable romantic option for Bella due to the Quileute phenomena of imprinting. Because Jacob does not imprint on her, Edward is Bella's only option. As a result, if the Edward/Bella union is to succeed, Bella *must* change, for all the reasons stated in the books. True, choice only exists if the person could have acted otherwise. In this case, Bella could not. Together, the "satellite" analogy, Bella's conformity to a masculine standard, and the lack of agency in her choices all highlight Edward's patriarchal authority over Bella.

Edward Is the World's Best Predator, Isn't He? Everything About Him Invites You In

When readers buy romance fiction, they are being sold more than just the book. The ideology of romance, exemplified by lessons of gender subjectivities and sexual difference in a patriarchal structure embedded in the patriarchal themes present in romance genre, is also being sold (Brown; Cooper). In their 2001 analysis of romance novels, Daniela Kramer and Michael Moore found that one marker of patriarchal ideology present in romance is aggressive behavior exhibited toward a spouse or partner. Kramer and Moore further observe that male aggression, in particular, "earns the respect and love of women" and, when it happens, "there is no questioning, analysis or attempt at insight" from the characters in the romance narrative. The presentation of violence as a sign of love in romance fiction is attractive which normalizes and legitimizes masculine power over females for the reader.

Edward would probably not be characterized by many readers as a batterer. However, he does engage in several behaviors indicative of male partner violence. As part of her "Getting a Firm Foundation" training, nationally known domestic violence trainer and consultant Lydia Walker has developed a list of seventeen behaviors seen in people who abuse their partners.[3] Walker cautions that if the person has several (three or more) of these behaviors, an increased potential exists for physical violence. Edward exhibits at least seven of these behaviors at different points in the *Twilight* saga. These are: jealousy; controlling behavior; quickly involving oneself in a relationship; unrealistic expectations of one' partner; blaming one's partner for one's own feelings; a "Jekyll/Hyde" personality; and the use of any force during a conflict.

Jealousy is displayed by several characters in the *Twilight* saga, but because we see the story through Bella's eyes and her eyes are firmly planted in Edward, it is his capacity for jealousy that is highlighted. In *Twilight*, for example Edward expresses his displeasure in many of Bella's potential suitors. While we are initially most acutely aware of Edward's dislike for Mike Newton and "the flare of resentment, almost fury" that he felt when Mike asked Bella to the school dance, it is the tension between Edward and Jacob that comes to the forefront as the story progresses. While Edward's jealousy of Jacob manifests itself in several ways, one of the more prominent ways is by controlling Bella's behavior. Walker defines controlling behavior as those actions that are attributed to a concern for a woman's safety and well being. In *Eclipse*, Edward continuously prevents Bella from visiting Jacob. First, he disconnects the cables to her car battery. Later, he manipulates Alice into participating in a kidnapping plot designed to keep Bella away from La Push. When he finally agrees to let her go, he does so only if he can take her there and pick her up himself.

This is not the first time we see Edward's controlling behavior which, Walker warns, is also frequently manifested in the abuser's lack of willingness to let a woman make personal decisions. After Edward rescues Bella from the Port Angeles thugs in *Twilight*, he tells Bella she needs to eat, even when she insists that she is not hungry. This behavior surfaces again in the last chapter when Bella is recovering in the hospital — Edward calls for the nurse to administer pain medication even though Bella states that she does not need them (*T* 477). Perhaps the most appalling example, though, is in *Breaking Dawn* when Edward attempts to arrange for an abortion for Bella without any discussion or her permission.

Another troublesome sign in the Bella/Edward relationship is how quickly it moves. Walker states that most battered women date or know their abuser for less than six months before they marry, live together, or get engaged. The events of the *Twilight* saga only span about two years: Bella moves to Forks in January and by March, Bella and Edward become a couple. By prom in May, Bella is ready to give up her mortality for Edward. The following summer finds Bella married to Edward — a choice, incidentally, that Edward consistently pressured Bella into making despite her vocalized misgivings about marriage. Moving quickly highlights the possessiveness of the controlling partner and their unrealistic assumption that their partner will meet all of their needs. Edward goes as far as even telling Bella, "You are my life now" (*T* 314).

Edward's unrealistic relationship expectations result in another of Walker's warning signs: he blames Bella for his inability to control his feelings. Edward is, of course, responsible for what he thinks and feels, but he uses his feelings to manipulate Bella. For example, in *Twilight*'s meadow scene, Edward drops his carefully constructed facade to show Bella the true extent of the danger he poses. He's frenzied as he explains how he could easily destroy her, and then blames Bella when he feels he has lost control. Later, when Bella and Edward kiss before meeting the rest of the Cullens for a game of baseball, he forcefully pulls himself off of her when he loses control and proclaims: "You'll be the death of me" (*T* 363).

Walker also suggests women look out for sudden mood changes in which one minute the controlling partner is really nice and the next minute he is out of control. She explains that explosiveness and moodiness are typical of people who abuse their partners since these behaviors can intimidate and frighten the victim and are reflections of the abuser's use of threats and manipulation to establish and maintain power and control. *Twilight* (certainly until Bella is rescued in Port Angeles by Edward in chapters eight and nine) is focused on Edward's odd behavior towards Bella that vacillates between amusement and pure contempt. At one point, his behavior causes Bella to say to Edward, "I can't keep up with you," and question him as to whether he has a "multiple personality disorder" (*T* 84, 82). Edward eventually makes his true feelings for Bella known. While he works hard to keep his emotions in-check around Bella, he's prone to the occasional swing.

The most dangerous of Walker's signs, however, is the use of physical force during a conflict. It is important to recognize that force is not limited to hitting or punching, it also includes holding a woman down, physically restraining her from leaving a room, or pushing/shoving her. In chapter five of *Twilight*, Bella faints during a blood-typing exercise in her Biology class. Edward convinces the school secretary to excuse them from class so that he can escort her safely home. Bella agrees, happy to get out of class, but is fully intent on seeing herself home. When Bella moves to the driver's seat of her truck, Edward physically restrains her by pulling the back of her jacket. Later, Bella is restrained again, this time by Emmett (under Edward's direction) as they rush to flee James after the baseball game. While trying to decide how to counter James' inevitable attack, Edward decides to take Bella away from Forks. When she protests, Edward orders Emmett to secure her by her wrists and forcibly strap her into the harness of the Jeep they are using to escape.

Edward may not cross the line into full-on batterer, but he comes dangerously close. Of course, some readers will see Edward as he is presented — as the ideal, romantic, doting boyfriend — and rationalize that his actions are justified because he had Bella's best interests in mind and because Edward, as a vampire, has physical and mental capabilities that Bella, as a mortal, does not possess. However, we cannot let Edward off the hook just because he is a vampire and not a living, breathing person. While personhood is certainly linked to humanity, one does not necessarily need to be human to be a person. According to Nicholas Michaud's essay in *Twilight and Philosophy: Vampires, Vegetarians, and the Pursuit of Immortality*, those who "demonstrate certain qualities such as consciousness and self motivated activity ... [or] capabilities such as practical reason and affiliation" should be granted the status of personhood (45). Edward's respect for the human soul, his choice to drink animal blood instead of human blood, and his attempt to assimilate into Forks' society demonstrate his desire to pass and be accepted as a person and not a vampire. Therefore, if Edward wants to enjoy the benefits of personhood in our society, we have to demand of him the same standards that we would expect from any other male in it, regardless of any supernatural power he may possess.

Physical violence is one method by which men control women and maintain their supremacy, but patriarchy does not need to be enforced by using violence alone. In this case, Edward's actions create an environment where Bella cannot love Edward without loathing herself. He demonstrates that, despite Bella's constant claim to the contrary, he is actually very far from perfect. Yet, Bella still sees herself as subordinate to him. She consistently reminds the reader — and herself— that she is not good enough for Edward. Because the Bella/Edward relationship is presented as fated and Edward's actions are justified as being for the benefit of Bella's safety, we permit Bella to respond in ways that would concern us if we saw it manifested in others close to us. We condone her continued disregard for her own personal safety. We allow her to isolate herself from her family and friends. We accept her explanations for her repeated injuries. Bella literally gives up her life for "love." Edward's controlling behavior coupled with Bella's justification of it creates a situation in which the female's subordination becomes not only acceptable to readers, but rational as well.

Can Romance Narratives Be Anything But Oppressive?

The abuse narrative present in the *Twilight* saga becomes especially problematic when viewed with an understanding of the romance genre. Romance as a genre is frequently characterized by the quest for an ideal heterosexual love relationship between a strong, dashingly handsome, young man and a beautiful, vulnerable, self-sacrificing young woman (Behm–Morawitz, Click, and Aubrey; Burnett and Beto). These qualities of romance stories are at the forefront of the *Twilight* saga. While these aspects of romance can be read as contributing to the perpetuation of patriarchal ideas about gender roles, romance can also be interpreted as the ultimate feminist genre. Catherine Asaro reminds us that the plots of most romance stories are centered on the desires of the heroine; her values are given priority and she always ends up getting what she wants. Bella spends four books telling us, the readers, that she wants to achieve immortality as a vampire and spend eternity with Edward while still being able to keep her best friend — and Edward's rival suitor — Jacob around. *Breaking Dawn* sees Bella fighting for her right to bear a child. She ultimately achieves all of this.

Asaro also asserts that romance novels are unique in that they adhere to the female gaze. Laura Mulvey's concept of the "male gaze" rests in the assumption that the audience is forced to view the action and characters of a filmic text through the perspective of a heterosexual man. Examples of its manifestation in filmic texts are seen in camera shots focusing on the curves of the female body, cleavage, or other sexualized positioning of women. In romance novels, however, the male form is the one under the heaviest scrutiny — its features extolled upon in great detail. In fact, the female heroine is frequently described with just enough detail to humanize her, while leaving enough information out of the picture so that the reader might insert herself into it. In *Twilight*, Bella frequently compares Edward to the mythical Greek god Adonis. Her description of his facial features is specific — he is perfect and angular with high cheekbones, a strong jawline, and a straight nose and full lips. His hair, which is always messy, is an unusual, eye-catching shade of bronze while his eyes are topaz. Bella, on the other hand, is described to the reader far more simply — she has long brown hair and brown eyes.

Texts presented through the female gaze are significant in two distinct ways. For one, that the heroine is presented as an "everywoman" can be seen as empowering to female readers who are often only presented with representations of "female characters that fade into the background unless they have qualities deemed 'important'" (Asaro). Readers are able to recognize aspects of themselves in the narrative. Also, it legitimizes female sexuality and debunks the myth that women don't notice men in "that" way. Physical attractiveness is just as important for females as it is for males. Female sexuality is further legitimized in romance in that the heroine is rarely punished for engaging in sexual acts and can frequently be seen as the initiator of such acts. In *Twilight*, for example, it is Bella who is eager to consummate the relationship she has with Edward, and Edward who is resistant to give in without being married.

Still, none of this negates the charge that the *Twilight* narrative is potentially harmful. Even though Edward arguably never crosses the line into domestic violence, his behavior is still troublesome. If we view the repeated consumption of romance narratives through the lens of George Gerbner's cultivation theory, then we can assume that, over time, romance narratives can potentially influence readers' interpretations of appropriate behavior for men and women in romantic relationships. In *The Killing Screens*, Gerbner emphasizes the effects of media consumption on the attitudes rather than the behavior of audiences. In short, heavy exposure is seen as fostering attitudes which are more consistent with the world of media than with the everyday world. Gerbner argues that media cultivates attitudes and values which are already present in a culture, normalizing and reinforcing the more dominant values, while making other underlying ideas more salient. In a society such as ours where masculine ideology is already privileged, where we already have historical struggles with creating safe, egalitarian spaces for women, and where we already struggle with violence and intimidation, Gerbner's theory tells us that extended consumption of the acts of oppression that we witness in the *Twilight* saga can normalize and legitimize the acts of oppression that we experience in our own lives. When control and abuse are made to be fun and entertaining, we run the risk of rationalizing and justifying it and fail to see the tragedy in it when we come across it in our real lives.

The role romance plays in preparing individuals for public life is even greater for young readers than what it may be for adults. Girls will use romances as an alternative to a romantic relationship when one has not yet presented itself. Romance novels act as safe spaces to gain insight on how to meet boys, what kinds of things they might say to them, and what dating is like. For them, romance novels act as beginner's manual for adolescence (Cherland and Edelsky; Christian-Smith; Willinsky and Hunniford).

Audiences appear to carry the lessons and desires cultivated through repeated exposure to romance narratives in their youth with them throughout their lives. For example, a generation ago, at the height of the coming-of-age teen romance flick, there emerged two archetypes for the ideal boyfriend — Jake Ryan and Lloyd Dobler. Jake Ryan, of course, was the cool, super-popular, super-rich, Porsche-driving, way-too-hot-to-be-in-high-school hunk who caught "Plain Jane" Samantha Baker's eye in the film *Sixteen Candles*. Lloyd Dobler, on the other hand, was an unpretentious, earnest, boombox-hoisting everyman who was thoroughly devoted to the super-smart Diane Court in the film *Say Anything*. It has been more than 25 years since *Sixteen Candles* was in theaters and 20 years since *Say Anything* was released, yet women coming of age in the 1980s and early 1990s report longing for their Jake or their Lloyd but never finding him (Stuever, *Real Men*; Steuver, *What*

I Did). There is evidence that the same desire audiences have for a relationship with Jake Ryan and Lloyd Dobler also exists for Edward Cullen, regardless of the age of the audience member. For example, on the discussion forum for the TwilightTeens.com fansite, for example, one can find a multitude of discussion threads in which young fans deliberate questions like "On a scale of 1 to 10, how lucky is Bella Swan [to be with Edward Cullen]?"; "Could you see yourself dating a guy like Edward?"; or "What do you like about Edward?" Additionally, Emily Reynolds' interviews and surveys with female adult readers of the *Twilight* saga also revealed their desires to be romantically linked with Edward. According to one of Reynolds' participants: "I would leave my husband for someone like that" (30). The difference is that seeking out a Jake Ryan or a Lloyd Dobler, though it may end in disappointment, is not likely to meet with a violent end. However, seeking out an Edward Cullen might.

Is It All Bad?

The point of this essay is not to vilify the *Twilight* saga or the readers that enjoy reading it, sometimes multiple times. Feminist media scholar Janice Radway was one of the first to take seriously the pleasure that women readers consistently seem to find in romance. According to her influential text *Reading the Romance*, women use romance as a way to set up a quiet space for themselves and are able to vicariously enjoy status positions and spaces of nurturing through the books that they do not enjoy in the real world. *Twilight* readers, too, use the novels to perform these functions in their own lives (Behm-Morawitz, Click, and Aubrey).

It is okay to enjoy things that are entertaining and fun — and, as Radway points out, sometimes it is even beneficial — but we should not dupe ourselves into believing that our choice of entertainment media does not also assist in formulating our ideas about our culture. Popular media help shape a worldview in audiences that re-inscribes dominant positions of power and authority (Althusser; Gitlin; Hall), which in Eurocentric cultures like ours is "white, patriarchal capitalism" (Fiske qtd. in Meyers 7). Patriarchy is the primary oppressor of females in a society (Firestone; Millett). Since patriarchy does not necessarily operate as an explicit, perceivable reality (meaning, we don't always recognize it when we see it), we must review the aspects of our culture — pop culture included — that perpetuate patriarchal ideology and cause it to be normalized. What are, in fact, dangerous ideas that devalue the female in society are too frequently seen as legitimate choices in the *Twilight* saga — choices made in the name of "true love" or in the face of supernatural forces. When presented through these lenses, Bella and Edward's relationship is seen as romantic and desirable, when in any other world it would be destructive.

We have to remember that patriarchy, while notable for marginalizing females, does not operate free from feminine influence (Enloe). Social systems are not made solely of men; women are also contributing members. As such, a patriarchal society relies on the participation of all members — men and women — to endure. Therefore, as destructive as Edward is in the *Twilight* narrative, the real danger exists when we fail to confront patriarchy and oppression when we encounter it. It is advantageous that *Twilight* appeals to readers across several generations because it can be used as a framework for encouraging discourse between adults and youth about how female oppression occurs in society.

NOTES

1. The film adaptations of the novels are very similar to the source texts, but there are some differences. For this reason, and because the narrative arc of the book series has reached its conclusion, this essay will focus primarily on the story of *Twilight* as presented in the novels.

2. Stephenie Meyer has taken this position in Q-and-A sessions when Bella's choices are challenged by readers (Meyer, Frequently Asked Questions).

3. The complete list of "Signs of a Battering Personality" can be found at http://www.lydiawalker.net.

WORKS CITED

Ang, Ien. *Watching Dallas: Soap Opera and the Melodramatic Imagination*. London: Methuen, 1985.

Asaro, Catherine. "A Quickie with Catherine Asaro on Feminism & Romance." *All About Romance: The Back Fence for Lovers of Romance Novels*. December 1997. Web. 10 July 2010.

Barthes, Roland. "The World of Wrestling." *Steel Chair to the Head: The Pleasure and Pain of Professional Wrestling*. Ed. Nicholas Sammond. Durham, NC: Duke University Press, 2005. 23–32.

Baumgardner, Jennifer, and Amy Richards. *Manifesta: Young Women, Feminism, and the Future*. New York: Farrar, Straus & Giroux, 2000.

Behm-Morawitz, Elizabeth, Melissa A. Click, and Jennifer Stevens Aubrey. "Relating to Twilight: Fans' Responses to Love and Romance in the Vampire Franchise." *Bitten by Twilight: Youth Culture, Media and the Vampire Franchise*. Eds. Melissa A. Click, Jennifer Stevens Aubrey, and Elizabeth Behm-Morawitz. New York: Peter Lang, 2010. 137–54.

Benjamin, Walter. *The Work of Art in the Age of Mechanical Reproduction*. New York: Classic Books America, 2009.

Brown, Mary Ellen. "The Politics of Soaps: Pleasure and Feminine Empowerment." *Australian Journal of Cultural Studies* 4.2 (1987): 1–25.

Burnett, Ann, and Rhea Reinhardt Beto. "Reading Romance Novels: An Application of Parasocial Relationship Theory." *Journal of Speech & Theatre* 13 (2000): 28–39.

Cherland, Meredith Rogers, and Carole Edelsky. "Girls and Reading: The Desire for Agency and the Horror of Helplessness in Fictional Encounters." *Texts of Desire: Essays on Fiction, Femininity, and Schooling*. Ed. Linda K. Christian-Smith. London: The Falmer Press, 1993. 28–44.

Christian-Smith, Linda K. "Sweet Dreams: Gender and Desire in Teen Romance Novels." *Texts of Desire: Essays on Fiction, Femininity, and Schooling*. Ed. Linda K. Christian-Smith. London: The Falmer Press, 1993. 45–68.

Clasen, Tricia. "Taking a Bite out of Love: The Myth of Romantic Love in the Twilight Series." *Bitten by Twilight: Youth Culture, Media and the Vampire Franchise*. Eds. Melissa A. Click, Jennifer Stevens Aubrey, and Elizabeth Behm-Morawitz. New York: Peter Lang, 2010. 118–34.

Cooper, Dianne. "Retailing Gender: Adolescent Book Clubs in Australian Schools." *Texts of Desire: Essays on Fiction, Femininity, and Schooling*. Ed. Linda K. Christian-Smith. London: The Falmer Press, 1993. 9–27.

Durham, Meenakshi Gigi. "Articulating Adolescent Girls' Resistance to Patriarchal Discourse in Popular Media." *Women's Studies in Communication* 22.2 (1999): 210–29.

Enloe, Cynthia. *The Curious Feminist*. Berkeley: University of California Press, 2004.

Firestone, Shulamith. *The Dialectic of Sex: The Case for Feminist Revolution*. 2003 ed. New York: Farrar, Straus and Giroux, 1970.

Gitlin, Todd. *The Whole World Is Watching*. Berkeley: University of California Press, 1980.

Hall, Stuart. "Encoding/Decoding." *Culture, Media, Language*. Eds. S. Hall, et al. London: Hutchinson, 1980.

Horkheimer, Max, and Theodor W. Adorno. "The Culture Industry: Enlightenment as Mass Deception." *Dialectic of Enlightenment*. 1944. London: Verso, 1997.

The Killing Screens: Media and the Culture of Violence. Dir. Sut Jhally. Perf. George Gerbner. Media Education Foundation. 2002. DVD.

Kramer, Daniela, and Michael Moore. "Gender Roles, Romantic Fiction, and Family Therapy." *Psycoloquy* 12.24 (2001): n. pag. Web. 10 July 2010.

McRobbie, Angela, and Trisha McCabe. *Feminism for Girls: An Adventure Story*. London: Routledge, 1981.

Mellencamp, Patricia. "Situation Comedy, Feminism, and Freud: Discourses of Gracie and Lucy." *Studies in Entertainment: Critical Approaches to Mass Culture*. Ed. Tania Modleski. Bloomington: Indiana University Press, 1986. 80–95.

Meyer, Stephenie. *Breaking Dawn*. New York: Little, Brown and Company, 2008.

_____. *Eclipse*. New York: Little, Brown and Company, 2007.

_____. "Frequently Asked Questions: Breaking Dawn." *The Official Website of Stephenie Meyer*. n.d. Web. 10 July 2010.

_____. *New Moon*. New York: Little, Brown and Company, 2006.

_____. "The Story Behind the Writing of New Moon." *The Official Website of Stephenie Meyer*. n.d. Web. 10 March 2010.

_____. *Twilight*. New York: Little, Brown and Company, 2006.

Meyers, Marian, ed. *Mediated Women: Representations in Popular Culture*. Cresskill, NY: Hampton Press, 1999.

Michaud, Nicolas. "Can a Vampire Be a Person?" *Twilight and Philosophy: Vampires, Vegetarians, and the Pursuit of Immortality*. Eds. Rebecca Housel and J. Jeremy Wisnewski. Hoboken, NJ: John Wiley and Sons, 2009. 39–49.

Millett, Kate. *Sexual Politics*. New York: Doubleday, 1971.

Modleski, Tania. *Loving with a Vengeance: Mass Produced Fantasies for Women*. New York: Routledge, 1982.

Mulvey, Laura. "Visual Pleasure and Narrative Cinema." *Media and Cultural Studies*. Ed. D. Kellner and M.G. Durham. Malden, MA: Blackwell, 2006. 167–91.

Radway, Janice. *Reading the Romance: Women, Patriarchy and Popular Literature*. Chapel Hill: University of North Carolina Press, 1984.

Reynolds, Emily. "Screams, Vampires, Werewolves and Autographs: An Exploration of the Twilight Phenomenon." Master of Arts Thesis. Department of Mass Communications, Brigham Young University, 2009.

Storey, John. *Cultural Theory and Popular Culture: An Introduction*. Harlow: Longman, 2009.

_____. *An Introduction to Cultural Theory and Popular Culture*. 2d ed. Athens: University of Georgia Press, 1998.

Stuever, Hank. "Real Men Can't Hold a Match to Jake Ryan of 'Sixteen Candles.'" *The Washington Post* 14 February 2004. Web. 10 July 2010.

_____. "What I Did For Lloyd — The Nerdy Romeo of 'Say Anything' Still Has a Place in Women's Hearts." *The Washington Post* 14 February 2006. Web. 10 July 2010.

Tuchman, Gaye, Arlene Kaplan Daniels, and James Benet, eds. *Hearth and Home: Images of Women in the Mass Media*. New York: Oxford University Press, 1978.

van Zoonen, Lisbet. *Feminist Media Studies*. London: Sage Publications, 1994.

Walker, Lydia D. "Signs of a Battering Personality." *"Getting a Firm Foundation" Training*. 2003. Web. 10 July 2010.

Wethington, Elaine. "Are Academic Opinions About Romance All Negative?" *All About Romance: The Back Fence for Lovers of Romance Novels* February 1999. Web. 10 July 2010.

Willinsky, John, and R. Mark Hunniford. "Reading the Romance Younger: The Mirrors and Fears of a Preparatory Literature." *Texts of Desire: Essays on Fiction, Femininity, and Schooling*. Ed. Linda K. Christian-Smith. London: The Falmer Press, 1993. 87–105.

Denial and Salvation
The Twilight *Saga and Heteronormative Patriarchy*

ASHLEY DONNELLY

> Are you willing to call your husband "Lord"? ... one that you have
> to follow, even when he makes bad judgments. Are you ready to
> do the most vulnerable thing a woman can do and submit yourself
> to a man, who you are going to have to follow in his faith, who is
> incredibly imperfect and is going to make mistakes? Can you do
> that? Can you call your husband "Lord"? If the answer is no, you
> shouldn't get married [Joyce 3].

Such a startling, outrageous demand for the submission and oppression
of women might seem like a part of a bizarre cult, but for a growing number
of conservative Christians the self-named Christian patriarchy movement is
very popular (Joyce 4–6). Scenarios such as the one detailed above are com-
monplace as "training" for those eager to commit to the lifestyle of this faction.
This movement, also known as "Quiverfull" (explored in detail in Kathryn
Joyce's 2009 *Quiverfull: Inside the Christian Patriarchy Movement*), guides the
lives of the Duggar family, the stars of the popular TLC series *19 Kids and
Counting.* Jim Bob and Michelle Duggar are now household names. Their
faces appeared on magazine covers, online news sources, and TV talk shows
when news of their 19th child's birth made national headlines. Their religious
beliefs and lifestyle choices were initially sensational when their show first
aired, but they have ultimately become an everyday part of popular culture
in the U.S. The passive acceptance of what many may see as antiquated and
intolerable roles for women and the popularity of media which perpetuates

and celebrates patriarchy and heteronormativity is a threat to the equality and humane treatment of not just women, but all of those that do not fit into the ideological restraints of heteronormative patriarchy.

Patriarchy is a system which is male dominated, male identified, and male centered, and within which women are subordinated (Bennett 55). Yet "not all men have gained equally from patriarchal structures" because patriarchal systems are inextricably linked with heteronormative ideals (Bennett 56). Heteronormative ideology is a system of beliefs that indicates or implies that there are only two distinct sexes (male and female) and two clear gender roles in which heterosexuality is the only "normal" sexual orientation, identifying all other forms of sexuality and/or gender as "abnormal." Heteronormative patriarchy identifies certain characteristics as "masculine" or "feminine," limiting humanity's ability to function holistically.[1] Emotions and nurturing, for example, are considered "feminine" and violence and aggression are considered "masculine." As will be discussed further in what follows fiction and other popular media reproduce these dogmatic divisions and, consequently, perpetuate a variety of social ills.

As this essay will argue, under the guise of vampire fiction, Stephenie Meyer's wildly popular *Twilight* series is grounded in heteronormative, patriarchal belief. The resulting tales perpetuate an ideology that celebrates the oppression of women and enforced conformity into restrictive gender roles. Her use of monsters and her manipulation of that which they traditionally represent effectively gives readers a moral lesson in denial, repression, and conformity.

The New Vampire

Traditional vampires of popular culture have threatened, repulsed, titillated, and enthralled us, and the penetration of fangs and the sensual suck of mouth on neck are the standard tropes of the glamorized blood/sex/euphoria relationship central to their allure. However, since the late 1990s/early 2000s, the sympathetic vampire, the angsty monster, tortured over his/her need to feed on humans, has become distinctly more common in popular fiction and film than the monstrous stereotype of the vampire as a vicious killer. The figure of the blood-abstinent vampire currently abounds in popular U.S. culture: Vampire Bill from Charlaine Harris's *Sookie Sackhouse* novels (now HBO's successful *True Blood* series), Stefan from the *Vampire Diaries*, Angel from *Buffy the Vampire Slayer*, Mitchell from BBC America's *Being Human* series, and Mick from *Moonlight,* to name but a few. These chiseled, brooding, sultry men and women deny their most basic nature, shunning the human blood that traditionally keeps them and their vampire kin alive and at their most powerful. Their reasons vary from one another's, but the basic claim overall seems to be that their blood abstinence is an attempt to live a redemptive, morally upright existence — one that will enable them to live peacefully among humans.

The new popularity of this particular manifestation of the vampire is a curious one. For so long the *typical* romanticized demon was a figure of danger, a threat, a shadowy menace preying on humanity which many critics have identified as a metaphoric symbol of a threat to established ideological boundaries, for example, heterosexuality or ethnocentricity, that permeate the subconscious of a culture.[2] Julia Kristeva identifies figures of horror (that which is "abject") as "the 'object' of primal repression" (12), which have traditionally served as an external means of dealing with that within human nature that we cannot accept. As Kristeva argues, "The abject confronts us, on the one hand, with those fragile states where man strays on the territories of animal. Thus, by way of abjection primitive societies have marked out a precise area of their culture in order to remove it from the threatening world of animals or animalism, which were imagined as representatives of sex and murder" (12–13). The abject figure of horror for pre-industrial societies and for mainstream, Western cultures today, allows for an external Othering of that which we choose not to accept about our own humanity. The vampire figure, for example, has, in some forms, served as a representation of animalistic sexuality — s/he hunts prey, attacks, and enjoys the physical pleasure of the assault in a completely carnal manner.

In her article "Vampires, Anxieties, and Dreams: Race and Sex in the Contemporary United States," Shannon Winnubst articulates the traditional position of the vampire as one that transcends the clear lines of sex and race established in U.S. culture over decades.

> The vampire is neither subject nor Other. The vampire, the crosser of boundaries extraordinaire, is forever haunting because he is forever beyond the grasps of straight white male subjectivity. The vampire infects his blood, alters his spirit and — damned most of all — exceeds his concepts. And, in exceeding them, he always carries the power to expose them, to expose them and their anxieties — about blood, about boundaries, about kinship and purity and control, about the racing of sex and the sexing of race [9].

For Winnubst, the traditional vampire monster threatens the straight, white male's position of power, allowing for an escapist fantasy not just for those oppressed, but for the oppressor as well. This is clearly evident in the homoerotic novels of Anne Rice's vampire series, for example.

Yet, as stated above, there has recently been a pronounced increase in the number of sympathetic vampire figures in popular culture. The *Twilight* saga is a notable example as most of *Twilight's* vampires (and werewolves) are "friendly" monsters, content to quench their thirst on beasts rather than humans. The saga is heaving with unsatisfied desire, both for blood and for sexual release. Meyer's emphasis on denial of both the sexual and the primal (blood and violence) goes well beyond the issue of basic moral order of which most blood abstinent vampires concern themselves. While many read the abstinence in the series as a guide to Christian morality for horny teenagers, there are arguably other latent messages associated with this emphasis on denial. Edward's denial not only controls his life choices, but Bella's as well, and this control over her decisions reflects the strong, patriarchal dominance of the tales. From Edward's nearly complete control of Bella's life to the acceptance of domestic abuse and the binding of females in the werewolf community,[3] men are frighteningly superior throughout the series. Edward's "moral" restraint indicates not only his ability to dominate his relationship with Bella, but also implies that masculine strength is needed to restrain the wild feminine, a theme present throughout the entire series, which clearly celebrates patriarchal dominance and heteronormativity.

In the *Twilight* saga, readers are presented with the character of Edward, a sexy, intelligent, wealthy vampire trapped forever in his 17-year-old body. At 108 years old, the gorgeous Edward remains a virgin. In fact, as he confesses to Bella, "in the last hundred years or so ... I never imagined anything like this. I didn't believe I would ever find someone I wanted to be with ... in another way than my brothers and sisters" (*T* 300–301). In keeping with the moral code of his "family," Edward does not drink the blood of humans, but instead quenches his thirst on the blood of animals. Through the symbol of "vampire" Meyer creates an atmospheric world that relies on the cultural and historical understanding of the tropes associated with this mythical creature — the danger and the blood/sex/euphoria relationship — but removes the threat from her main characters, making them fantastical yet practically human. They do not threaten established boundaries or cross racial or gender lines. They do not challenge the established moral codes of the Judeo-Christian ethic.

Critics and commentators have latched onto Edward's denial, many lauding the message of self-control they believe Meyer articulates. For example, Jennifer L. McMahon states that "Edward, rather than being prey to his impulses, embodies our wish to subject our appetites to rational control" (203), placing him in contrast to traditional vampire figures who, she argues, "articulate the anxiety we have about appetites.... They are made monsters by their surrender to impulse, and they personify our latent fear that conceding to appetite will compromise our being and endanger other people" (202).

While McMahon and others identify the ethical issues surrounding Edward's and the other blood-abstinent vampires' denial, other critics have focused on the sensuality created by the tension of refusal in the series. Christine Seifert calls it "abstinence porn," suggesting that, to some extent, "*Twilight* actually convinces us that self-denial is hot."

The Sublimation of Desire and Heteronormative Conformity

Edward, the Cullens, the Denalis, the similarly-vegetarian friends of the cullens who live in Alaska, have chosen to deny their most basic urges, shunning the consumption of human blood and hunting only animals, though it renders them slightly less powerful. They have mastered the very urges that drive their existence, just as Edward is master over his sexual urges. The manifest message of the novels is clearly one of self-control and self-sacrifice for the good of others. Yet below the surface of the series the connection between the denial of blood and the denial of sexuality becomes more complex when paired with an emphasis on sublimation of desires and a strong message of heteronormative conformity. Underscoring this message is the often discussed threat of eternal damnation. Edward (and others) assumes that their monstrous nature excludes them from salvation and dooms them to hell, should they ever *really* die. But for Edward, his salvation is not simply tied to his vampirism, but also to worldly deeds, which is why he denies Bella her carnal desires. For Edward, pre-marital sex will ruin their "shot at heaven, or whatever there is after this life" (*E* 453). He equates unsanctified sex with murder in terms of how damaging it would be to Bella's soul, a theme that helps establish the moral undercurrent of the entire *Twilight* series.

The vampires sublimate their urge to feed with animal blood and their urge to fight with friendly wrestling and family baseball. The Quileute wolves channel their aggression and desire for violence by sequestering themselves and fighting amongst themselves. Sublimation works as a way for them to distance themselves from their monstrous natures, because, as Jacob says in *New Moon*, "who wants to be a nightmare, a monster?" (345). Sublimation and denial allow them to blend in and function in society, not as aberrations but as "normal" citizens. This strong, behavior-modifying ideology echoes other ideological platforms throughout history, but most contemporarily the movement of "*therapy* of homosexuality" in which men and women with "unwanted" homosexual urges can be "reformed" and pursue the "ideal family form" of "traditional model of man-woman marriage" (Narth, n.p.).

Noteworthy critics of sexual politics have explored the effects of heteronormative ideologies. Adrienne Rich, in her controversial essay "Compulsory Heterosexuality and Lesbian Existence" argues that compulsory heterosexuality, the forcing of sexual roles onto individuals through the disallowing of difference in a culture, leads to enforced, damaging conformity for those who are Other in that system. "The retreat into sameness — assimilation for those who can manage it — is the most passive and debilitating response to political repression, economic insecurity, and a renewed open season on difference" (204). Yet most established cultural systems remain fundamentally heteronormative, forcing those Othered by that system into uncomfortable conformity or into the role of "monster."

In his seminal 1993 collection *Fear of a Queer Planet*, Michael Warner establishes a basis for what is now known as "queer theory," bringing together scholars who tackle the subject of queer politics and social theory. In *Fear*, Warner articulates the overarching implications of heteronormative ideology. In his introduction he highlights the foundational work of Eve Kosofsky Sedgwick when he argues that heterosexual ideology:

> in combination with a potent ideology about gender and identity in maturation ... bears down in the heaviest and often deadliest way on those with the least resources to combat it: queer children and teens. In a culture dominated by talk of "family values," the outlook is grim for any hope that child-rearing institutions of home and state can become less oppressive [xvi].

The assertion that Othered youth are especially vulnerable to the consequences of a stringent heteronormative worldview articulates the need for a critical exploration of the heteronormative message in Meyer's books, especially as the series is truly a global phenomenon for teens, tweens, and adults alike. However, as much as it captivates its adult audience, it is indeed adolescent fiction, featuring high school-aged characters and teenage romance and its influence could be, arguably, most powerful on adolescents and young adults, many of whom are not yet secure in their sexuality or gendered identity. Regardless of age, many readers may take on Meyer's ideals of heteronormative patriarchal dominance, which are unfortunately not uncommon in mainstream culture.

In the world of and around Forks, Washington, all of the characters are identified as heterosexual. There are no characters living outside of (or not clearly desiring) the male/female pair bond. It is not through any direct statement of anti-gay rhetoric that Meyer emphasizes this heteronormative ideology, but through a very clear lack of inclusion. This lack of inclusion perpetuates the "overarching, relatively unchallenged aegis of a culture's desire that gay people *not be*" (Sedgewick 79). To further emphasize the importance of the heterosexual lifestyle, nearly all of the characters are united in a male/female pair bond, a bond with specific gender roles for each partner. The single characters expend their energies lamenting their single status and attempting to woo a mate. Though Bella's parents were divorced, both eventually "correct" their single states and pair up with another. Harry Clearwater's wife, Sue, is even shifted from single widowhood back to the role of mate with Charlie by the end of the series. The end "goal" for each pair bond appears to be marriage, preferably early marriage as most of the characters enter into this state as teenagers (or vampires appearing to be teenagers). The nature of "imprinting," which will be discussed in greater detail below, essentially mimics the arranged marriage of children, dictating the life-partner choice of those affected often even before puberty. Yet there are characters in the series that are not in clearly identifiable pair bonds. These characters are all clearly identified as Others, and marked in some way. This strong emphasis on labeling Otherness works with the exclusion aspect of Meyer's texts to emphasize patriarchal heteronormative ideals.

Marking Good and Evil

The emphasis in the *Twilight* series on the dichotomy between "good" and "evil" is established by identifying who wants to live "normally" among humans (the "good") and who wants to remain apart from them (the "evil"). The "good" vampires and werewolves deny their primitive drives for blood and violence whereas the "evil" vampires choose to follow their instincts and live as predators. In order to further clearly identify which side the characters are on, Meyer marks them in physical ways. The "good" vampires have golden eyes that go dark when they are hungry; the "evil" vampires have glowing red eyes. The werewolves, though frightening and bestial in wolf form, are depicted in the Western, cultural ideal masculine form when they walk as humans.[4] Through this large, muscular form, Meyer seems to be assuming that her audience will be able to associate them with the culturally ubiquitous trope of the super-fit super hero. The masters of the Volturi viscerally disturb Bella with their "paper-thin" white skin and "dull crimson eyes" in contrast to the almost angelic beauty of the Cullens. In addition to physical markings of Otherness, the characters on the side of "evil" do not, overall, subscribe to the heteronormative pair bonds to which the "good" characters so readily attach. The initial villains, James, Victoria, and Laurent, appear in a group of three with their "deep burgundy color" eyes that are "disturbing and sinister" (*T* 376). They are described as animals rather than humans, in stark contrast with the family baseball game upon which intrude. Bella introduces Victoria and James as follows:

The woman was wilder, her eyes shifting restlessly between the men facing her, and the loose grouping around me, her chaotic hair quivering in the slight breeze. Her posture was distinctly feline. The second male hovered unobtrusively behind them, slighter than the leader, his light brown hair and regular features both nondescript. His eyes, though completely still, somehow seemed the most vigilant [376].

In this passage the use of words like "wilder," "chaotic," "feline" and "male" are reminiscent of how one would identify feral creatures, clearly marking this trio as Other, emphasizing their lack of humanity. It is possible that their ménage is an allusion to "deviant" sexuality. The other villains of the series, the Volturi, are also identified as a group rather than by their relationships. Victoria's newly made rogue vampires in *Eclipse* live singly, disconnected from others, and are also described as frightening feral creatures with no remnants of humanity. The fearsome Maria of Jasper's story initially appears with two other women before reaching her pinnacle of power, when she then leads an army with a strong core of exclusively male soldiers. Through physical appearance and relationship status, Meyer's characters fall clearly into categories of "good" and "evil," creating a very distinct message that the good guys are attractive and joined with another in heterosexual relationships and the bad guys are physically different and live in alternative relationship situations, underscoring the message that the only "right" way to live is within a narrowly defined patriarchal heteronormative worldview.

Marking Gender Roles

A strict, heteronormative, patriarchal worldview, as stated above, implies two clearly defined gender roles. In these roles, actions, emotions, and characteristics become gendered, with certain attributes labeled as "feminine," others "masculine." This socialized division of gender both supports and perpetuates the system of patriarchy, exalting the masculine and suppressing the feminine. In the *Twilight* series, Meyer consistently emphasizes the need to suppress the wildness of femininity and this is achieved through patriarchal oppression. The most obvious and frequently discussed example of patriarchal oppression is evident in the relationship between Edward and Bella in which Edward is controlling and dominant in every aspect. Their first dinner together, which occurs after Edward's valiant rescue of Bella from a band of men intent on violating her virtue, includes this exchange:

"Drink," he ordered.
   I sipped my soda obediently, and then drank more deeply, surprised at how thirsty I was. I realized I had finished the whole thing when he pushed his glass toward me.
   "Thanks," I muttered, still thirsty. The cold from the icy soda was radiating through my chest, and I shivered.

"Are you cold?"
"It's just the Coke," I explained, shivering again.
"Don't you have a jacket?" His voice was disapproving [*T* 169].

From the very beginning of their relationship Bella is portrayed as weak, submissive, and almost childlike in her truculence. Edward, her savior, is powerful, dominant, knowledgeable, and protective. This simple exchange is illustrative of the very clear patriarchal dynamic and heteronormative role-play that dominates the series. In their essay "Undead Patriarchy and the Possibility of Love," Leah McClimans and J. Jeremy Wisnewski explore the issue of patriarchy in the series focusing on the relationship between Bella and Edward (see also Miller's paper, this anthology). They offer a very clear explanation of patriarchal society, which is useful in exploring the control dynamic between the two characters.

> Patriarchal societies support inequality between men and women: Men are strong and rational; women are weak and silly. For many feminist theorists, controlling behavior is a consequence of patriarchy: Men will try to control those situations in which their dominance is threatened. Controlling behavior, however, also reinforces systems of domination and subordination, in that women whom men attempt to control are taken to be in *need* of control — in need of guidance, protection, and oversight [169].

Edward clearly believes Bella, who has made it to the age of seventeen without his assistance, is in need of his protection. He's constantly pointing out her physical clumsiness and fighting with her over her lack of fear and overconfidence in the face of danger — even when that danger is Edward himself. He wants her, seemingly for her own protection, to be cowed. "You *need* a healthy dose of fear," he tells her. "Nothing could be more beneficial for you" (*T* 216). In an effort to "protect" Bella, he dictates the limits of their physical contact, he monitors her movements, he keeps her away from her best friend, and he even seeks to dictate the situation of her death. Though arguably a strong, intelligent female character, Bella regularly capitulates to Edward's rule, aiming to make him happy and, ultimately, assume her role as his wife. Bella, though she chafes at the limits Edward puts on her freedoms, consistently recognizes Edward's overprotection and controlling nature as concern for her, not as domineering or mildly sociopathic. The romance of his concern is intended to override the restrictive consequences on Bella's life and the message Meyer implies is that men must step in, dominate, and protect and women should capitulate, understanding that it is for their own good.

In a clear position of traditional patriarchal power, the heads of household (or clan or tribe) are all men. Charlie, Carlisle, Sam, Billy, Aro, Marcus, and Caius feature prominently, their word serving as that which dominates.[5] The masculine leader role is supported consistently by a female in the role of wife (or surrogate wife). The role of wife is traditionally presented throughout the *Twilight* series: Esme is Carlisle's doting homemaker, "mother" to the Cullens. Emily, scarred from a run-in with her werewolf fiancé, which will be discussed further below, serves as mother and domestic servant to the werewolf pack. In fact, her only role and defining characteristics seem to be that of domestic servant. Bella describes her days with Emily as such:

> Emily was a cheerful person who never sat still. I drifted behind her while she flitted around her little house and yard, scrubbing at the spotless floor, pulling a tiny weed, fixing a broken hinge, tugging a string of wool through an ancient loom, and always cooking, too. She complained lightly about the increase in the boys' appetites from all their extra running, but it was easy to see she didn't mind taking care of them [*NM* 350].

As a very young woman, the still unmarried Emily seems to have been completed by taking on her role as den mother.

Even Bella, as a teenager, steps into the domestic role in her father's house, cooking and cleaning without complaint. When Bella finally leaves, Sue Clearwater steps in, resolving both her position as widow and Charlie's position as a lone man. Our first clear indication of her new role comes as she is shown feeding and caring for others in Charlie's kitchen. Bella is clearly pleased with her presence, "glad someone was trying to keep him from starving due to his lack of cooking ability" (*BD* 513). Though a bachelor for several years, Charlie was never able to learn to cook for himself. Sticking closely to the rigidly defined gender roles within more extreme examples of heteronormative patriarchy (such as the Christian patriarchy movement discussed earlier), he does not cook as it is implied that such domestic labor is for women alone.

The two women in the novels on the side of "good" that do not conform to their gendered expectations — Bella's mother Renee and Leah Clearwater — are shown as problematic. Renee is shown as flaky, almost simple, and unable to really care for herself. At the beginning of *Twilight*, Bella describes her concern for leaving her mother, which emphasizes her weakness:

> I felt a spasm of panic as I stared at her wide, childlike eyes. How could I leave my loving, erratic, harebrained mother to fend for herself? Of course, she had Phil now, so the bills would probably get paid, there would be food in the refrigerator, gas in her car, and someone to call when she got lost, but still... [4].

Renee, who left Charlie in what is described as a heartless, selfish fashion, abandoning her role as wife, is depicted as clearly defective — fun and harmless, but simple-minded and unable to care for herself and others. She does not fit into the female gender role subscribed to by those in a heteronormative, patriarchal system. By labeling her Other in this way, Meyer is able to work around the fact that Charlie and Renee are divorced but still "good" characters: Something is clearly "wrong" with Renee and though Charlie was victimized by her leaving, his manhood is not in question because she is so Other.

Leah, the first female werewolf in the tribe's history, though she is shown as fast and strong and capable, is also described as difficult, confrontational, and emotional, suggesting that when women move into masculine territories they become, to put it bluntly, bitches. She's aggressively competitive and defensive, trying to assert her place in the male wolf pack. Once removed from her traditional place of house and home, ousted by Sam's imprinting on Emily, Leah causes problems, reinforcing the oppressive, patriarchal system of gender roles. Othered by her new role in this traditionally masculine world, Leah is normalized by Meyer by her victimhood — her heart was broken and the role of wife was ripped away from her through no fault of her own. However, according to Edward, "she's making life exceedingly unpleasant for the rest of them. I'm not sure she deserves your sympathy" (*E* 417).

Imprinting Heteronormative Patriarchy

Though the focus of most of the criticism of the problematic gender issues in the novels has centered on Edward and Bella's relationship, the werewolf community's "imprinting" and reactions to abuse are deeply troubling and require more attention. The tradition of imprinting is a part of Meyer's creation of the werewolf legacy in the Quileute tribe (in no way connected with any actual legends from the tribe itself). At some point in a werewolf's life, he (having always been male, until Leah) may one day see a female and recognize instantly that she will be his mate for life. There is no room for question and no way out for the chosen wolf. As romantic as this may seem to some on first read, because of its notions of soul mates and eternal love, it is truly a disturbing issue. With imprinting, the female technically has a choice but it is assumed she would never want to decline the male wolf's attentions. According to Jacob, "it's hard [for women] to resist that level of commitment and adoration," intimating that it is truly futile for women to attempt to resist the attentions of a determined man (*E* 123). She is passive, chosen and bound by *his* destiny. What's even more disturbing is that this "imprinting" can often occur with children, even infants. These young girls are bound to grown men before they even have a sense of self; destined to become wives and mothers with no real chance to date or explore themselves before making a lifetime commitment. Though Meyer insists this has no pedophiliac implications, that the relationships between the men and girls are strictly platonic until they reach an appropriate age, it is still a troubling notion. Even if there is nothing sexual involved in the relationship, it still deprives the children involved of any semblance of a normal life. They do not have any control over their sexuality or their future relationships, yet this is idealized in the novels as romantic and spiritual. Coupled with the push for early marriage throughout the series, a clear message of patriarchal control through the institution of pair bonding is created, leaving no room for a woman's individual control over her destiny.

Through the series-wide acceptance of imprinting and the clear ideology that the appropriate gender role of women is a domestic one, the way is paved for an ideology that tolerates violence against women. In heteronormative patriarchy, men are considered the physical sex, with manhood and masculinity linked to violence, aggression, and physical dominance.[6] The relationship between hostility and masculine identity can be seen in the tales of the Judeo-Christian God, the ultimate patriarch. "The dominant notion of *god* in the Abrahamic patriarchal religions is an all-male being whose defining characteristics seem to be omnipotence, jealousy, righteousness, judgment, and dominance" (Caputi16). If, as many religious followers claim, we, as humans, are made "in His image," then it makes sense that the male gender should be as dominant and aggressive as his God. In patriarchal, heteronormative societies, many allowances are made for masculine violence as men fulfilling their God-given role to protect and fight.

The men of the *Twilight* series, inundated with religious themes and symbols, are no exception. Through the relationship of Emily and Sam, readers are offered a lesson in the tolerance of domestic abuse. Once in an established relationship with Emily, the newly minted wolf Sam loses control and attacks her, scarring her for life. The claw marks on her face mar her beauty and serve as a reminder that the wolves inside the men can never be completely trusted. Emily accepts both the scars and the role she must play in keeping everyone calm. Bella is told repeatedly how dangerous the young wolves are and the implication is that it is her and all of the women's responsibility not to rile them up. "Hanging out with werewolves has its risks" (*NM* 330), she is told before being introduced to the scarred Emily. Aside from Sam's apparent remorse, in the text there is no further apology and no shame. The passive acceptance of such a doctrine is deeply unsettling, clearly reminiscent of the social adage that men are not to be held responsible for their actions and that it is a woman's role to keep them under control and accept the abuse they offer should they lose their cool. It undermines a woman's right to live unabused in her home, clearly reinforcing a system of patriarchal control.

Beyond the werewolf community Meyer reminds readers again and again that men are dangerous. From the gang of men in Port Angeles in *Twilight* to the marriage bed in *Breaking Dawn*, our heroine Bella is at constant risk from the seemingly innate violence of men. Once Edward has ensured that they are bound by traditional matrimony, he reluctantly allows Bella to indulge her carnality and they make love on their honeymoon. She awakes the next morning covered in bruises atop a bed with ruined pillows. "So," she asks Edward, "why exactly did you decide to ruin Esme's pillows?" to which Edward responds, "I don't know if I decided to do anything last night.... We're just lucky it was the pillows and not you" (*BD* 95). Clearly, even in the traditional role of wife, a woman needs to beware of man's passions. As Edward is well aware, serious damage is possible if he gives into temptation and allows himself to indulge his desires instead of denying them. Thus after their initial encounter, he attempts to reassert his control and deny Bella's and his own desires.

Females, according to the series, need this control. Bella is a liability to herself, needing Edward's help to not injure herself or wander into dangerous situations. Edward treats her desires as silly and irrational and takes it upon himself to dictate her life decisions. Her lust must be controlled and he charges himself with protecting both her life and her virtue. "Bella is not in control of her body, as abstinence proponents would argue; she is absolutely dependent on Edward's ability to protect her life, her virginity, and her humanity" (Seifert).[7] But once this control has been lost and their desires indulged, a new threat emerges for Bella. After two nights of sex, Bella conceives a daughter that threatens her very life.

When their daughter Renesmee is born, she is the potential epitome of the wild feminine, out of control of her urges and desires. She grows at an alarming rate, tearing Bella apart from the inside out. Once she is cut from the womb, effectively ending Bella's human life, she is a threat to others because of her inability to control her thirst and a threat to the entire Cullen clan by her very existence. Renesmee is the first character on the side of "good" in the series that has the potential to cross boundaries. She is half human, half vampire and proves to be, though endearing and loving, monstrous in her unabashed desire for blood. Though her family loves her, she is dangerous and unstable, and no one is completely convinced that she will not continue to be a liability. Things are safer, Meyer tells us, when they conform to standards and norms and when boundaries are not crossed, reiterating the need for heteronormative, patriarchal control.

The first three books of the series laboriously explore the denial of passions, so when *Breaking Dawn*, the last of the series, begins with Edward and Bella's consummation of their marriage, it may appear as though Meyer's emphasis on denial has been undermined. This consummation, however, even though it occurs within the bonds of matrimony, proves to be destructive.

Bella is physically harmed by Edward's brute strength, their relationship is strained because of his emotional awkwardness afterward, and, ultimately, Bella receives a death sentence through the conception of Renesmee. The capitulation to their desires does, in the end, doom Bella to an agonizing death. Rather than reward the couple with the bliss of carnal pleasure for waiting to have sex, it can be read that Meyer reinforces the message that sex and passion are dangerous and frightening, completing the moral lessons of the sanctity of denial, the genius of patriarchal leadership (Edward was right all along), and the heteronormative worldview that requires weak, vulnerable women to be protected by a male partner.

The end of the series sees Edward, Bella, Renesmee, the rest of their vampire kin, and a newly imprinted Jacob preparing to head off into the wilds of South America to search for answers to the mystery that is Renesmee. Rather than a picture of domestic bliss and a happy-ever-after ending, the newly formed family seems to experience happiness tinged with anxiety over the fate of the newest member. Having given in to their lust, Bella and Edward created a monstrosity, an actual physical incarnation of the potential threat of Otherness.

Conclusion

Stephenie Meyer's *Twilight* series is undoubtedly entertaining. Through this madly successful phenomenon, the world has embraced Edward, Bella, Jacob and the entire cast of fantastical characters. Meyer's manifest messages about true love, self-sacrifice, and self-control are laudable for young adult fiction, particularly in a world so saturated with over-sexualized material aimed at tweens and teenagers who are already bombarded with media that trivializes sex in general. Yet the underlying, latent ideology of the series is capable of strongly influencing an entire generation of young readers and filmgoers, not to mention the vast adult audience captivated by the novels and movies. By constructing the world of Forks and the relationships in her series as she has, Meyer is perpetuating an exclusively heteronormative, patriarchal worldview that relies not only on the continued (some may say renewed) oppression of the female gender and femininity in general, but also, by equating difference with "evil," has insinuated that those who do not conform to such social norms are not only labeled as Other, but denied eternal salvation.

The *Twilight* series is part of a disturbing trend of anti-feminist popular media that has been on the rise since the Reagan-Bush–era, according to author Kellie Bean (see Shachar's essay, this anthology). It was during the Reagan administration that society began to:

encounter women in the public domain making the confusing claim that women no longer require the services of the women's movement, and no longer need concern themselves with those issues which feminism has always cared so deeply, like equal pay, daycare, abortion rights, sexual harassment, and domestic violence [10].

The ever present influence of the "emphatically patriarchal, seriously conservative, willfully biased capitalist" mainstream media has indeed spread doubt about a need for a feminist fight in contemporary Western culture (10). Fiction like the *Twilight* series, which romanticizes conformity and restrictive gender roles, similarly champions patriarchal conservativism. The world-wide popularity of Meyer's series and its now ubiquitous presence in popular culture illuminates the ease with which audiences are willing to accept the physical, emotional, and sexual dominance of men over women, the exclusion of all peoples that do not abide by the heteronormative pair-bonding dichotomy, and the restrictive moralizing of heteronormative patriarchy. To allow such "entertainment" to escape critical attention would ensure that these oppressive ideologies ingrain themselves in the collective subconscious.[8]

NOTES

1. In their explanation of sex vs gender, Josephson and Tolleson-Rinehart clarify that "sex is the characteristic of the biological being; gender is the socially constructed aspect of the self" (4). They also note the fallacy of the assumption that sex is dichotomous by pointing out that at least one percent of humans are born as intersexual (4).

2. For example, see Judith Halberstam's "Technologies of Monstrosity: Bram Stoker's *Dracula*." *Victorian Studies* 36.3 (Spring 1993): 333–352.

3. There are readers/fans that debate the charge of "domestic abuse" amongst werewolves and their partners. See section "Imprinting Heteronormative Patriarchy" for further discussion.

4. Billy, the wizened leader of the Quileute tribe, is the only adult character on the side of good not in a heterosexual pair bond. He is, however, in a wheelchair, physically marking him as Other, "allowing" for the difference.

5. The Denali clan *is* run by a woman, but she is merely alluded to and does not feature in the novels.

6. See Jackson Katz's *Tough Guise* for an intriguing look at masculinity and violence.

7. This is a particularly noteworthy point for a discussion on the lack of lesbian identities in the novel. Though female friendships are fetishized, the idea of lesbianism is avoided completely. In the ménage a tois of James, Victoria, and Laurent, there are two men, but only one woman. This is one area of research that deserves more research and more focus than the confines of the above article allow.

8. For further commentary on heteronormativity and the *Twilight* series, please see "A Very Queer Refusal: The Chilling Effect of the Cullens' Heteronormative Embrace" by Kathryn Kane, *Bitten by Twilight: Youth Culture, Media, and the Vampire Franchise (Mediated Youth)* by Melissa A. Click, Jennifer Stevens Aubrey, and Elizabeth Behm-Morawitz.

WORKS CITED

Bean, Kellie. *Post-Backlash Feminism: Women and the Media Since Reagan-Bush*. Jefferson, NC: McFarland, 2007.

Bennett, Judith M. *History Matters: Patriarchy and the Challenge of Feminism*. Philadelphia: University of Pennsylvania Press, 2006.

Caputi, Jane. *Goddesses and Monsters: Women, Myth, Power, and Popular Culture.* Madison: University of Wisconsin Press, 2004.

Joyce, Kathryn. *Quiverfull: Inside the Christian Patriarchy Movement.* Boston: Beacon Press, 2009.

Kristeva, Julia. *Powers of Horror: An Essay on Abjection.* Trans. Leon S. Rodrigues. New York: Columbia University Press, 1982.

McMahon, Jennifer L. "Twilight of an Idol: Our Fatal Attraction to Vampires." *Twilight and Philosophy: Vampires, Vegetarians, and the Pursuit of Immortality.* Eds. Rebecca Housel and J. Jeremy Wisnewski. Hoboken, NJ: John Wiley and Sons, 2009. 193–208.

McClimans, Leah, and J. Jeremy Wisnewski. "Undead Patriarchy and the Possibility of Love." *Twilight and Philosophy: Vampires, Vegetarians, and the Pursuit of Immortality.* Eds. Rebecca Housel and J. Jeremy Wisnewski. Hoboken, NJ: John Wiley and Sons, 2009. 163–176.

Meyer, Stephenie. *Breaking Dawn.* New York: Little, Brown, 2008.

_____. *Eclipse.* New York: Little, Brown, 2007.

_____. *New Moon.* New York: Little, Brown, 2006.

_____. *Twilight.* New York: Little, Brown, 2005.

NARTH National Association for Research and Therapy of Homosexuality. 25 February 2010 <http://www.narth.com/index.html>.

Rich, Adrienne. "Compulsory Heterosexuality and Lesbian Existence." 1980. *Adrienne Rich's Poetry and Prose: Poems, Reviews, and Criticism.* Eds. Barbara Charlesworth Gepi and Albert Gepi. New York: W.W. Norton and Company, 1993. 203–223.

Sedgwick, Eve Kosofsky. "How to Bring up Your Kids Gay." *Fear of a Queer Planet: Politics and Social Theory.* Ed. Michael Warner. Minneapolis: University of Minnesota Press, 1993. 69–81.

Seifert, Christine. "Bite Me! (Or Don't)" BitchMagazine.com. 2008. 27 May 2008 <http://bitch magazine.org/article/bite-me-or-don't>.

Tolleson-Rinehart, Sue, and Jyl J. Josephson, eds. *Gender and American Politics: Women, Men and the Political Process.* New York: M.E. Sharp, 2000.

Warner, Michael, ed. *Fear of a Queer Planet: Politics and Social Theory.* Minneapolis: University of Minnesota Press, 1993.

Winnubst, Shannon. "Vampires, Anxieties, and Dreams: Race and Sex in the Contemporary United States." *Hypatia* 18.3 (Autumn 2003): 1–20.

It's a Wolf Thing

The Quileute Werewolf/Shape-Shifter Hybrid as Noble Savage

NATALIE WILSON

The word werewolf literally means "man-wolf."[1] This etymological origin is particularly interesting in terms of how the *Twilight* saga grafts certain components of werewolf lore onto the notion of the shape-shifter, a concept found in Native American and Nordic lore, as well as in super-natural and fantasy texts across the ages. Historically, the hybrid of human/animal has many racialized and class connotations, with certain cultures, ideologies, and peoples associated with the human (and sometimes god-like) and others associated with the animal, the beastly, the savage, and particularly, with the supposedly id-driven wolf. While werewolf lore tends to be more negative in its representations of these hybrids, presenting werewolves as cannibalistic, ferocious beasts that threaten humanity, shape-shifting legends to do with wolves proffer more celebratory depictions of the wolf/human hybrid.[2] This shift in representation can be linked to the *Twilight* saga, which itself moves from presenting Jacob and the Quileute as modern-day werewolves (in the first three books) and then redefines them as shape-shifters (in the final book of the series).[3]

In the same way that werewolves are textually presented as more dangerous and negative in literature and lore, while shape-shifters are generally depicted as more noble and glorified, the *Twilight* texts move from a representation of the Quileute wolves as a danger to the Cullens and Bella to the closing representation of them as noble protectors. Along the way though, the texts also rely on racialized and class-based representations that echo the negative conception of werewolves *and* of indigenous peoples.[4] As argued by Kristian Jensen in her paper "Noble Werewolves or Native Shape-Shifters,"

Meyer's Quileute shape-shifters are a new creation: like the European werewolves they partially retain their humanity, and they exhibit the traits of mythical shape-shifters or guardian spirits, but they also display the mental afflictions of the lycanthrope. A closer look at Quileute and nearby indigenous peoples' shape-shifter rituals and ceremonies reveals how Meyer appropriates some American Indian beliefs, but in a manner that promotes the Noble Savage idea [94].

As I explored extensively in an earlier essay, the saga uses Quileute legend to frame the wolves as Noble Savages who become the assimilated protectors of the Cullens.[5] To what extent Meyer consciously draws on historical werewolf lore and Quileute legend to present us with a saga that is highly problematic in terms of its representation of race and class is up for debate. Such arguments about authorial intent are largely moot points though, as the famous essay by literary theorist Roland Barthes "The Death of the Author" makes clear. The important factor is not what the author may or may not have intended, but what the text itself actually reveals and represents.[6]

It is my contention that the *Twilight* saga draws on both werewolf and shape-shifter legends in order to present us with a tale that works to glorify whiteness and wealth on the one hand, and to perpetuate notions of indigenous people as noble but beastly savages on the other.[7] However, the werewolf/shape-shifter hybrid depiction that Meyer enacts relies more heavily on werewolf lore than on shape-shifter legends, resulting in a presentation that is more negative than glorifying. Rather than the wolf as regal protector that is found in indigenous myths, we have aggressive and animalistic wolves who fight amongst themselves and harm others, or, modern descendents of the werewolf. While the werewolf was often a very negative figure in lore, the wolf itself is positively depicted across many cultures. In Norse mythology, the wolf symbolizes victory. In Asian lore, wolves sometimes guard the entrance to the celestial realm. In particular, wolves are positive figures in much Native American mythology. To several tribes (such as Mohawk, Navajo, Hopi, Cheyenne, Pawnee, Blackfeet, Quileute), the wolf is known as a protective spirit or honored ancestor and is associated with loyalty and intelligence.[8] Though the common phrase "lone wolf" indicates otherwise, wolves are regarded for their communal natures and play primary roles in many indigenous creation myths, such as that of the Quileute.[9] The wolf is sometimes presented as divided between spirit and body, or as being part of both the physical and mythical worlds, though in much legend this is not given the same negative spin as the human/animal divide of werewolf tales.

In contrast, the werewolf is associated with murder, rape, cannibalism and incest. Variously attributed to making pacts with the devil or due to brain malfunction, werewolf identity has historically been associated with evil, insanity, poverty, and outsiderdom.[10] According to Kate Orenstein, the pre-modern werewolf was "an historical villain" presented as a literal predator of humans (93). Given that literal attacks by wolves were widespread in mainland Europe in the 16th and 17th century, it is not surprising that lore of the time includes a figure — the werewolf— that accounted for these attacks. And, in keeping with the ideological beliefs of the time that held aristocracy above peasants, as well as the fact that peasants were more prone to attack due to their outside labor and their less-safe housing, the lore also came to associate poverty with the wolf. As Orenstein writes, "the wolf became a symbol of peasant hardship. To have 'the wolf at the door' signified desperate poverty and hunger" (94). In effect, the werewolf came to serve as a warning, instilling fear and encouraging social conformity, a "means of controlling Europe's isolated rural population" (Orenstein 102).

The mid 1500s through the early 1600s involved many "werewolf trials," the most famous of which is that of Stubbe Peter, who claimed he made a pact with the devil and became a werewolf. As Orenstein documents, "In the heyday of these trials, any woman or man who bucked social norms might be accused of being a witch or werewolf" (103). The "hunting" of werewolves in Europe, as with witch-hunts, were largely about people excluded or seen as socially transgressive.[11] While women were the predominant targets of witch accusations, men were most often accused of being werewolves. Such accusations were leveled at "men living on the fringes of society: beggars, loners, hermits ..., the mentally ill" and often included allegation of rape, incest, cannibalism, and homosexuality (Orenstein 103). These trials, and the werewolf tales that supported them, were, Orenstein argues, a warning to "peasants on the edge" that "issued in no uncertain terms to the hermit, the outcast, or just the average peasant man — to keep in line" (103). While werewolf trials seem outlandish today, the cases were taken very seriously at the time. Indeed, as documented by James Twitchell, between 1520 and 1630, 30,000 cases of wolf transformations were reported in France alone (210). Twitchell notes the eradication of the wolf population in Europe accounts for the decline in both number and popularity of werewolf tales. In other words, once death by wolf became far less common, the tales themselves no longer haunted the public imagination to the same extent.

However, tales of lycanthropy didn't die out entirely. During the Victorian era, for example, werewolves inhabited many Gothic narratives. Weres were usually depicted as both good and bad, both human and beast — or as a representation of the divided self, the id verses the ego.[12] Stephen King, arguing "the face of the real Werewolf" is Edward Hyde, provides a provocative reading of *The Strange Case of Dr. Jekyll and Mr. Hyde*, interpreting the tale as an exploration of the split between the Dionyson (or the animal/wolf side of humanity associated with the id) and the Apollonian (or the mind/moral side of humanity associated with the ego) (78). King argues "the horror tale generally details the outbreak of some Dionysian madness in Apollonian existence," noting "the horror will continue until the Dionysian forces have been repelled and the Apollonian norm restored again" (368). We can see werewolf tales functioning in this way with the wolfish monsters representing the dangers of those who subvert societal, threaten the status quo, or who are Otherized due to ethnicity or class.[13] This conception of the wolf as an Other is present, for instance, in the ethnic Othering of the Vikings who the Anglo-Saxons called "wolf-skinned" (partly due to the fact they wore wolf pelts in battle). This naming is especially interesting in relation to the Old English Poem "Wulf and Eadwacer."

"Wulf" is a German and English surname. One origin theory of the name is that it might have been derived from the appearance or personality of the original bearer of the name (a practice that was common in medieval times). Thus, "Wulf" is the name of one of the male lovers of the poem, but we might also read this "Wulf" as wolf-like, especially as he is often interpreted as the Viking lover who the Anglo-Saxon speaker of the poem has born a child with, the "wretched welp" that must be sacrificed in the woods. Hence, the lament in the poem can be read as a mournful warning against miscegenation, or, when one sleeps with wolf-like lovers, tragedy and monstrous births ensue. In relation to *Twilight*, we might read Bella as the sorrowful Anglo-Saxon female caught between these two men. Interestingly enough, a translation by Dolores Warwick Frese calls the Anglo-Saxons "corpse-greedy warriors," a fitting description for vampires. Alas, in the saga itself, Renessmee is the child of Edward and Bella and thus not a "wretched welp," but a human/vampire hybrid presented as infantile perfection. Just as we might read the Cullen vampires as the Apollonian minds and the wolves as the Dionyson bodies (drawing on King's reading of *Jekyll and Hyde*) so too might we interpret Edward as the Anglo-Saxon lover (especially given Carlisle's English roots) and Jacob as the ethnically Otherized Viking.

While I am not suggesting Meyer intentionally drew on literary texts exploring the wolf (or "wulf"), her tales undoubtedly incorporate lore that frames the wolf as the dangerous Other — an other that is ethnically and/or socioeconomically constructed as lesser and evil. That she does so is not surprising as werewolves are traditionally framed as evil and, due to a variety of factors, the wolf as evil (as codified in European lore and modern werewolf tales) is a far more common depiction than the wolf as totem protector (as found in much indigenous lore). Given that indigenous peoples were framed as animals in order to justify colonization, it makes sense that their reverence for the wolf is lost in mainstream cultural narratives. In other words, showing animals as intelligent protectors (as wolves are often framed in indigenous lore) works against the human/animal hierarchy that colonization relies upon. The *Twilight* saga echoes the common representation of the wolf (and the indigene) as lesser (rather than as a higher spiritual protector and guide). As such, the saga's representation of ethnic Others contributes to the long historical tradition of linking the wolf to those framed as poor, savage, uncivilized, evil, and so on. Or, as Orenstein puts it, the werewolf is "a dangerous outcast, a social misfit, and a warning of the consequences of that status" (100).

Jacob, our modern day "wolf-skinned" boy, is indeed an outcast — not only from the angelic Cullen vampire family, but also from mainstream Forks society. He is also a misfit within his own society, a wolf rebel who challenges the hierarchy of the pack. When he questions the alpha wolf's decision to destroy Bella's unborn child and lights out on his own in *Breaking Dawn*, we might interpret his long sojourn in wolf form as a representation of the consequences of bucking social norms. In other words, if you don't follow the rules, you will end up alone and all fours. More generally, the male Quileute wolves are presented as dangerous — to Bella, to the Cullens, to Quileute women. They are depicted as gang-like outsiders who others suspect of being drug users or dealers (as when Bella and Quil discuss the "cult" and wonder if they are using "Drugs or something" in "The Cult" chapter of *New Moon*). These werewolf/shapeshifters are presented in vastly different ways to the vampires — they are not the perfectly white, wealthy Cullens nor the powerful, aristocratic Volturi — they "live on the res" in tiny houses, apparently can't afford much clothing let alone the types of shiny cars the Cullens have by the dozen, and they are consistently associated with stereotypes of the "noble savage" (as explored in detail in my previous paper, "Civilized Vampires verses Savage Werewolves").

In addition to the association with the racial/socio-economic Other, werewolves in lore are also associated with the devil — an association that has of course been used historically to de-base certain peoples and cultures and to justify the need for their colonization/religious conversion. As noted by werewolf scholar Brian Frost, werewolves were traditionally depicted as the embodiment of evil, as "the most terrible of all Satan's bond slaves" and as the "emblem of treachery, savagery, and bloodthirstiness" (3). A common theory of wolf transformation claims that it stems from making a pact with the devil, as in the famous Stubbe Peter text which reads, "The Devil gave unto him a girdle, which, being put about him, he was straight transformed into the likeness of a greedy devouring wolf" (Orenstein 88.) Today, this concept has trickled into our lexicon, as when we say "speak of the Devil" (which is equivalent to the Latin phrase "lupus in fabula" or "wolf in the fable") (Orenstein 93). Wolves of course also feature prominently in Christian mythology, as in the Sermon on the Mount where Jesus warns, "Beware of false prophets, which come to you in sheep's clothing, but inwardly they are ravening wolves" (Matthew 7:15). In terms of *Twilight*, Jacob can be read as the "ravening wolf." If we note other wolf warnings of the bible, such as that in Luke 10:3 ("Go your ways: behold, I send you forth as lambs among wolves") or Acts 20:29 ("For I know this, that after my departing shall grievous wolves enter in among you") we might also interpret Bella as the lamb among wolves, who, when Edward departs, though not "fed to the wolves," is at least put in their vicinity. Or, in other words, when god/Edward departs, Jacob, the ravening wolf inculcates himself into her life, tempting her to consider a wolf-future, as she does when she pictures an alternate life with him, complete with human/wolf babies.

While Jacob represents a very earthly, bodily future for Bella, Edward represents a celestial one — one where Bella can be immortal and join the eternal Cullen family.[14] Indeed, we can read Edward as a vampire–Christ incarnate — a white god who has died and come back to life to save Bella, our white lamb/virgin Mary. Edward's associations with all-seeing golden eyes, with immortality, and with perfection ally him with a god. In the series, Bella repeatedly refers to Edward as god-like and angelic, emphasizing his whiteness. In *Twilight* alone, she claims Edward has "the face of an angel," "the voice of an archangel," and relates that "I couldn't imagine how an angel could be any more glorious" (19, 311, 241). She also refers to him as "my perpetual savior," as a "godlike creature," and notes he "looked like a god" (166, 292, 65). Thus, while Jacob is the beastly (were)wolf, Edward is the vampire-god — this dualistic representation of Bella's two suitors not only animalizes one and deifies the other, it also reifies whiteness as next to godliness, a trend documented by Richard Dyer is his study *White*. As Dyer argues, the Christian concept of god has "been thought and felt in distinctly white ways for most of its history" and this "gentilising and whitening of the image of Christ and the Virgin" has been used as a "ready appeal to the God of Christianity in the prosecution of doctrines of racial superiority and imperialism" (17).

For her part, Bella accords to "the image of the glowingly pure white woman," an image which Dyer reads as related to the Virgin Mary and Eve (17, 29). As Dyer asserts, "In Western tradition, white is beautiful because it is the colour of virtue. This remarkable equation relates to a particular definition of goodness ... purity, spirituality, transcendence, cleanliness, virtue, simplicity, chastity" (72). Arguing all concepts of race are also concepts of bodies, Dyer contends that "Black people can be reduced (in white culture) to their bodies and thus to race, but white people (are not) reducible to the corporeal" (14). Noting white people are associated with transcendence and spirituality and non-white people are allied to immanence and corporeality in the Western imagination, Dyer's work offers a fruitful approach to examine the white/dark and spiritual/bodily binaries the *Twilight* saga circulates around. While the white hero and heroine of the saga are consistently allied with transcendent, eternal love, the Quileute characters are connected to mortality, immanence, and the body. They are focused on for their darkness and their corporeality is emphasized. For example, when Bella first sees Jacob and his friends at La Push, she describes them as "all tall and russet-skinned, black hair cropped short" with "strikingly similar hostility in every pair of eyes" (*E* 263, 323). Billy Black, the only disabled character in the saga, is also quite literally relegated to immanence. The films, by presenting him as needing others to manipulate his wheelchair, further the representation of him as a helpless body. Jacob, in different ways, is also relegated to the body. For him, it is presented as natural to be naked — he is, after all, an animal (both literally via the werewolf narrative and figuratively as a "savage" Native American).

The fact the wolves are never fully clothed doesn't escape Bella's attention (nor the fans). Indeed, at one point, Bella asks Jacob, "Is it really so impossible to wear clothes...?" (*E* 215). While the explanation the text offers, that shape shifting makes wearing clothes difficult, is plausible, the film adaptations' obsessive focus on the half-naked "wolf pack" smacks of objectification. Though it is still relatively rare to see semi-naked white males in film, this is not the case for non-white males — a trend with a long history, as noted by Dyer: "In the Western, the plantation drama and the jungle adventure film, the non-white body is routinely on display" (146). As Dyer reminds us, "Clothes are bearers of prestige, notably of wealth, status, and class: to be without them is to lose prestige" (146). In other words, the wolves may be "hot" without shirts, but this representation further animalizes them. Moreover, for working class, wolves-of-color like Jacob (like working class men of color in the real world) power has to be enacted through the physical body. As masculinity scholar Jackson Katz argues, "For working class males, who have less access to more abstract forms of masculinity-validating power (economic power, workplace authority), the physical body and its potential for violence provide a concrete means of achieving and asserting manhood" (135). In fact, we might argue that the Quileute are forced to become wolves in order to access power. Their shape-shifting allows them not only to assert power, but also provides the opportunity for them to legitimate their identities as "properly masculine" — an assertion that is necessary because powerful white males (who are the vampires of *Twilight*) render their identities as Other, as lesser.

In the saga, Jacob and other Quileute characters russet-colored skin and black hair are associated with animality — an association with religious as well as colonial roots. Jacob's representation as a wolf links him to the beasty that threatens god's lambs in the bible. In addition to this connotation, might we also read the Mormon view of indigenous peoples as coming into play in the saga given the author's devout Mormonism? Once again, I am not suggesting that Meyer *intentionally* drew on Mormon ideology in her saga, but rather, that as a devoted follower of the faith, her religious beliefs cannot help but *seep* into her texts to at least some degree.

As explored in detail in my book *Seduced by Twilight*, the Book of Mormon names Native Americans a cursed race (Brodie 83). Joseph Smith's scripture solved the origin of Native Americans and blacks, presenting each as uniquely "cursed" and separate from whites (Brodie 172). Referring to this factor as leading to "the discrimination that is the ugliest thesis in existing Mormon theology," Mormon scholar Fawn Brodie notes that Smith's religion promised a sort of equality, but one that was based on skin color. Once "cursed" dark-skinned people accepted Mormonism they would become *white* (174, 93). In brief, the Book of Mormon contains the history of two warring races, not vampire and werewolf as in *Twilight*, but white and non-white: one a "fair and delightsome people," the other a "wild and ferocious, and a bloodthirsty people; full of idolatry and filthiness ... wandering about in the wilderness, with a short skin girded about their loins, and their heads shaven" (Book of Mormon, Enos 20). Smith named these two races the Nephites, who were "peace-loving and domestic," and the Lamanites, who were "bloodthirsty and idolatrous" (Brodie 43–4). These two races supposedly fought for 1,000 years, with the evil, dark-skinned Lamanites eventually killing off the white Nephite race. In a reversal of genocide, the darker-skinned Lamanites were said to have slaughtered the Nephites, leaving only Moroni, son of the heroic Nephite leader Mormon, who would eventually lead Smith to the gold plates that contained the Book of Mormon.[15]

Smith's scripture abounds with references to white-skinned people as good and pure (much like *Twilight*) and to dark-skinned people as "loathsome," "filthy," and "full of idleness and all manner of abominations" (Book of Mormon, Nephi 12:23). While those with white skin are "exceedingly fair and delightsome" those cursed with dark skin are "not ... enticing unto my people," indeed this is why God "did cause a skin of blackness to come upon them" (Book of Mormon, Nephi 5:21). Yet, if these cursed people accept God (and more specifically Mormonism) "their scales of darkness shall begin to fall from their eyes; and many generations shall not pass away among them, save they shall be a pure white and a delightsome people" (Book of Mormon, Nephi 30:6). These racialized beliefs resulted historically in Mormons' thoroughly documented history of "framing Indians for crimes" committed by Latter Day Saints (Krakauer 245). In addition to disguising themselves as Natives and committing murder and theft, Mormon leaders also encouraged Natives to attack gentiles with promises they would share their plunder (Krakauer 213). Thus, not only does Mormon scripture codify racism as ordained by God, Mormon practice reveals that cultural exploitation was an acceptable practice. What, however, does all this have to do with *Twilight*?

For starters, we can note the almost obsessive emphasis on the Quileute as "russet-colored," a designation that echoes the white/non-white dichotomy in the Book of Mormon.[16] We might also read the Quileute wolves as "cursed," with their ancestral history of shape-shifting (and indeed, Jacob views his fate as a curse). In contrast, the Cullen vampire life is presented as blessed and opulent. While the Cullens are depicted as exceedingly "white and delightsome," Quileute wolves are forced into a life of servitude wherein they lack free choice. And, if we read the Cullens as persecuted Mormons, forced to migrate further and further west before finding their virtual Zion in Forks, we might interpret the Quileute as the descendents of the dark-skinned Lamanites who, if only they will accept Mormon/vampire ways, will be able to become themselves a "white and delightsome" people instead of russet-skinned shape-shifters (much like Jacob has assimilated into the Cullen clan by the series close). These Mormon underpinnings of the saga combined with the use of werewolf and shape-shifting lore provide readers with a tale in which the wolf/Other is presented as racially, spiritually, and socio-economically inferior.[17]

In addition, *Twilight* furthers the representation of Native peoples as savage (a representation necessary to both colonial and religious conversion projects). Robert F. Berkhofer, in *The White Man's Indian: Images of the American Indian from Columbus to the Present*, argues that over four centuries of imagery has sedimented the notion of the "good Indian" as someone who "was hospitable to invaders and whites, was thought to be strong, noble, calm, and brave, and assumed to live a life of liberty, simplicity, and innocence" (28). The "bad Indian," on the other hand, was associated with nakedness, lechery, polygamy, and promiscuity, was thought to be cruel to captives, take part in constant warfare, and mistreat women. Meyer draws on both of these traditions, presenting the Quileute as a brave and noble people, and championing those who are kind to whites (such as Jacob, Seth, Billy). Yet her saga is infused with the stereotypical legacy of the "bad Indian" as well — the wolf boys are violent, their people are given a history of polygamy via the story of the third wife, they are shown to be unnecessarily prejudiced against the good Cullens and eager to wage war against them, and, via the storyline of Emily and Leah especially, they are shown to mistreat women. In effect, the saga, like most media representations of Native peoples furthers the trope of the Noble Savage. Stuart Hall argues this concept functions as "a very ancient grammar" and has traces across media where indigenous peoples are depicted as "cunningly plotting the overthrow of 'civilisation'" (22). In *Twilight* this "ancient grammar" appears both in the unreliability of the wolves (which is shown in particular in relation to how they cannot initially control their "phasing," or when the turn from wolf to human, nor their anger) and to the Quileute's desire to overthrow the peaceable Cullens.

Along similar lines, Elizabeth Bird explores "the fabrication of the Indian by White culture," in which Natives "are akin to primitive children — in a rude state of nature they are nobly innocent, but when crossed they will turn wild and uncontrollable" — much like the Quileute wolves who are "nobly innocent" as they hang out by the La Push campfire, but who become "wild and uncontrollable" at various instances throughout the saga (3). Bird contends that white stories about indigenous people tend to promote the concept of the Noble Savage, arguing "these stories, at a mythic level, explain to Whites their right to be here and help deal with lingering guilt about the displacement of Native inhabitants" (2). Using Bird's schema, might we argue that *Twilight* justifies the rights of the white, Mormon Cullen vampires to inhabit Forks, while simultaneously suggesting that the Quileute people *benefit* from their presence (as when, by the end of the saga, the Quileute become their allies and Jacob symbolically assimilates/converts to whiteness/Mormon identity)?

While Meyer denies any conscious intent to depict themes of Mormonism in her saga and also insists her inclusion of the Quileute came about due to her visit to Forks and discovery of their legends, it nevertheless cannot be denied that representing a real indigenous people *as* werewolves (and co-opting Quileute legend to do so) is problematic. Indeed, Meyer readily admits that she had concerns about her depiction of the Quileute, suggesting that at some level she was aware of the troubling ramifications of using their legends (and possibly also aware of how her depiction echoes the Book of Mormon's framing of indigenous people as cursed).[18] In fact, Meyer's comments in Question and Answer sessions with fans (archived at stepheniemeyer.com) reveal that she had some sense she was taking liberty with another culture's legends and history. For example, when asked why she chose certain settings, Meyer shares, "I was nervous about what the real life citizens of Forks would think, and more especially what the real life people of La Push would think — I'd taken some rather big liberties with their fictional history, and I wasn't sure if they would find it amusing or irritating."[19] Again, Meyer reveals an awareness that her "liberties" might be taken as an affront. What she does not seem aware of though, is how said liberties build upon a history of appropriation in the name of white, colonial interests and how they also jibe with her religion's belief in indigenous people as a cursed race.

Further, as pointed out by Cynthia Willis-Chun, Meyer fails to recognize her use of Quileute legends as cultural theft. Her framing of Quileute legend as "fictional history" is especially troubling in its suggestion that such history and legends are "mere fairytales" (one wonders how she might react if Mormonism were framed as such!) (Willis-Chun 273). Further, the fact Meyer is so vague in interviews regarding her research into Quileute history and culture frames her "great interest" in Native American culture as disingenuous (Jensen 95). As Jensen documents,

> While for the most part Meyer invents Quileute legends to serve her narrative, an investigation into several of the region's myths about Kwatee reveals many tribal motifs that she may have, whether consciously or unconsciously, incorporated into the series.... The detailed origin story that Bella hears in *Eclipse* is clearly a retelling of the story, "Q'wasti' and the Wolves" [98–9].

Although Meyer acknowledges that she read the Quileute origin myth, she does not cite this nor any other myths as sources, nor fully acknowledge how, where, or how much research she did. Given that she is using the sacred beliefs of a culture, such an omission is rude at best, and a form of cultural appropriation bordering on plagiarism at worst — an appropriation that sediments for generations to come the fictionalization of a real people as werewolves. Here, it is interesting to note that Meyer expanded her focus on the Quileute characters of the saga at the request of her editor in order to "add cultural complexity" (Jensen 95). The problem with this trajectory of the narrative is that it does not so much add "cultural complexity" as it does Otherizing stereotypes drawn both from unacknowledged indigenous tales and existing racialized ideologies.

Meyer's well known stories about dreams inspiring the *Twilight* series are also interesting here — just as dreams are filled with our subconscious longings, beliefs, and desires, so is writing — thus, while she might not have meant to appropriate Quileute history nor include a racialized, colonialist view (and, we must remember, only veered in this direction at her editor's request) she nevertheless does. The result is a saga that renders the oppression colonialism relies on and the white privileges it fosters invisible. To be fair, Meyer's sociohistorical positioning cannot help but shape her knowledge, as well as her depiction of Native culture. Or, as Sherman Alexie argues, "when non–Indians write about us, it's colonial literature. And unless it's seen that way, there's a problem."[20] Yet, Meyer does not seem aware of this colonial view, rather, she frames herself as an innocent fan of Quileute mythology.[21] Yet, as Jensen argues, Meyer's Quileute wolves are "more a product of her imagination and of the romantic and patronizing Western stereotype of the 'Noble Savage,' than of a faithful attempt to represent the Quileute culture (92). Such non-native co-optation of indigenous lore tends to distort Native legends and culture and results in the perpetuation of negative stereotypes. As Rob Schmidt of the blog *Newspaper Rock* writes,

> Non-Natives have a long history of borrowing Native legends, stories, concepts, beliefs, and practices. And then simplifying them, changing them, sometimes bastardizing them beyond recognition. The result is a mishmash of mistakes and stereotypes amid nuggets of actual information.

In Meyer's case, one of the founding legends of the Quileute as being descended from wolves is 'bastardized' into depicting Quileute people as werewolves. One of the few printed accounts of this legend reads as follows:

> Then kwati, the Transformer, went on and reached the Quileute land. He saw two wolves. There were no people here. So kwati transformed the wolves into people. And he told these people, "For this reason you Quileute shall be brave, because you come from wolves. In every manner you shall be strong," said kwati [Andrade 85].

Notice that the legend emphasizes the strength and bravery of the Quileute. The saga, though, emphasizes their violence and animality. The traditional colonial stance that Meyer's work conforms to translates into the white characters in the series, be they vampire or human, being presented as more civilized — the non-white Quileute, in contrast, are eroticized, animalized and turned into contemporary Noble Savages. Just like the government agent sent to La Push in 1883 who gave Quileute children names from the bible and American history (effectively erasing their own culture and history), so does the series stamp a new name on Quileute cultural legend — werewolf. This designation has been so effective that fans repeatedly ask about werewolves in Quileute legend, an action that understandably dismays tribal storytellers.[22] Further, this representation has led some writing about the series to present the Quileute NOT as a real tribal nation, but as a fictional creation of Meyer's. For example, Lois Gresh in her companion guide to the series writes, "The Quileute tribe in the *Twilight* Saga is an ancient werewolf pack, and they have always hated vampires literally to the death" (88). Though Gresh is writing about the saga, her failure to emphasize that the Quileute are a real people is problematic, especially given the number of fans I regularly encounter that do not realize this is the case.

Due to the racialized and socio-economic Othering underpinning werewolf lore and legend discussed above, the saga also has to be considered in relation to how it grafts such lore onto Native American mythology and Quileute identity. Via this grafting, Meyer de-politicizes the long historical tradition of appropriating indigenous legend by deploying them in a fictional werewolf and vampire tale — or, in effect, turning a real people and their legends into a fictional representation. In the saga, the Quileute become fantasy characters, super-natural werewolves, rather than the real historical tribe that suffered greatly due to colonization and westward expansion.

Alas, just as Jacob is slowly "civilized" by the Cullen clan and forced to adopt their ways, so too are we as readers "colonized" by the saga — from now on, we will associate Quileute with werewolves. While Meyer certainly may not have intentionally or consciously considered the race, class, and belief contexts when placing the working-class-wolf-of-color as the inferior romantic rival, we, as astute readers, must take these contexts into account. One also wonders why her editor, who, as previously noted, suggested the expanded focus on the Quileute characters, did not question the racialized representation this focus resulted in. As Dyer argues in his book *White*, ideologies are best thought of as "a way of seeing the world that serves particular social interests" (83). The ideology of *Twilight* serves at least in part to champion and bolster white privilege and to keep the wolfy Other firmly in his half-naked place.

NOTES

1. Brian J Frost, *The Essential Guide to Werewolf Literature*, 5.

2. For an exploration of changing conceptions and theories about the werewolf, see Chantal Bourgalt du Coudray's *The Curse of the Werewolf*.

3. See Kristian Jensen's "Noble Werewolves or Native Shape-Shifters?" which also charts this shift.

4. As Bourgault du Coudray notes, "material relating to the werewolf in every period has been informed by prevailing cultural values and dominant ways of knowing and speaking about the world" (2). Thus, we might read *Twilight*'s depiction of wolves in relation to current cultural values and how they reflect white privilege on the one hand and the erasure of indigenous people (both literally and in narrative) on the other.

5. See my "Civilized Vampires Versus Savage Werewolves: Race and Ethnicity in the *Twilight* Series."

6. As I argue in my book *Seduced by Twilight*, Meyer rather consistently denies she was penning any sort of Mormon screed, let alone writing with any sort of purposeful authorial intent.

7. As I argue both in "Civilized Vampires and Savage Werewolves" and in *Seduced by Twilight*. Jensen's essay also compares wolves and shape-shifters. While Jensen focuses on use of Quileute legends and the representation of the Quileute as "noble werewolves," I am more interested in the racialized results of this use.

8. See Jensen 102. See also Andrade, "Quileute Texts." Admittedly, sometimes the wolf is sinister, as in some "skin-walker" tales. See Jensen 94.

9. Jensen cites the lone wolf phrase as coming from werewolf lore and notes it "expresses loathing toward the violent outider or outlaw" (93).

10. See Bourgault du Coudray's first chapter for a detailed exploration of the shifting explanations of the causes of lycanthropy which moved from superstitious lore and legend to more scientific explanations based on brain malfunction (11–43). Du Coudray also notes the tendency to associate werewolves with poor or underclass (45).

11. For an account of how witch trials worked to construct notions of the Other, see Breuer's *Crafting the Witch: Gendering Magic in Medieval & Early Modern England.*

12. Frost xi. See also Bourgault du Coudray, Chapter 1, 11–43.

13. See Bourgault du Coudray's Chapter 2 for a detailed discussion of how werewolf tales were used to contrast notions of "good citizens" with those Otherized due to poverty, race, and ethnicity (44–64).

14. For example, see my chapter "The Soul of the Vampire: Sparkly Mormons, Female Eves, and Unconverted Wolves" in *Seduced by Twilight.*

15. Ibid.

16. Bourgault du Coudray's work reveals the turn to werewolf has often been depicted as a turn to being darker-skinned, 86–87. Thus, turning to wolf is also presented as a turn towards becoming a person-of-color, reifying the conflation between people-of-color and animality.

17. The depiction of the Quileute as werewolves is interesting in relation not only to the racialization of the werewolf, but also in regards to werewolves themselves have sometimes been put into racialized hierarchies. For example, Bourgault du Coudray notes a short story from 1898 that constructed a hierarchy of werewolves that place Native Americans at the bottom of the scale, or, in other words, as the most savage and animalistic, 46.

18. When asked by a fan if she had "any negative recourse for the fictional portrayal of their tribal members as werewolves," Meyer answered: "I was pretty worried about this myself. However, to this point I've had nothing but positive feedback from Native Americans, both Quileute and otherwise. I actually got a letter on MySpace from a girl who is the daughter of one of the council members (she titled her message Quileute Royalty), and she loved the werewolf thing. The common theme in the positive feedback that I've gotten is that the Native Americans I've heard from like that my Quileute characters are fully formed characters whose ethnicity is just one aspect of who they are, rather than their main feature." From "Stephenie Meyer Answers Questions from *Twilight*MOMS Members: Part 2" *Twilight Moms,* 17, August 2010, <http://www. *Twilight*MOMS.com/media/interviews/stephenie-meyer/stephenie-meyer-answers-questions-from-*Twilight*MOMS-members-2/>.

19. John Granger, "Stephenie Meyer *New Moon* Q and A: The Volture," *Forks High School Professor,* 18. November 2009, 17 August 2010, <http://fhsprofessor.com/?p=311>.

20. Sherman Alexie, interview, *Atlantic Unbound,* June 2001. 17 August 2010 <http://www. theatlantic.com/past/docs/unbound/interviews/ba2000–06–01.htm>.

21. As here: "The Story Behind the Writing of *New Moon*," *The Official Website of Stephenie Meyer,* 17 August 2010, <http://www.stepheniemeyer.com/nm_thestory.html>.

22. Anita Wheeler, "*Twilight* Legends Panel," TwiCon, Dallas, August 2, 2009.

Works Cited

Alexie, Sherman. Interview. *Atlantic Unbound* June 2001. Web. 17 August 2010 <http://www.the atlantic.com/past/docs/unbound/interviews/ba2000–06–01.htm>.

Andrade, Manuel J. "Quileute Texts." *Columbia University Contributions to Anthropology* 12 (1931): 1–211.

Barthes, Roland. "Death of the Author." *Image, Music, Text.* Trans. Stephen Heath. New York: Hill and Wang, 1978. 142–48.

Berkhofer, Robert F., Jr. *The White Man's Indian: Images of the American Indian from Columbus to the Present.* New York: Vintage Books, 1978.

Bird, Elizabeth S. "Constructing the Indian, 1830s–1990s." *Dressing in Feathers: The Construction of the Indian in American Popular Culture.* Oxford: Westview Press, 1996. 1–12.

Bourgault du Coudray, Chantal. *The Curse of the Werewolf: Fantasy, Horror, and the Beast Within.* London: I.B. Taurus, 2006.

Breuer, Heidi. *Crafting the Witch: Gendering Magic in Medieval & Early Modern England*. New York: Routledge, 2009.

Brodie, Fawn M. *No Man Knows My History: The Life of Jospeh Smith*. 2nd ed. New York: Vintage Books, 1995.

Dyer, Richard. *White*. London, Routledge, 1997.

Frese, Dolores Warwick. "Wulf and Eadwacer: The Adulterous Woman Reconsidered." *Religion and Literature* 15, 1 (Winter 1983): 1–22.

Granger, John. "Stephenie Meyer *New Moon* Q and A: The Volture." *Forks High School Professor*, 18 November 2009. Web. 17 August 2010 <http://fhsprofessor.com/?p=311>.

Gresh, Lois H. *Twilight Companion: The Unauthorized Guide to the Series*. New York: St. Martin's Griffin, 2008.

Hall, Stuart. "The Whites of Their Eyes: Racist Ideologies and the Media." *Gender, Race, and Class in Media*. Eds. Gail Dines and Jean M. Humez. Thousand Oaks, CA: Sage, 1995. 18–22.

Jensen, Kristian. "Noble Werewolves or Native Shape-Shifters?" *The Twilight Mystique: Critical Essays on the Novels and Films*. Eds. Amy M. Clarke and Marijane Osborn. Jefferson, NC: McFarland, 2011.

Katz, Jackson. "Advertising and the Construction of Violent White Masculinity." *Gender, Race, and Class in Media*. Eds. Gail Dines and Jean M. Humez. Thousand Oaks, CA: Sage, 1995. 133–141.

King, Stephen. *Danse Macabre*. New York: Everest House, 1981.

Krakauer, John. *Under the Banner of Heaven*. New York: Doubleday, 2003.

Meyer, Stephenie. *Breaking Dawn*. New York: Little, Brown, 2008.

_____. *Eclipse*. New York: Little, Brown, 2007.

_____. *New Moon*. New York: Little, Brown, 2006.

_____. *Twilight*. New York: Little, Brown, 2005.

Orenstein, Catherine. *Little Red Riding Hood Uncloaked*. New York: Basic Books, 2002.

Schmidt, Rob. "The Problem with Quileute Werewolves." *Newspaper Rock: Where Native America Meets Pop Culture*. 23 October 2008. Web. 17 August 2010 <http://newspaperrock. bluecorncomics.com/2008/10/problem-with-quileute-werewolves.html>.

Twitchell, James B. *Dreadful Pleasures: An Anatomy of Modern Horror*. Oxford: Oxford University Press, 1985.

Wheeler, Anita. "*Twilight* Legends Panel." TwiCon, Dallas, 2 August 2009.

Willis-Chun, Cynthia. "Touring the Twilight Zone: Cultural Tourism and Commodification on the Olympic Peninsula." *Bitten by Twilight: Youth Culture, Media, and the Vampire Franchise*. Eds. Melissa A. Click, Jennifer Stevens Aubrey, and Elizabeth Behm-Morawitz. New York: Peter Lang, 2010. 261–79.

Wilson, Natalie. "Civilized Vampires Versus Savage Werewolves: Race and Ethnicity in the *Twilight* Series." *Bitten by Twilight: Youth Culture, Media, and the Vampire Franchise*. Eds. Melissa A. Click, Jennifer Stevens Aubrey, and Elizabeth Behm-Morawitz. New York: Peter Lang, 2010. 55–70.

_____. *Seduced by Twilight*. Jefferson, NC: McFarland, 2011.

Violence, Agency, and the Women of *Twilight*

ANNE TORKELSON

Stephenie Meyer's enormously popular *Twilight* saga uses the framework employed in many vampire narratives, that of the intellectually superior male vampire paired with a weak, vulnerable human female, which consequently "represent[s] the male as virtually unassailable in terms of power" (Brown).[1] In the *Twilight* saga, the framework expands to male supernatural beings/ female humans, which includes Jacob and Sam in the male-female power structure. As Caitlin Brown argues in her article "Feminism and the vampire novel," this framework denies Bella the power afforded to the saga's central male characters (par. 6).

Brown's article is one among many feminist critiques of the *Twilight* saga. Since *Twilight*'s 2006 publication, scholars, book reviewers, journalists, and fans have discussed the gendered power imbalance prevalent in the novels, criticizing their glorification of an unhealthy romantic relationship (North; Rice), the fall of mankind allegory in which Bella represents the Eve-like temptress and Edward the keeper of her virginity (Brown; North), the violent anti-abortion message (Seifert), and, once *Breaking Dawn* hit bookstores in 2008, Bella's abandonment of her family and educational ambition to fulfill the patriarchal ideal of young marriage and motherhood (Rice). Many reviewers also criticize episodes of physical violence against Bella in the novels, particularly the kissing scenes between Bella and Jacob, the brutal consummation of Bella and Edward's marriage, and the fatal pregnancy Bella insists upon carrying out. Abuse and violence is the primary focus in Rebecca Housel's "The 'Real' Danger: Fact v. Fiction for the Girl Audience," in which Housel examines the control and emotional cruelty within Bella's relationship with Edward.

No published reviews or analyses, however — not even Housel's essay — discuss the violent histories of *Twilight*'s other female characters, namely the three women of the Cullen clan and Emily Young, at length.[2] Given the global epidemic of violence against women, this notable gap in the *Twilight* critical conversation deserves serious attention.[3] Also missing is an in-depth dialogue on rape culture — a culture prevalent in American society, where Meyer, many of her readers, and *Twilight*'s main characters live — and the novels' perpetuation of its myths. Examining the episodes of violence against Bella in the larger context of violence against other women in the books reveals an imbalance of power relations that extends beyond Edward and Bella to the series' other male-female relations.

Many critics also identify anti-feminist messages in the *Twilight* novels without examining the responses of everyday readers. Print culture historian Jonathan Rose would say these critics are committing the "receptive fallacy," where the critic does not study readers' responses to a book but assumes that whatever the author wrote, or whatever the critic finds in the book, is the message that the common reader takes away (Rose 49). In today's digital age, the multitude of online blog posts, fan forums, and articles on the *Twilight* saga provides insight into actual readers' experiences with the novels, but also poses a challenge in that it is unfeasible to locate, read, and analyze all or even the majority of the reader responses. Nevertheless, an analysis of *some* readers' experiences, chosen from a wide variety of experiences shared on popular *Twilight* fan sites and online articles, shows that the *Twilight* saga perpetuates myths of rape culture, normalizes and romanticizes violence against women, and reinforces a power structure that denies female agency and positions male dominance as the natural social hierarchy. Finally, a look at how readers are beginning educate other readers on these issues provides a possible solution to the issues the *Twilight* saga poses.

Bella, Jacob, Edward, and the Perpetuation of Rape Culture

A rape culture is not simply a culture in which rape exists. As defined by *Transforming a Rape Culture*, a rape culture:

> is a complex of beliefs that encourages male sexual aggression and supports violence against women. It is a society where violence is seen as sexy and sexuality as violent. [...] In a rape culture both men and women assume that sexual violence is a fact of life, inevitable as death or taxes [vii].

The feminist blog *Shakesville* expands this definition to one that many female readers will recognize:

Rape culture is 1 in 6 women being sexually assaulted in their lifetimes. [...] Rape culture is telling girls and women to be careful about what you wear [...] where you walk, when you walk there [...] if you're alone [...] if it's dark [...] to always be alert always pay attention always watch your back always be aware of your surroundings and never let your guard down for a moment lest you be sexually assaulted and if you are and didn't follow all the rules *it's your fault* [McEwan].

In short, rape culture supports male-female power imbalances and even promotes violence against women through a multitude of rape myths, such as that victims are responsible for what happens to them and that violence against women by men is acceptable because "boys will be boys." Yet, violence against women is a worldwide issue, not limited to certain cultures, countries, or groups of women ("How Widespread is Violence Against Women?"). Even a few minutes skimming *Shakesville* or *The Curvature* blog, which documents and discusses the legal cases, media coverage (or lack thereof), and rhetoric surrounding such violence, provides a shocking and bleak picture of how widespread rape culture is today.

Out of the scenes between Bella and Edward or Bella and Jacob, three in particular reinforce rape culture and its myths. One scene is the first kiss between Jacob and Bella in *Eclipse*, which critics identify as sexual assault (Rice; Wilson, "Civilized Vampires"), a reading fully supported by Jacob's actions and Meyer's diction. Despite Bella's verbal and physical protests, Jacob kisses Bella "angrily, roughly," his lips "forc[ing]" hers open, his hand gripping her neck and preventing her escape (330). Jacob ignores her when she fights back and when she shuts down in self-defense. When Bella asks if he is finished, he responds with a smile.

Then, in a rare moment of agency, Bella punches Jacob in the mouth. The novel quickly reverts this female power back to the structure of male dominance, however, when Bella accepts a ride home from Jacob, who banters and whistles, his conscience completely at ease with his assault on Bella moments before. Bella's easy forgiveness echoes rape culture's "boys will be boys" mentality, which Charlie also reinforces when he condones Jacob's actions with a congratulatory, "Good for you, kid" (336). Like Adrienne Rich's description of people living in a culture dominated by male power, the *Twilight* saga's characters have been socialized to feel that "male sexual 'drive' amounts to a right" (37). Bella is not praised for her self-defense, nor does Jacob face any consequences; Bella is viewed by all — including herself— as a prize to be conquered, an object to cater to Jacob's sexual needs. Though she does recognize Jacob's actions as assault, it is not until nearly 100 pages later, and she downplays it through her language and attitude. Instead of asserting her right to her own body, she tells Jacob she doesn't "count" the kiss as a kiss and "think[s] of it more" as an assault (476). When Jacob responds with a flippant, "Ouch! That's cold," she merely shrugs.

The message of the seriousness of Jacob's actions clearly doesn't reach him, either. Later in *Eclipse*, he once again assaults Bella in a scene that reinforces rape culture in yet another way. In this scene, Jacob emotionally manipulates Bella into kissing him by threatening to harm himself unless he gets his way. This coercive tactic effectively leaves Bella without true choice, powerless to do other than he demands. The scene uses rape-evoking language: Jacob "take[s] advantage" of the situation, kissing Bella "with an eagerness that was not far from violence" (526). He holds her by the roots of her hair while the other hand, Bella narrates, "grabbed roughly at my shoulder, shaking me, then dragging me to him. [...] [Jacob] yanked me forward, bowing my body against his" (526). When Bella fights back and Jacob continues, Bella excuses him, saying that he "misunderstood" her struggles (527). In "Compulsory Heterosexuality and Lesbian Experience," Rich writes that young women and men are taught that the sex drive of the adolescent male "once triggered cannot take responsibility for itself or take no for an answer" (47). Jacob, who Bella defends as "too strong to recognize" that her resistance isn't consensual passion, again forces himself on Bella, "clutching frantically" at her waist (*E* 527).

Just as Bella starts to gain physical control, she begins returning the kiss (527), suddenly enjoying Jacob's assault on her and deciding that she loves but doesn't deserve him. Echoing Bella's reaction and the experiences of real women across the country, Pamela R. Fletcher writes in "Whose Body Is It, Anyway?" that "[w]e didn't define what they did to us as rape, molestation, or sexual abuse. We called it love" (432). Jacob's actions and Bella's physical response and internal dialogue participate in what Rich calls the "mystique of the overpowering, all-conquering male sex drive" that is "rooted [in] the law of male sex right to women" (Rich 47); Jacob and Bella have internalized the cultural message that it is normal and acceptable for men to claim sexual power over women and that women desire this power imbalance. Later, blaming her emotional turmoil on herself, Bella supports another rape myth that women who are abused and violated invite, desire, or deserve the violence done to them.

Some readers share this mentality.[4] Out of approximately 75 posts answering the question "Was it okay of Bella to ask Jake ... [to kiss her]" on the *Twilighters.org* message boards, more than half express annoyance with Bella and feel that she wronged Edward. While many posts criticize Jacob for tricking Bella, just as many blame her, and some do both: "deep down she probably knew he was manipulating her and she let him" (Pretty_Face). In another thread called "Do you think Jacob was wrong to trick Bella?" common responses such as "it's immature but he is only young" (Aimeeee) and "yes I think it was wrong of him but I can understand why he did it" (TashiCullen) simultaneously accuse and excuse Jacob. Another comment perfectly captures the "boys will be boys" mentality and illustrates the prevalence and cultural acceptance of sexual assault: "Yes it was wrong for Jacob to trick her in that way. But he did truly did love her and lust for her, so he acted as many other teenage boys would" (Hopelessly_hopeful). Whether readers are bringing their own beliefs and experiences to the books or internalizing the scenes' normalization of rape culture myths, the *Twilight* saga clearly reinforces these myths for readers.

Bella's *Breaking Dawn* wedding night, perhaps the most anticipated scene in the series, also perpetuates rape myths. In the morning, Bella finds herself covered in bruises — only after Edward draws attention to them — feeling as if her "bones had all become unhinged at the joints" (88). Bella's attitude toward her injuries, however, is even more disturbing than the injuries themselves. First, Bella expected the injuries and worse, knowing that sex with Edward would endanger her life (70). This attitude perpetuates the rape myths that sexual violence is sexy and desired by women. When Bella discovers her injuries, she justifies and downplays her pain in multiple instances, such as by saying she has had worse, calling her swollen and bruised face "fine," and explaining that her skin "marked up easily" (89). She is also covered in feathers from the pillows Edward destroyed in his passion; "We're just lucky it was the pillows and not you," he tells her (95). Bella shies away from the danger and brutality of the sexual experience to focus on how "wonderful and perfect" it was (92). Physically battered, she only thinks of Edward, hiding her bruises to spare his feelings and worrying that he might not have enjoyed himself (71). A second romp results in another scene that eroticizes abusive sex through violent images such as more bruises, shredded lingerie strewn across the sheets, and a destroyed headboard. This scene sends the same message prevalent in pornography: that women are "natural sexual prey to men and love it," that physical abuse is erotic, and that "enforced submission and the use of cruelty [...] is sexually 'normal'" (Rich 40).

As *Twilight*'s fan responses show, readers are not immune to this message. One writes, "If I was Bella and I woke up the next morning covered on feathers and bruises shaped like his hands, I'd be ecstatic!" (IsabellCullen) while another muses, "Bella was all smacked up with bruises and still begging for more. Must have been even better than I imagined" (Yuliya). Other fans buy merchandise celebrating violent sex, such as the "Edward Can Bust my Headboard, Bite My Pillows, and Bruise My Body ... Anyday!" t-shirt (Stein). On one *Twilighters.org* forum thread lamenting the scene's lack of sexual detail, one reader comment is particularly telling. In an apparent defense of how little description of the sexual acts the *Twilight* books include, the reader posts that she wouldn't want her thirteen-year-old cousin, a *Twilight* fan, reading material that is "too graphic" (ILoveJasper). Apparently, many readers don't view or recognize descriptions of romanticized assault and eroticized, violent sex as "too graphic" or harmful for young women.

The Other Women of Twilight

Beneath the surface, scenes between Bella and her romantic interests reveal a disturbing perpetuation of rape culture myths. Even more troubling is that Bella is not the only female character in the *Twilight* saga to evoke these myths. A closer look at *Twilight*'s other female characters, their histories, and their relationships with men exposes a pattern of violence against women, rape culture, power imbalances, and a lack of agency that runs throughout the novels. Reader responses to the stories of Emily, Esme, Alice, and Rosalie allow analysis of how readers reject or accept and internalize these messages.

Emily's Story

In "Creating Redemptive Imagery: A Challenge of Resistance and Creativity," Sandra Campbell argues that "our popular images and stories present women as subordinate, objectified as sexual bodies, which are considered the domain for male aggressive sexuality and, ultimately, violence" (144). She also argues that in popular culture, violence has no significant consequences, which "allows the creation of sensational, extreme images" that visually emphasize physical violence while detaching it from its physical or emotional effects (145). These beliefs underlie the story of Emily Young, whose face and arm are permanently scarred from an incident in which Sam lost his temper and lashed out at her as he changed into wolf form. The werewolves and even the vampires treat violence as an unfortunate, and perhaps inevitable, consequence of this form transformation. Jacob explains, "Sam lost control of his temper for just one second ... and she was standing too close" (*NM* 345). His rhetoric implicates Emily in the violence; instead of holding Sam fully accountable for his assault on Emily, it is Emily who is responsible. This simple, subtle sentence supports the rape myth that women are to blame for violence against them. Even Edward's warning to Bella about werewolves resembles an excuse: "Werewolves are unstable. Sometimes, the people near them get hurt. Sometimes, they get killed" (*E* 18).[5]

Descriptions of Emily emphasize her scars, dissociating the physical impact of the violence from the pain it caused; the attack has left her face disfigured by "three thick, red lines, livid in color though they were long healed" (*NM* 331) that pull her face into a "permanent grimace" (*NM* 331). The novels do not ignore the psychological consequences of the violence on Sam; when it comes to Emily, however, they only note the scars that have "ruined" (*NM* 333) her beauty and do not address any physical pain or emotional damage she suffers. When readers discuss Emily's scars on *Twilighters. org*, most defend Sam and Emily's love, calling the violence an accident and criticizing Emily. Writes one reader,

> They were maybe argueing or he could have been argueing with someone else. [...] Emily was standing to close, so in a way it is slightly her fault. She knows wolves are dangerous when annoyed or feeling strong emotions, she should have left whatever was bugging Sam and walked away [H;teamswitzerland].

Another reader responds, identifying how the comments perpetuate a rape culture myth (though the reader doesn't use the term "rape culture"):

> You seem to be saying that it's Emily's fault that she got hurt? Isn't that like *blaming a victim of abuse*? Being a wolf doesn't give Sam the best excuse, a person can have anger management issues but that doesn't mean it's alright for them to hit people. Does being unable to control himself make it acceptable for him to lash out at Emily [Kendra, emphasis mine].

Other readers continue to defend Sam, with comments such as, "You want the very best for the one you love, but there will be times when you accidentally hurt them" (AamMilk). In some readers' minds, the violence done to Emily was not only an inevitable accident — part of normal, everyday life — but was partially her fault.

As in many cases of violence against women, those who know the truth behind Emily's scars protect Sam, her assailant, by inventing a cover-up story that a bear attacked her. Bella, and thus readers, learn what really happened from Jacob and Edward. Emily never discusses the event or her scars; men control her story. Emily even ends up comforting Sam for the violence done to her, playing into what Rich calls society's false consciousness of the "demand that women provide maternal solace, nonjudgmental nurturing, and compassion for their harassers, rapists, and batterers" (49). Bound in her relationship by Sam's imprinting and by *Twilight's* society of compulsory heterosexuality,[6] Emily is ultimately a silent victim of domestic abuse, unable to leave her abuser.

Esme's Story

Powerlessness and domestic violence are themes that also run in Esme's story, though interestingly, Esme's untold history is also one of female agency. According to Meyer on the *Twilight Lexicon* website ("Personal Correspondence #1"), Esme married an abusive man and remained in the marriage to appease her parents. When she became pregnant, she ran away from her husband and home, fleeing again when her parents learned of her location. A self-sufficient single mother, she supported herself through a teaching job. The *Twilight* saga doesn't show readers this strong, courageous Esme that refuses to accept the violence done to her and controls her own destiny, however; instead, they deny Esme power and present only the side of her story in which Carlisle decides her future. In *Twilight*, Esme tells Bella how she had jumped off a cliff after losing her infant (interestingly, the same action Bella takes after Edward leaves her). Barely alive, Esme was brought to the morgue where Carlisle was working, and Carlisle turned her. Edward explains to Bella that Carlisle would only change a dying human into a vampire and "would never do that to someone who had another choice" (*T* 288). But the inability to choose does not equal consent, just as the inability to choose sexual activity — whether through alcohol or unconsciousness — does not provide license for action.[7] Without considering whether Esme would choose a transformed life of immortality and drinking blood, Carlisle took control of her future, transforming her out of loneliness and his own desire for a mate. Furthermore, Carlisle doesn't question whether Esme, once a vampire, would choose to become his mate, and Esme happily and unquestioningly accepts a man's control of her fate and his desire for her as his sexual partner. This power imbalance is noted by readers. On the *Twilight*MOMS.com fan forum thread titled "Carlisle: Selfish or Savior?" the 77 comments range between those who recognize that Esme had no choice in becoming a vampire —

> It is not up to Carlisle to think "she'll get over it" and change her. Imagine being Esme, going through 3 days of agonizing pain, only to wake up completely different, craving human blood and still grieving over your lost child.

— to those who argue that Carlisle is not selfish because he changed Esme out of loneliness and love for her. While perhaps putting Carlisle's actions in a more understandable light, this latter view still denies Esme agency and choice.

Alice's Story

A teenager in the 1920s, Alice lived in an insane asylum at the time of her transformation, committed and abandoned by her family because she had visions. A historical approach to Alice's human story suggests a number of abuses she likely suffered in the asylum, including beatings, immobilization, choking, straight jackets, smothering and suffocation, hydrotherapies, and even forced sterilization (Geller 10). While many readers may not have extensive knowledge of women in asylums in early 20th-century America, they do know from the novels that Alice was given shock treatments and kept in a "black hole of a cell" for so long, presumably so accustomed to abuse, that she didn't even notice the excruciating pain of becoming a vampire (*T* 447–48). But when discussing Alice's forced institutionalization ("Chapter 10: The Visitor"), few readers mention this violence that Alice endured. Perhaps like Alice, they are so accustomed to abuse against women that they don't even notice it or find it worth mentioning.

Likewise, little reader discussion exists on the overwhelmingly unequal, gendered power relations in Alice's human history. Alice has no agency or choice in her own story, but is acted upon by men; she is desired by a man, hunted by a man, set free by a man, and changed into a vampire and thereby saved by a man. As a vampire, Alice exercises agency in trying to find out more about her past and her family. Her lack of memory of the asylum and the scant information she uncovers, however, serve to keep her silenced about the violence she suffered. She cannot give voice to her abuses; even her story is first told by a man, as the tracker James reveals Alice's history — just as he is about to kill Bella for sport. Without any memory of her human life, Alice is not physically or emotionally affected by the violence done to her, which reinforces the myth that violence against women has no consequences. She actually benefits from her transformation by the development of her psychic powers, which in turn supports another rape myth that compensation can negate violence. As a vampire, she is a prevailing figure. She possesses enormous power in her visions, chooses Jasper for her mate, and decides to become part of the Cullen family. But as a human, like Esme, she was abused, powerless, and transformed without a choice. Her human story perpetuates the dominant narrative of male power and female submissiveness as the natural social order, a power imbalance so normalized that it fails to catch readers' attention or interest.

Rosalie's Story

Rosalie's agency as a vampire is similarly troubled by her human history. Rosalie was a teen in the 1930s when her fiancé and his friends beat her, raped her, and left her for dead. Carlisle found her and changed her because it was "too much waste" (*E* 93). Whether this "waste" is one of a life or of beauty, readers are unsure ("So Much Waste?"). Again taking a woman's future into his own hands, Carlisle explains, "I couldn't just let her die" (*E* 93). While Carlisle's reasoning may seem caring and respectful of human life, he is actually violating Rosalie's choice to become immortal. He also treats her as a sexual reward, transforming her in order to create a mate for Edward. Many readers point out Rosalie's declaration that if given the choice, she would not have become a vampire (*NM* 534). Other readers defend Carlisle's actions on the basis that he transformed Rosalie out of love for Edward and a desire for his happiness ("Carlisle: Selfish or Savior?"), supporting the books' objectification of Rosalie.

Rosalie's story — and Rosalie herself — also perpetuates rape culture myths. Rosalie accepts partial blame for her attack; because she was beautiful, she was expected to marry a man for his high social standing instead of for love, which led to her involvement with her fiancé. But whether Rosalie married the right or wrong man, for the right or wrong reasons, she and Bella both fail to recognize that she is not responsible for what happened to her. Rosalie's story, through its focus on her physical beauty, supports the rape myths that only young, attractive women are raped and that female victims are to blame for what happens to them because of their appearance, being in the wrong place at the wrong time, saying the wrong thing, or getting involved with the wrong man.

Though Rosalie does perpetuate this myth, she is the one female vampire who doesn't accept her new fate without question. Once she realized what she had become, she "knew that my life was ended, and there was no going back for me" (*E* 94) and admits to Bella that at times, she has hated the life of a vampire and would trade "everything I have" to be in Bella's human position (*E* 96). Like Alice, she demonstrates agency as a vampire. Once turned, she tells Bella, she used her strength and cunning to kill her attackers. Rosalie takes her place among woman warriors, females avenging the wrongs done against them and their families (Clarke 398). Rosalie does not use a literal weapon but embodies D. A. Clarke's description of a woman with a sword:

> She is no one's property. A crime against her will be answered by her own hand. She is armed with the traditional weapon of honor and vengeance, implying both that she has a sense of personal dignity and worth, and that affronts against that dignity will be hazardous to the offending party [394].

In "A Woman with a Sword," Clarke sees "potential value in fiction and film on the theme of women taking violent means of vengeance on rapists and femicides," which asserts female honor and carries a certain "shock value" (402). Violent female vengeance, she argues, shocks the audience into considering *why* they are shocked at the "idea of vigilante women hunting down men" and not by the "images of men hunting down, overpowering, and hurting women [that] surround us" (402). Rosalie's story of vengeance is shocking in *Twilight's* world of submissive, powerless women, and is also empowering. Rosalie did not let her attackers evade justice, and she carried out that justice herself. Tempted by her attackers' blood, she exercised enormous control in not drinking it and allowing it inside her. Though violence against men by women is hardly the solution to rape culture, Rosalie's agency is welcome among readers, who celebrate her revenge with comments such as, "I have grown to love Rosalie. [...] She is strong, loyal and protective. Besides, she got her vengance and I've got to love that" (Tamia) and "I loved the fact that she seeked revenge in the first place" (Jaxman007).

As a vampire, Rosalie also breaks free of the male-dominated power structure when she chooses Emmett for her mate and when she stands with pregnant Bella against the rest of the coven's wishes, acting as her protector. Taking this agency into account, the *Twilight* saga seems to suggest a positive and much needed message that women victims of violence and abuse can survive and reclaim power for themselves. That Rosalie only exhibits agency after she has gained superpowers, however, complicates this message. For all of Rosalie's power, it is only power that is transferred to her, supernaturally, by a man, without her consent. Just as in the stories of Esme and Alice, Rosalie does not *become*, but is *made*, a vampire. As a human woman, she undergoes brutal violence and is left without the choice or ability to determine her future.

Impact of Twilight on Readers

How do these messages, participating in a wider culture of violence and male dominance, impact the millions of *Twilight* readers? While Jonathan Rose illustrates the "receptive fallacy" (49) and the need for the critic to consider reader responses, Campbell provides room for the critic to analyze these responses when she argues that the "process of image internalization works outside rational thought;" unknowingly, people absorb "the values represented in contemporary icons, perpetuating their underlying beliefs" (143). Similarly, Justin Lewis states in the 2001 documentary *Mickey Mouse Monopoly* that the media influences the way we think by "creating a certain environment of images that we grow up in and we become used to. And after awhile, those images will begin to shape what we know and what we understand about the world." What Lewis calls a "slow, cumulative effect" is already impacting *Twilight* readers. In their study of female fans of the saga, documented in "Relating to *Twilight*: Fans' Responses to Love and Romance in the Vampire Franchise," Elizabeth Behm-Morawitz, Melissa A. Click, and Jennifer Stevens Aubrey find that some fans draw upon *Twilight* relationships, particularly that of Bella and Edward, to form expectations for and evaluate their own romantic relationships.

That not all readers notice or critically examine the novels' patterns of male dominance, denial of female agency, and violence against women does not prove that readers are not affected by these meta-narratives, but rather suggests that the novels reinforce norms and messages already prevalent and established in our society and popular culture. Many readers point out that they are able to distinguish fantasy from reality and do not learn negative messages from the books, while other readers challenge this view. For example, one commenter affirming the article "Top 20 Unfortunate Lessons Girls Learn From *Twilight*" writes,

> You may think teenage girls won't take any life lessons from these books, but they will and they have. I deal with fans of the series on a daily basis, and it is ridiculous the kind of things that these girls learn from the series. I know of many girls who will acknowledge Edward's abusive tendencies but will immediately defend him, "Yes he's abusive and does a lot of bad things, but he does it because he loves her!" In many a fan's mind, if the act of abuse has love as its motivator then it's absolutely okay and forgivable. If you don't believe me, then you haven't been around enough of the fans.

Another reader, "jack," takes his response a step further by suggesting how we can respond to these negative messages: "Teenagers are going to see questionable things. Our duty is not to stifle the exposure to these ideas rather to give the kids the critical thinking skills to enjoy the entertainment without letting it adversely influence them." Jack recognizes that the issues of violence against women and denial of female agency in the *Twilight* saga do not merit banning or condemnation of the books. Instead, they illustrate the need for discussion on popular literature and a more critical dialogue about the *Twilight* saga in particular. While critics continue to write feminist diatribes on the saga, the *Twilight* books "do not represent a failure of feminism, but rather a golden opportunity to evaluate where we can focus on outreach" (Peterson). In "Twihard With a Vengeance: Why *Twilight* Is a Boon for Young Women," Latoya Peterson asks, "[h]ow often do we get a non-personal opportunity to talk about issues with obsessive relationships?" She notes that the popularity of the *Twilight* saga and franchise will one day end, providing an opening for adults to "influence the great *Twilight*-after" through encouraging readers to guide Bella via fan fiction and by recommending similar books with "more progressive leanings." I would expand Peterson's thoughts to add that adults — and peers — do not have to wait to take this opening until after *Twilight*'s popularity dies down, but can and should critically discuss the saga's issues while it remains active in the minds and hearts of so many readers. The more subtle ways in which the *Twilight* saga reinforces rape culture myths and denies agency to its other female characters are given little voice in *Twilight* conversations, and considering that an estimated one in five women around the world will become the victim of a rape or attempted rape during her life and that young women — the *Twilight* saga's main fan base — are "disproportionately victims of domestic violence and rape" in America, these conversations are greatly needed. As Peterson and increasing numbers of critics and fans are realizing, the *Twilight* saga's bestselling, record-breaking popularity among readers of multiple generations offers a prime opportunity for critical evaluation, discussion, and education on issues in the books — including the perpetuation of rape culture myths, the normalization and romanticization of violence against women, and the reinforcement of a male-dominated power structure — that continue to draw criticism and that have yet to be fully explored.

NOTES

1. While most vampire stories use this framework, vampire literature does not include influential works featuring female vampires. Of note are Johan Wolfgang von Goethe's *The Bride of Corinth* (1797), Sheridan Le Fanu's *Carmilla* (1872), Anne Rice's *The Queen of the Damned* (1988), and Jewelle Gomez's *The Gilda Stories* (1991).

2. At the time of writing this essay, academic *Twilight* criticism is just beginning to emerge in print. While criticism discussing the other women of *Twilight* in depth may exist, I have not found any to date.

3. See UNICEF's 2000 report "Domestic Violence Against Women and Girls" for more information.

4. Reader response analysis took place in early 2010. No doubt many additional message board postings and blog comments have appeared since then. Readers' comments often contain errors in spelling and grammar. Throughout this essay I present the comments as they originally appeared.

5. In addition to supporting rape culture myths, Edward's warning contains negative racial implications. See Wilson's "Civilized Vampires" for an investigation of race and ethnicity in the saga and an analysis of how Meyers' treatment of the Cullens and the Quileutes perpetuate white privilege and indigenous stereotypes.

6. Adrienne Rich introduced the phrase "compulsory heterosexuality" and explained the concept in her 1980 essay "Compulsory Heterosexuality and Lesbian Experience." For more on heteronormativity in the *Twilight* saga, see Wilson's "Homophobia and Twilight" and Kathryn Kane's "A Very Queer Refusal."

7. U.S. laws consider people in an altered state of consciousness to be unable to legally give consent for sexual activity.

WORKS CITED

AamMilk. "Re: Bella, Jacob, Renesemee & Love/Imprinting." *Twilighters message boards*. Twi-lighters.org, 11 July 2009. Web. 9 December 2009.
Aimeeee. "Re: Do you think Jacob was wrong to trick Bella?" *Twilighters message boards*. Twi-lighters.org, 18 May 2009. Web. 9 December 2009.
Behm-Morawitz, Elizabeth, Melissa A. Click, and Jennifer Stevens Aubrey. "Relating to Twilight: Fans' Responses to Love and Romance in the Vampire Franchise." *Bitten by Twilight: Youth Culture, Media, & the Vampire Franchise*. Eds. Melissa A. Click, Jennifer Stevens Aubrey, and Elizabeth Behm-Morawitz. New York: Peter Lang, 2010. 137–154. Print.
Brown, Caitlin. "Feminism and the Vampire Novel." *The F-Word* 8 September 2009. Web. 1 December 2009.
Buchwald, Emilie Scott, Pamela R. Fletcher, and Martha Scott Ross, eds. *Transforming a Rape Culture*. Minneapolis: Milkweed Editions, 1993. Print.
Campbell, Sandra. "Creating Redemptive Imagery: A Challenge of Resistance and Creativity." *Transforming a Rape Culture*. Eds. Emilie Scott Buchwald, Pamela R. Fletcher, and Martha Scott Ross. Minneapolis: Milkweed Editions, 1993. 142–52. Print.
"Carlisle: Selfish or Savior?" *TwilightMOMS Forums*. TwilightMOMS.com, 24 January 2009. Web. 4 December 2009.

"Chapter 17 — The Visitor." *Twilight Lexicon Discussion Forums.* Twilight Lexicon, 17 August 2008. Web. 11 December 2009.

Clarke, D. A. "Woman with a Sword: Some Thoughts on Women, Feminism, and Violence." *Transforming a Rape Culture.* Eds. Emilie Scott Buchwald, Pamela R. Fletcher, and Martha Scott Ross. Minneapolis: Milkweed Editions, 1993. 395–404. Print.

Click, Melissa A., Jennifer Stevens Aubrey, and Elizabeth Behm-Morawitz, eds. *Bitten by Twilight: Youth Culture, Media, & the Vampire Franchise.* New York: Peter Lang, 2010. Print.

Fletcher, Pamela R. "Whose Body Is It, Anyway?" *Transforming a Rape Culture.* Eds. Emilie Scott Buchwald, Pamela R. Fletcher, and Martha Scott Ross. Minneapolis: Milkweed Editions, 1993. 429–41. Print.

Geller, Jeffrey L., and Maxine Harris. *Women of the Asylum: Voices from Behind the Walls, 1840–1945.* New York: Anchor-Doubleday, 1994. Print.

H;teamswitzerland. "Re: Bella, Jacob, Renesemee & Love/Imprinting." *Twilighters message boards.* Twilighters.org, 10 July 2009. Web. 9 December 2009.

Hopelessly_hopeful. "Re: Do you think Jacob was wrong to trick Bella?" *Twilighters message boards.* Twilighters.org, 30 May 2009. Web. 9 December 2009.

"How Widespread Is Violence Against Women?" United Nations Department of Public Information. February 2008. Web. 14 May 2010. PDF file. <http://www.un.org/en/women/end-violence/factsheets.shtml>.

ILoveJasper. "Re: Who Enjoys A Little Pillow Biting??" *Twilighters message boards.* Twilighters. org, 28 January 2009. Web. 11 December 2009.

IsabellCullen. "Edward Was Probably Disapionted." *Twilighters message boards.* Twilighters.org, 4 October 2009. Web. 10 December 2009.

Jack. "There has been a lot of energy ..." [Weblog comment.] 29 November 2009. "Top 20 Unfortunate Lessons Girls Learn From 'Twilight.'" John Scott Lewinski. *The Best Article Every Day.* 25 November 2009. Web. 10 December 2009. <http://www.bspcn.com/2009/11/25/top-20-unfortunate-lessons-girls-learn-from-twilight/>.

Jaxman007. "Confusion About Rosalie's History — Can Anyone Help?" *Twilight*MOMS *Forums.* *Twilight*MOMS.com, 19 June 2009. Web. 11 December 2009.

Kane, Kathryn. "A Very Queer Refusal: The Chilling Effect of the Cullens' Heteronormative Embrace." *Bitten by Twilight: Youth Culture, Media, & the Vampire Franchise.* Eds. Melissa A. Click, Jennifer Stevens Aubrey, and Elizabeth Behm-Morawitz. New York: Peter Lang, 2010. 103–188. Print.

Kapoor, Sushma. "Domestic Violence Against Women and Girls." *Innocenti Digest* No. 6, June 2000. UNICEF Innocenti Research Centre. Web. 30 May 2010. PDF file. <http://www.unicef-irc.org/cgi-bin/unicef/Lunga.sql?ProductID=213>.

Kendra. "Re: Bella, Jacob, Renesemee & Love/ Imprinting." *Twilighters message boards.* Twilighters.org, 11 July 2009. Web. 9 December 2009.

Kulwick, Cara. *The Curvature: A Feminist Perspective on Politics and Culture.* N.p., 27 February 2010. Web. 27. February 2010.

Lewinski, John Scott. "Top 20 Unfortunate Lessons Girls Learn From 'Twilight?'" *The Best Article Every Day.* 25 November 2009. Web. 2 December 2009. <http://www.bspcn.com/2009/11/25/top-20-unfortunate-lessons-girls-learn-from-twilight/>.

McEwan, Melissa. "Rape Culture 101." *Shakesville.* 9 October 2009. Web. 5 December 2009.

Meyer, Stephenie. *Breaking Dawn.* New York: Little, Brown, 2008. Print.

_____. *Eclipse.* New York: Little, Brown, 2009. Reprint edition. Print.

_____. *New Moon.* New York: Little, Brown, 2006. Print.

_____. *Twilight.* New York: Little, Brown, 2005. Print.

Mickey Mouse Monopoly: Disney, Childhood & Corporate Power. Dir. Miguel Picker. Prod. Chyng Feng Sun. Media Education Foundation, 2001. Videocassette.

North, Anna. "Breaking Dawn: What to Expect When You're Expecting ... A Vampire." *Jezebel.* 7 August 2008. Web. 20 November 2009.

"Personal Correspondence #1." *Twilight Lexicon.* Twilight Lexicon, 3 November 2006. Web. 20 November 2009.

Peterson, Latoya. "Twihard with a Vengeance: Why Twilight Is a Boon for Young Women." *Jezebel.* 27 November 2009. Web. 12 December 2009.

Pretty_Face. "Was it okay of Bella to ask Jake ..." *Twilighters message boards.* Twilighters.org, 22 June 2009. Web. 28 February 2010.

"Re: Bella, Jacob, Renesemee & Love/ Imprinting." *Twilighters message boards.* Twilighters.org, 3 April 2009. Web. 4 December 2009.

Rice, Kellen. "'Twilight' Sucks ... And Not in a Good Way." *Blast: Boston's Online Magazine.* B Media Ventures, 16 April 2008. Web. 20 November 2009.

Rich, Adrienne. "Compulsory Heterosexuality and Lesbian Existence." *Blood, Bread, and Poetry: Selected Prose 1979–1985.* New York: W.W. Norton, 1986. 23–75. Print.

Rose, Jonathan. "Rereading the English Common Reader: A Preface to a History of Audiences." *Journal of the History of Ideas,* Vol. 53.1 (1992): 47–70. University of Pennsylvania Press. JSTOR. Web. 4 December 2009. <http://www.jstor.org/stable/2709910>.

Roxana. "Great article. Don't listen to the Twitards ..." [Weblog comment.] 30 November 2009. "Top 20 Unfortunate Lessons Girls Learn From 'Twilight.'" John Scott Lewinski. *The Best Article Every Day.* 25 November 2009. Web. 10 December 2009. <http://www.bspcn.com/2009/11/25/top-20-unfortunate-lessons-girls-learn-from-twilight/>.

Seifert, Christine. "Bite Me! (Or Don't)." *Bitch: Feminist Response to Pop Culture.* Bitch Media, 20 January 2009. Web. 20 November 2009.

"So much waste?" *TwilightMOMS Forums.* TwilightMOMS.com, 27 January 2009. Web. 4 December 2009.

Stein, Sadie. "Actual Men Threatened by Sparkly Vampire." *Jezebel.* 17 November 2009. Web. 9 December 2009.

Tamia. "Confusion About Rosalie's History—Can Anyone Help?" *TwilightMOMS Forums.* TwilightMOMs.com, 2 May 2008. Web. 11 December 2009.

TashiCullen. "Re: Do you think Jacob was wrong to trick Bella?" *Twilighters message boards.* Twilighters.org, 19 May 2009. Web. 9 December 2009.

Tntwilightmom. "Carlisle: Selfish or Savior?" *TwilightMOMS Forums.* TwilightMOMs.com, 24 January 2009. Web. 9 December 2009.

"Violence Against Women in the United States: Statistics." National Organization for Women. 1995. Web. 14 May 2010. <http://www.now.org/issues/violence/stats.html>.

"Was it okay of Bella to ask Jake ..." *Twilighters message boards.* Twilighters.org, 5 January 2009. Web. 9 December 2009.

Wilson, Natalie. "Civilized Vampires Versus Savage Werewolves: Race and Ethnicity in the *Twilight* Series." *Bitten by Twilight: Youth Culture, Media, & the Vampire Franchise.* Eds. Melissa A. Click, Jennifer Stevens Aubrey, and Elizabeth Behm-Morawitz. New York: Peter Lang, 2010. 55–70.

_____. "Homophobia and Twilight." *Seduced by Twilight.* 5 November 2009. Web. 10 December 2009. <http://seducedbytwilight.wordpress.com.>

Yuliya. "Re: Who Enjoys A Little Pillow Biting??" *Twilighters message boards.* Twilighters.org, 28 January 2009. Web. 10 December 2009.

Un-biting the Apple and Killing the Womb
Genesis, Gender, and Gynocide

LINDSEY ISSOW AVERILL

The now iconic cover of Stephenie Meyer's *Twilight* features a pair of pale white female hands cradling an unbitten apple. These hands stretch out towards the viewer, extending away from the woman's body, as if offering or giving away the apple. Blood red, round, ripe and fertile, the apple deeply contrasts the fine white wrists, impregnating them with a sense of nakedness, a certain vulnerability. We know this apple as belonging to Snow White's evil stepmother, the symbol of the first Judeo-Christian sin, the icon of enchanting sexuality. This unbitten apples serves as the emblem of that which lures us away from socially constructed morality. On her website, Meyer explains that this apple "represents [the] 'forbidden fruit,'" from Genesis (www.stephe-niemeyer.com). The apple links us to the cultural myth of female evil, a link that originates with Eve's fortuitous bite. Repeatedly, coming across the image of the *Twilight*'s cover in person and via the media, I found myself wondering what exactly do these supposedly innocuous teen books have to do with Eve and her apple? And, more importantly, if this apple on the cover of *Twilight* is Eve's "forbidden fruit" then why is she giving it away before she's sunk her teeth into its skin?

As a feminist, I have many bones to pick with Meyer's representations of Bella and Edward's love. In their article, "Undead Patriarchy and the Possibility of Love," Leah McCliman and J. Jeremy Wisnewski offer an understanding of Edward's behavior towards Bella, saying, "Edward *can* be very controlling. Feminists for some time have recognized the controlling relationship as one of the consequences of patriarchy" (165). "Taking a Bite out of *Twilight,*"written by Carmen Siering, notes "infantilized" Bella "is merely an object in the *Twilight* world. Bella is a prize not a person, someone to whom things happen, not an active participant in the unfolding story" (51). Bella functions purely as the object and recipient of Edward's desire, a "blank slate, with few thoughts or actions that don't center on Edward" (Siering 51). Christine Seifert author of, "bite me! (or don't)," recognizes an intense demonization of sexuality, particularly female sexuality and femaleness. She explains that Edward's opinion and desire dominates Bella's life, arguing that in *Twilight* we see a world where "when it comes to a woman's virtue, sex, identity, or her existence itself, it's all in the man's hands" (25). As you can see, feminists generally seem to agree that Edward and Bella's relationship functions within patriarchy's cultural code: Bella is the object of Edward's agency.

While I tend to agree with the assessments that feminists have gleaned from readings of Meyer's books, the image of the un-bitten apple continues to plague me. Traditionally the Adam and Eve myth serves as a cautionary tale meant to alert Judeo-Christian men to the wayward and tantalizing wiles of female sexuality. However, this understanding of the Adam and Eve creation story conceals one of the key moments of mythic female agency — and the symbol of that agency is the bitten apple.

This essay will explain how Meyer's *Twilight* series acts as a re-telling of the Adam and Eve myth, casting Bella/Eve as a willing participant in a male-centric worldview, perpetuating a return to the consciousness of the male-god's Garden of Eden, or rather a consciousness where the female body and female fecundity are completely erased, while male reproduction remains intact. Specifically, the female vampires and half-vampires in the *Twilight* series do not possess the life sustaining and nourishing capabilities of the female body, which arguably are largely the biologically defining elements of the female sex. To be clear, I am not arguing that women are meant to be mothers or that fecundity is the defining factor of femininity, rather, I wish to emphasize that the ability to nourish and gestate a fetus is a biological function of the female form, not the male form. Meyer's novels clearly represent the vampire form as superior to the human form, and a contingency of Meyer's brand of vampirism is the elimination of female reproductive power. This elimination forces an understanding of female reproduction as a limitation of the female form.

To truly understand a conversation concerning representations of Eve and her apple in the *Twilight* series, it is necessary to understand the patriarchal construction of the Adam and Eve myth, learn how Meyer's vampires represent the perpetuation of the patriarchal and Judeo-Christian worldview represented in Genesis, and finally to detail the violent results of representing Bella/Eve as a willing participant in the patriarchic worldview. Like Genesis, Meyer's novels emphasize the aspects of hegemonic masculinity as the desired norm, undermine female agency and underline masculine norms by shifting the source of creative/procreative power from female to male, thereby confirming male dominance and eliminating female agency and biological form.

Biting the Apple: Eve as Feminine Agency

In *Goddesses and Monsters*, a collection of essays that examines collisions of female mythic history and contemporary popular culture, Jane Caputi explains that within the Adam and Eve myth "linger the stray memories of the earthly paradise ... and the daring originality of the woman" (235). Despite the Judeo-Christian male-god's rules, Eve bites the "forbidden fruit," and in doing so she reclaims the bodily power of procreation and creation, which the male-god of Judeo-Christianity absconded from female body. It is this choice that empowers Eve and in turn all women. The biting of the apple is Caputi's moment of "daring originality" (235). It is the moment when Eve/woman says, "NO! I will not listen. I will not be merely 'a helper suitable' for Adam I am more than man's helper. I am woman, a powerful, sexual, creative piece of the whole." To overturn this moment and render the apple unbitten would reposition Eve as nothing more than "helper," a subordinated part, made from and ruled by a man (Gen 2:22). Thus, in the *Twilight* saga, leaving the apple un-bitten turns back the mythic clock, giving Meyer the opportunity to tell a tale in which woman/Eve opts *not* to act, or rather chooses to submit, and in turn lose her right to female procreative power.

The Biblical creation myth, a human origin story, involves a Judeo-Christian male-god that speaks the world into being, an act of his powerful male intellect, not a gestating womb.[1] This male-god created all the plants and animals, then he created man (Adam), and from man he created woman (Eve).[2] Once all of the creating was done, the male-god gave man power over the earth, all its green and beastly inhabitants, dependant on one rule: don't eat from the tree of good and evil because it will kill you, i.e., no apple biting. Supposedly, all was well until the Biblical moment of Eve's transgression. Simply put, the snake "more subtile than any beast" says to Eve, "Go ahead, eat the fruit; it won't kill you," and, after close inspection and thought, Eve decides the fruit is good; she gives it to Adam and they eat (Gen 3:1). I want to make specific note of the fact that Eve does chat with the serpent, who makes an argument, but no one forces the apple on Eve. She, of her own volition, decides that the "tree was good for food" (Gen 3:6). Of course, this decision is the reason that she is traditionally blamed for man's downfall. But what if the tree was GOOD for Eve?

In order to understand what Caputi calls the "altering of the central creation myth" we must look to the ancient and often overlooked symbolism within the Adam and Eve story (235). Snake and woman have a long and linked symbolic history, which many feminists argue informs and supports Eve's decision to bite the apple. In the *Woman's Dictionary of Symbols and Sacred Objects* Barbara Walker notes that the serpent is "one of the oldest symbols of female power" (387). In the *Monstrous-Feminine* Barbara Creed similarly offers, "Some ancient cultures also associated the full moon and a woman's monthly bleeding with the snake. All three ... move through stages in which the old is shed and the new reborn" (64). Barbara Mor, author of *The Great Cosmic Mother: Rediscovering the Religion of the Earth*, connects the female, particularly the pre–Christian figure of the mother goddess to the serpent; "Great live snakes were everywhere kept in the Goddess's temples during the Neolithic. In wall paintings, bas-reliefs, statues, she was often represented carrying snakes in her upraised arms or coiled around her. Or, she was imagined as a serpent herself, with a woman's body and a snake's head" (57).

Like the snake, the fruit tree is also linked to a mythic image of female power. Merlin Stone, author of *When God Was a Woman*, explains that the mother goddess was identified as "the original Creatress, and the patroness of sexual pleasures," and that the asherim, a fruit tree was "a symbol identified with the worship of the Goddess" (217, 175). Stone notes that this tree and its fruit were included in the Biblical creation story specifically to condemn the practices of those who worshipped the goddess; she writes "the symbolism of the tree of forbidden fruit ... clearly represented in the myth as the provider of sexual consciousness, was included in the creation story to warn that eating the fruit of this tree had caused the downfall of humanity" (217). Similarly, Gerda Lerner tells us "the tree of life with its fruit—the cassia, the pomegranate, the date, the apple—was associated with fertility goddesses" (195). And, Walker further enlightens, explaining, "Eve's fruit of knowledge used to be the goddess's sacred heart of immortality, all over the Indo-European culture complex. The Goddess's many western paradises grew the apples of eternal life" (*The Woman's Encyclopedia of Myths and Secrets* 48). With this information, it becomes clear that the knowledge the "forbidden" fruit is the knowledge of the woman/mother, the sexual knowledge of creation and human immortality through birth.

Arguably, the fruit was good for Eve not only because it was linked symbolically to a history of female knowledge and potency but also because the male-god's Eden is a space in which the female is rendered deviant and subordinate. Feminist theologians, such as Mary Daly and Carol Christ, are quick to point out that the creator in Genesis, the Judeo-Christian male-God, is, well, male. Christ explains, "religious symbol systems focused around exclusively male images of divinity create the impression that female power can never be fully legitimate or wholly beneficial" (212). In other words, the nature of a male-God is that a female can never live up to the image of that God, and "she can never have the experience that is freely available to every man and boy in her culture, of having her full sexual identity affirmed as being in the image and likeness of God" (Christ 212). There is an inherently sexist structure to the existence of a male-God: the female is not constructed in God's "likeness," so therefore her form is perceived as less than the male. Belief in an all powerful male-God perpetuates male dominance. Daly explains "exclusively masculine symbolism for God, for the notion of the divine 'incarnation' in human nature, and for the human relationship to God reinforce the sexual hierarchy" (4). We think of God as a man; we refer to him as "He," "Him" and "the Father"; men play him in movies, and therefore, men are like God. Women are not men and therefore not like God; they are construed as less than God and in turn, less than men.

The Adam and Eve myth continues to reinforce the subordination of woman to man by silencing a woman's role in the creation of life. The Bible says, "In the beginning God created the heaven and the earth" (Gen. 1:1), "God created man in his own image" (Gen 1:27), and then the kicker, while Adam slept God took Adam's rib and from it "made he a woman, and brought her unto the man" (Gen 2:22). It is worth noting that by creating Eve from Adam's rib, there is the natural subordination of her to him because she is a part of him and therefore not an independently formed being, but even more interesting is the image of male-God as creator of all things.[3] Mor notes that is a "very interesting biological reversal," because woman and her womb, who we all know to be responsible for creating life on Earth, play no part in the creating (276).[4]

In *The Creation of the Patriarchy,* a book that thoroughly details the historic rise of patriarchy as the dominant social construction, Lerner argues that a man-powered creation myth separates woman from her original position of "universal-fertility" (180). She explains that in Genesis, "There is no longer any maternal source for creation of the universe and for life on earth nor is there any indication that creativity and procreativity are linked. Quite to the contrary. God's act of creation is entirely unlike any thing humans can experience" (180). What Lerner is getting at is that this type of male-creation rises above the earthly creation, placing man (not woman) above procreativity. Specifically, man has emerged from a place beyond menstrual blood, semen, and the grunts and gyrations of the sexual body, indeed, the body is functionally erased within Biblical creating myths.

The Adam and Eve myth renders the power of female sexuality, the power to create and procreate, infertile and clears the way for an un-sexed man of the mind, and a subordinated feminized body. However, by biting the apple Eve reclaims the female body's power of creation and procreation. In Genesis 3:16 God doles out Eve's personal punishment for biting the apple, saying, "with pain you will give birth to children." And so, because Eve bites the apple the female power of creation and procreation is returned to its rightful owner — the female. Eve becomes the woman who reclaimed her feminine body, a biblical feminist.

Un-biting the Apple: Choosing Patriarchy's Worldview

The *Twilight* series presents us with a re-envisioned Eve, wherein Biblical feminist Eve is completely obliterated in Meyer's novels because Bella, a modern day Eve, chooses not to defy the male-God rules. For women in the saga the results are catastrophic — in short, biological womanhood and its creative and procreative powers are functionally erased. Understanding how the *Twilight* saga supports the gendered dualisms detailed in *Genesis* and heightens the Biblical female oppression by leaving woman without agency requires an examination of the "monstrosity" of Meyer's vampires because we need to understand what Bella is choosing when she chooses to be one of them.

Vampires have a long symbolic history of representation as monsters, but the human-friendly vampires of the *Twilight* series cannot be viewed or classically examined as monsters because, like well-behaved human followers of the Judeo-Christian worldview, they control their deviance via metaphorical "vegetarianism" (*T* 188). Because Carlisle Cullen, Edward's father (i.e., siring vampire), is religious and the son of a "clergyman," Edward and all the other Cullens were raised to refrain from consuming human blood because they perceive it as evil and un–Christian (*NM* 35). In other words, they desire human blood but repress this desire because their Christian religion dictates that the desires of the body contradict Christian constructs of goodness. Edward lives up to this Christian ideal by resisting the temptations of the body. In his case he resists the desire for Bella both in the Biblical and the ravenous sense, i.e., both his physical and sexual appetite.

Edward's particular brand of monstrosity, vampirism, makes his restraint a very powerful affirmation of what Judeo-Christian patriarchy deems acceptable sexual behavior. The deviance most often associated with the vampire is one of a sexual nature. When Bella makes note that Edward is "bizarrely moral for a vampire" she is pointing out the oddity inherent in Edward's existence (*E* 536). Cynthia Freeland, author of *The Naked and the Dead*, explains, "The vampire violates the norms of femininity and masculinity, as alleged through heterosexual desire to marriage…. Sexuality is rife in the vampire genre … Vampires are polymorphously perverse: In their search for blood they can find physical intimacy with a person of almost any gender, age, race or social class" (124). Through Freeland's understanding we can see that the classic vampire dissolves sexual gender boundaries, with no regard for patriarchic "heterosexual desire to marriage and procreation" (124). So, a vampire such as Edward who so aptly represses this deviance not only condemns bodily desire but also all forms of non-heteronormative sexuality. He refers to repressing his blood thirst as a "life of abstinence," markedly tying his refrain from feeding on human blood to a sex act; one that falls outside of what Judeo-Christianity deems acceptable for heteronormative body (*T* 342). Edward is the self-repressing vampire, the epitome of sexual bodily repression, which is of course an ideal of Christianity, and in particular the ideal with which Eve tussles.

No one would deny the "conflation of [Edward's] vampiric and carnal urges," so we can easily see how Edward's avoidance of his personal temptation is a metaphor for avoiding the sexual knowledge of the forbidden fruit however, this metaphoric resistance is emphasized by the fact that Edward also resists sexual temptation to consummate his relationship with Bella (Seifert 25); Edward tells Bella that he desires her sexually, saying "I am a man" (*T* 311), but he will not sleep with her because to have a "shot at heaven" they must follow the Judeo-Christian "rules" and maintain their "virtue" until marriage (*BD* 453). Having the willpower to resist Bella's blood and her body proves that Edward is a "model of" Christian behavior. Edward presents as better/stronger than the urges, the temptations of his body. He represses his own deviance, his bodily desires, by exercising Christian restraint.

This can be taken one step further: the vampire takes what he wants, acquires his victims, holding their bodies close, pressing lips and teeth to their necks, biting, breaking the skin, pulling the blood, allowing it to rush and pool against the curl of his tongue. We understand that this is a sex act. But it's not the patriarchal penis entering, dominating or violating the vagina. The vampire's violating sex organ, his mouth, has much more in common with the vagina than it does the penis. The mouth is not giving or leaving of bodily fluid; it is accepting, taking of bodily fluid. The vampire's lips, tongue and tissues envelop the object. In fact, this vagina is the aggressor, taking whatever it wishes; it resonates as the toothy vagina, the vagina dentata.

And of course the vagina dentata is the culmination of "men's fear of sex, expressing the unconscious belief that women may eat or castrate her partner during intercourse," or rather the dangers of the unruly, uncontrolled powers of female sexuality (Walker 1034). If we accept that vampires exist as the revolt of feminine sexuality, then it could be possible to read Edward as a as repressor of unchecked female sexuality, exactly what Biblical feminist Eve revolts against.

Whether or not you are willing to see Edward the repressor of empowered female or non-heteronormative sexuality, it is clear that Meyer has imposed a mythic reversal by creating Christian, non-human-blood-seeking vampires, and in doing so she effectively eliminates the monstrosity of the vampire, making the vampire a vehicle of repression rather than subversive monstrosity. Nothing about Edward says deviance or subversive; he resonates as hegemonic masculinity. He's super-white, Christian, male, wealthy, virile and heterosexual. He's violent and controlling and envisions Bella as unable to care for herself. He views himself as smarter than humans and more sophisticated than werewolves. He is a vision of patriarchy's elite. He is *not* a "revolution against norms established by the patriarchic institutions of religion, science, law and the nuclear family" (Freeland 124). Edward is a celebration, a revering, of this repression. He is not a monster, an Other, that needs to be conquered; Edward is the oppressor and repressor. He and his family serve as protection against the Other, the deviants — those that function on a non–Judeo-Christian framework, for example Bella and the Quileute — and in turn the Cullens resonate as metaphorically enhanced typical patriarchal forms of race, gender and sexuality.

The perks of the heightened patriarchal existence of being a "good" Judeo-Christian vampire abound. Edward has the extended knowledge of 100+ years of life as a high school/college aged male. He is uber civilized, an intellect and a musician. He hears the thoughts inside other vampires'/people's minds. These thoughts are "babbled like a gush of river inside" Edward's head (*T* 1), allowing him to know their inner feelings and motivations, much like an omnipotent Judeo-Christian God. He can rip "a two-foot thick branch from the trunk of a spruce," and run fast enough to circle a large meadow in "half a second" (*T* 264). Edward also has a heightened beauty, "everything about [him] invites [humans] in —[his] voice ... face ... even [his] *smell*" (*T* 264). In fact all of Meyer's vampires represent the epitome of human beauty and flawlessness. Meyer describes the faces of the Cullen clan as they enter the lunchroom, "They were faces you never expect to see except perhaps on the airbrushed pages of a fashion magazine. Or painted by an old master as the face of an angel. It was hard to decide who was the most beautiful"

(*T* 19). Also among these superhuman qualities exists, what I'll call uber-romantic-dominating-maleness, a love before life, knight in shining armor mentality, which when combined with extreme beauty, unconditionally serves male-centric view by luring in unsuspecting females and is completely irresistible to teenage girls, including Bella. Edward's god-like presence, his flawless beauty and his heightened abilities, make him more "divine" than humans and undeniably fascinating. Suddenly, his earth is an immortal's playground, ripe for the taking, much like how one might imagine life in male-God's Eden.

When Bella chooses Edward, she chooses everything that Edward implies—the rules and patriarchic order of the male-God—and his supernatural qualities heighten the intensity of him as metaphor for this worldview. In other words, Meyer's monsters' manipulative power over the audience/reader resides in the inaction of their "evil," allowing them to exist more in the realm of hegemonic superhero/superman than villain, more male-god than she-devil. Once we recognize the context of this herculean act of restraint, defined as his "goodness," Edward's superhuman abilities become the perks, the cool benefits of living a heightened moral existence in the world of the Judeo-Christian male-God.

Captivated by Edward, Bella is willing to shed her human life and her female reproduction for the life of the vampire; i.e., overturn the agency that Eve symbolically represents, or un-bite the apple. Her action or rather her *inaction* is represented by the apple on the cover of *Twilight*. Meyer openly explains that the apple on the cover of *Twilight* is linked to the Adam and Eve myth, the apple from Genesis. She explains that for her the image of the apple "says: choice" (www.stepheniemeyer.com). *Twilight*'s unbitten apple does not imply that the choice has been made but rather that there is a choice to make—Eve's choice, the choice to defy the male-God and reject the systematic subordination of a dualistically constructed culture, or to bend to the will of the male-God and accept a position of subservience. It is my understanding that like the choice to bite or not bite the apple was Eve's choice; it is also Bella's choice. Initially, Bella seems to be a woman with agency, a woman like Eve, but at the conclusion of *Eclipse*, Bella chooses a "definition of right" that matches Edward's Judeo-Christian worldview (Meyer 619).[5] With this choice Bella shifts her agency (and the agency of the actual biting) to Edward and in doing so she gains some access to the power/domination that Edward and his family imply; however, the mythic power of the female form that Eve reclaimed evaporates because with Edward's bite, Bella is reborn in Edward's image with her biological female form systematically eliminated.

Killing the Womb: Gynocide in Twilight

Much like *Genesis*, Meyer's construct of the vampire eliminates the procreative and creative powers of the female body, gifting creative powers to the male sex. Meyer's female vampires cannot create life. Their bodies exist in an unchanging stasis and although they desire blood, without it they would not die. In particular, Meyer's vampires have no life-sustaining bodily needs, their bodies are impenetrable, they don't get hurt, they don't get sick, they don't sleep, they don't drink human blood — they are quintessentially non-body, or rather all mind. Their bodies no longer function in the human sense, the bodily sense, and one would assume not in the reproductive sense; however, this is only true for the female vampires.

Meyer's vampires have sex with each other, but their sex does not culminate in reproduction because the female vampire cannot carry a fetus. Rosalie, Edward's sister, who did not choose to be a vampire, explains to Bella that although she is happy with her vampire husband Emmett, she remains unfulfilled because she can never have children. She says, "there will never be more than two of us. And I'll never sit on a porch somewhere, with [my husband] gray-haired by my side, surrounded by our grandchildren" (*E* 167). What Rosalie is missing is not family. (The Cullens are a large family: a mother, a father, three brothers, two sisters, Bella will make a third sister, and they have cousins that live in Alaska.) Rosalie yearns "for her own little baby" (*E* 156). Rosalie longs to create, in the bodily sense. She wants to carry a child in her womb, to gestate and to nourish. As a vampire, a female can bite a human and create another vampire, but it will never have a heartbeat, never breathe, never grow or give birth; it will never be part of the cycle of life and reproduction because its body is unchanging and therefore unable to create.

Unlike the female vampires in Meyer's saga, a male vampire can still create life but only when they mate with human females. Before she becomes a vampire, Edward and Bella have sex and he impregnates her. Bella realizes the reason the female vampire womb is barren; it will not take a pregnancy because it cannot change. Bella explains:

> Of course Rosalie could not create a child, because she was frozen in the state, which she passed from human to inhuman. Totally unchanging. And human woman's bodies had to *change* to bear children. The constant change of a monthly cycle for one thing and then the bigger changes needed to accommodate a growing child, Rosalie's body couldn't change.... But [Bella's] could [*BD* 126].

The womb of the vampire is "frozen ... unchanging." The human womb is not; it still possesses the power to "*change*." This power that Bella mentions, the "*change*" that enables women to have children, the potent creative power of the fecund female form, which the Judeo-Christian male-God usurps in the Genesis creation myth, is lost to Meyer's female vampires. Meyer also hinges the male vampire's ability to reproduce to change. In Meyer's world human males and male vampires have no such "cycles of fertility" (*BD* 126). So, unlike their female counterparts, their fertility continues. Bella says human men "pretty much stayed the same from puberty to death," so male vampires would still be fertile because their fertility is not based on change (*BD* 126). It is worth noting that the claim Meyer makes in regard to the male body not requiring "change" to produce sperm is a false assertion. Like the cycles of menstruation, sperm require functioning and producing systems. It is equally interesting that Meyer disregards or elevates male reproduction above this need for change, rendering male fertility as not of the living body, much like the male-God's spoken powers of creativity.

When male vampires mate with human females, who do cycle because they are still functioning female bodies, male vampires can reproduce; however, the life they create does not affirm the reproductive feminine form. This lack of affirmation is two-fold. Firstly, half-vampire offspring always kill their human female mothers during birth; they tear their way out of the womb. Secondly, this male power to create mimics the creative force of the Judeo-Christian male-God, a creative power that passes from one male to another, leaving female offspring infertile. Naheul, the only known half-human/half-vampire male is able to create vampires with his venomous bite but his three female siblings "cannot" (*BD 737*). Like the other females, Bella and Edward's half-vampire daughter Renesemee is not "venomous," and we can assume that she cannot carry a child because once she reaches maturity she will enter a state of stasis, like the vampires around her, one where she will continue through immortality un-"changed" (*BD* 736). Renesemee becomes the ultimate culmination of subordination of the female-creative power to the male (*BD* 454). She can create neither human, nor vampire, nor anything in-between. Eve's "punishment" for disobeying the male-God is repealed, and we return to the Garden of Eden where the only life-creating power that remains is male-creative force, the male-God.

Twilight's complete annihilation of the biological reproductive function of the female body reads as what Mary Daly and Andrea Dworkin refer to as gynocide. In *Our Blood*, Dworkin defines gynocide as "the systematic crippling, raping, and/or killing of women by men. Gynocide is the word that designates the relentless violence perpetuated by the gender class men against the gender class women" (16). Dworkin notes examples of gynocide: Chinese foot-binding, witch burning, and systematic rape of women in Bangladesh by invading soldiers and their continued rape by husbands, brothers and fathers who believe the initial rape rendered the victim unclean. Gynocide is any violent act committed systematically against women by the patriarchal culture that renders them subservient and subordinated.

The *Twilight* series constructs a vampire culture steeped in a patriarchal Judeo-Christian worldview; this culture is understood as the ultimate existence, but in order for a woman to take part in this existence she must relinquish the female creative body; she must kill her womb. This is an act of gynocide, an act of violence perpetrated systematically against that which is biologically female by that which is philosophically male. Thus the world of Meyer's fertile male vampires elevates the social order of the patriarchy and portrays female reproduction as a hurdle to overcome. Meyer celebrates the vampire state, an overt patriarchal worldview, and portrays it as perfection so much so that her readers are literally rooting for Bella's change, rooting for Bella's death and the death of her biologically female state, rooting for gynocide.

Both Genesis and the *Twilight* series undermine feminism(s) and underline the tradition of hegemonic masculinity by shifting the source of creative/procreative power from female to male, thereby confirming the limiting construction of the female form. The all male creativity and procreativity of Meyer's vampires echoes the male-god's creation in the Garden of Eden. *Twilight*'s destruction of female-creative power erases Eve's transgression and strips young women from access to the female form as a source of empowerment.

Through the Judeo-Christian lens, the "good" choice, Bella's choice, was to deny the serpent and forgo the apple, leaving it unbitten, much like the apple on the cover of Meyer's *Twilight*. Through the feminist lens this unbiting maintains male-oriented domination, or rather a world constructed in a male-centric worldview, a world where inherent sexism reigns and wholeness or equality can never be reached, a world where the female form is systematically eliminated, a world riddled in gynocide. Unlike Bella's choice, Eve's action questioned and looked to overturn the patriarchal worldview. While Eve's choice did not undo patriarchy, it honored the female biological form and its creative and procreative strength. Unlike Bella's choice, Eve's actions created the space in which women and men might begin to envision a world that honors both feminine and masculine qualities and male and female bodies as potent and creative.

NOTES

1. In Christian theology, God's procreative force is specifically intellectual, and this force is recognized as the supreme or dominant creative/controlling force. God brings life into the world with his voice. God's power is the power of "the word" or the *logos* (John 1:1–9). Language

or "the word" is a function of the intellect, not the body. John Granger, author of *Spotlight: A Close-up Look at the Artistry and Meaning in Stephenie Meyer's Twilight Saga,* notes that in Christian belief the *logos* or the word "is the uncreated aspect of our minds" that links all; it is "the Creative Principle." He explains that Christian theology would have us believe that "fostering the *logos* faculty within us" allows us to recognize others who are conceived of our "inner principals (logoi)" (85). Granger tells us "Christian natural theology teaches us that this *logos* recognition is the only way we can know anything at all" (Granger 85). In other words, the perceptions/products of the inner intellect or the controlling spirit, i.e., the perceptions/products of the *logos,* are the only perceptions/products that truly matter. Hence, the demonization of the body — particularly the female body — as creative force.

2. There are readings of the Adam and Eve creation myth, which detail an understanding of *'adam* as "an androgynous creature," a representative of human rather than either sex (Stone 65). In his article "The Garden of Eden and the Heterosexual Contract," Ken Stone explains that queer readings of the Adam and Eve creation myth rely on the use of the Hebrew word *'adam,* "the generic term for humanity" rather than the "sexually differentiated terms *'ish* (man) and *'ishah* (woman)," which are not used in "the Yahwist text until Genesis 2:23, after the creation" of Eve (64).

3. Genesis 1:27 notes a secondary creation myth: "So God created man in his own image, in the image of God created he him; male and female created he them." This version makes no reference to an apple or the name Eve, but it also relies on male parthogenesis.

4. The tradition of male parthogenesis does not begin in Genesis, but rather much earlier, for example the birth of the Greek goddess Athena. Learner explains "to prevent his own overthrow, [Zeus] swallows his wife ... and by assimilating into himself [his wife's] power ... [he] can give birth to Athena, who springs full-grown from his head" (205). Symbolically, being born from the head can equate to being born from the male mind or intellect. Also, in more modern history there are noted technological attempts, both fictional and nonfictional, to shift the procreative power away from the womb, such as a text like Mary Shelley's *Frankenstein,* or a scientific procedure like human cloning. Rosi Braidotti, author of *Nomadic Subjects,* notes that these attempts are artifacts or "male techniques," i.e., products of intellectual science not maternal creation (87).

5. The film version of *Eclipse* revises this exact moment, rendering a more empowered version of Bella. The difference between the two scenes is that Bella explains her reasoning for "choosing" to follow Edward's worldview. She argues that with Edward and his family she feels more accepting of herself than prior to knowing them. While feminists might argue with this reasoning, perhaps noting it as a symptom of her submission to his abuse or at the very least pointing out that a woman should not discover herself through the eyes of her lover, the film version of Bella provides us a spark of recognition that this life or death decision requires some deep thought and consideration on the part of the woman who is choosing.

WORKS CITED

Beauvoir, Simone de. *The Second Sex.* New York: Random House, 1952. 114–24. Rpt. in *Theorizing Feminisms: A Reader.* Eds. Elizabeth Hackett and Sally Haslanger. New York: Oxford University Press, 2006.

Braidotti, Rosi. *Nomadic Subjects: Embodiment and Sexual Difference in Contemporary Feminist Theory.* New York: Columbia University Press, 1994.

Caputi, Jane. *Goddesses and Monsters.* Madison: University of Wisconsin Press, 2004.

Christ, Carol L. "Why Women Need the Goddess: Phenomenological, Psychological and Political Reflections" *Heresies: A Feminist Publication on Art and Politics.* 1978. 211–19. Rpt. in *Theorizing Feminisms: A Reader.* Eds. Elizabeth Hackett and Sally Haslanger. New York: Oxford University Press, 2006.

Creed, Barbara. *The Monstrous-Feminine: Film, Feminism, Psychoanalysis.* New York: Routledge, 1993.

Daly, Mary. *Beyond God the Father.* Boston: Beacon Press, 1973.

Dworkin, Andrea. *Our Blood: Prophecies and Discourses on Sexual Politics*. New York: Perigee Books, 1976.

Freeland, Cynthia A. *The Naked and the Undead: Evil and the Appeal of Horror*. Boulder, CO: Westview, 2000.

Granger, John . *Spotlight: A Close-up Look at the Artistry and Meaning of Stephenie Meyer's Twilight*. Allentown, PA: Zossima Press, 2010.

Halberstam, Judith. *Skin Shows: Gothic Horror and the Technology of Monsters*. London: Duke University Press, 1995.

The Holy Bible, King James Version. University of Virginia Library. Electronic Text Center. 12 April 2009 <http://etext.virginia.edu/toc/modeng/public/KjvGene.html>.

Lerner, Gerda. *The Creation of Patriarchy*. New York: Oxford University Press, 1986.

Lorber, Judith. *Gender Inequality*. Oxford: Oxford University Press, 2010. Print.

Meyer, Stephenie. *Breaking Dawn*. New York: Little, Brown, 2008. Print.

Meyer, Stephenie. *Eclipse*. New York: Little, Brown, 2007. Print.

Meyer, Stephenie. *Midnight Sun*. 28 August 2008. 25 February 2009 <http://www.stepheniemeyer.com/midnightsun.html>.

Meyer, Stephenie. *New Moon*. New York: Little, Brown, 2006. Print.

Meyer, Stephenie. *The Official Website of Stephenie Meyer*. 30 March 2009 <http://www.stepheniemeyer.com/twilight_faq.html#bella>.

Meyer, Stephenie. *Twilight*. New York: Little, Brown, 2005. Print.

Mor, Barbara, and Monica Sjoo. *The Great Cosmic Mother: Rediscovering the Religion of the Earth*. 1987. New York: HarperCollins, 1991. Print.

Seifert, Christine. "bite me! (or don't)." *Bitch* Winter 2009: 23–25. Print.

Siering, Carmen. "Taking a Bite Out of Twilight." *Ms.* Spring 2009: 50–2. Print.

Stone, Ken. "The Garden of Eden and the Heterosexual Contract." *Take Back the Word*. Eds. Robert Goss and Mona West. Cleveland, OH: Pilgrim Press, 2000. Print.

Walker, Barbara G. *The Woman's Dictionary of Symbols and Sacred Objects*. San Francisco: Harper Collins, 1988.

Walker, Barbara G. *The Woman's Encyclopedia of Myths and Secrets*. San Francisco: Harper Collins, 1983.

Wisnewski, J. Jeremy, and Leah McCliman. "Undead Patriarchy and the Possibility of Love." *Twilight and Philosophy*. Hoboken, NJ: John Wiley & Sons, 2009. 163–75. Print.

Wood, Robin. *Hollywood from Vietnam to Reagan ... and Beyond*. 1986. New York: Columbia University Press, 2003. Print.

Young, Iris. "Humanism, Gynocentrism, and Feminist Politics," *Women's Studies International Forum*. 1985. 174–86. Rpt. in *Theorizing Feminisms: A Reader*. Ed. Elizabeth Hackett and Sally Haslanger. New York: Oxford University Press, 2006. Print.

About the Contributors

Heather Anastasiu lives just south of Austin, Texas and is pursuing an M.A. degree in literature at Texas State University. Her creative writing has been published or is forthcoming in *Gargoyle, Blue Earth Review* and *Permafrost* among others. Her first novel for young adults, *Glitch*, recently sold in a three-book deal to St. Martin's Press (forthcoming).

Lindsey Issow Averill (M.F.A. Emerson College, 2005) is the chair of English and communications at Keiser University and a Ph.D. student in comparative studies at Florida Atlantic University. Her research focuses on mythic representations of women, sexuality, popular culture, feminist care ethics and ecofeminism. Her interaction with the *Twilight* saga was spurred by questions of how representation either hinders or bolsters young women's overall sense of physical and emotional empowerment.

Ashley Benning graduated from California State University Northridge with a B.A. in film production and an M.A. in English literature. Her thesis focused on representations of age in the *Harry Potter* Series. Ashley was chair of the Teaching *Twilight* workshop at TwiCon 2009, where she also presented a paper, "There Is No Team Jacob," on the Vampire Mythology panel. She is currently a language arts teacher in the Los Angeles area and writes YA fiction.

Ashley Donnelly is an assistant professor of telecommunications at Ball State University. Her research centers on U.S. popular culture, specifically gender and media studies. As a cultural critic and mother, the overwhelming popularity of the *Twilight* series concerned her, as its ideological messages for and about young women, she believes, have largely been overlooked in mainstream media in favor of a fixation on romance and fantasy.

Tanya Erzen is an associate professor of comparative religious studies at Ohio State University. Her work has appeared in *The Nation*, the *Boston Globe*, the *Washington Post* and academic journals such as *American Quarterly* and *PMLA: Publications of the Modern Language Association*. She is the author of *Straight to Jesus: Sexual and Christian Conversions in the Ex–Gay Movement* (University of California Press, 2006), which won the Gustave O. Arlt award and the Ruth Benedict prize. Her book about religion, post-feminism and the social worlds of *Twilight* fans is forthcoming.

Jessica Groper received her master's and Ph.D. degrees from Claremont Graduate University with an emphasis in Victorian English literature. Her dissertation focuses on depictions of epilepsy in the novels of Charles Dickens, George Eliot, and Wilkie Collins. She became interested in writing about the *Twilight* books when she saw how much prejudice there was against them because of their popularity with women and young adults. Her work identifies *Twilight*'s place in a literary tradition that reaches back into the nineteenth century.

Melissa Miller (M.A., Georgia State University, 2006) is an instructor and Ph.D. student in communications at Georgia State University. She studies the portrayal of gender, race, class and sexual orientation across various media and genres. Her dissertation examines how Meyer's *Twilight* saga plays a role in the way women identify with socially constructed ideals of femininity.

Ananya Mukherjea is a feminist medical sociologist and a longtime scholar of *Buffy the Vampire Slayer* and other vampire and Gothic fictions. She has published and presented on the topics of HIV/AIDS advocacy and community organizing; international sex work policy; the social and public health politics of flu pandemics; and masculinity, gender identity, and sexuality in popular culture. She is the editor of the book *Understanding Emerging Epidemics: Social and Political Approaches* (Emerald, 2010). Mukherjea is an assistant professor at the City University of New York's College of Staten Island and a member of the International Whedon Studies Association.

Colette Murphy is a scholar of popular culture and literature. In December 2010, she completed her master's thesis, "True Love's Bite: The *Twilight* Saga as Fairy Tale and Media Virus." She has been a lecturer in literature, composition, and public speaking and is a freelance writer. In addition to teaching and research, she spends much of her time writing fiction and plays. She is online at *http://colettemurphywrites.blogspot.com*.

Maggie Parke is the head of development for Elfin Productions and, concurrently, is earning her Ph.D. in event film adaptation and fan management at the National Institute for Excellence in the Creative Industries at Bangor University, Wales. She was a visiting researcher on the set of the first *Twilight* film in 2008 and has been involved in such events as the Leicester Square premiere in London and the TwiCon Fan Convention, where she was the programming chair. She was the media manager for *Vampire Baseball* in Portland, Oregon, and has published in the *Journal of Gaming and Virtual Worlds*, the online journal *InMedia Res*, and the British Council's American issue of the *Wales International Consortium*. Her blog can be found at *imstillwandering.blogspot.com*, and her website is *www.maggieparke.com*.

Hila Shachar is an honorary research fellow in the Department of English and Cultural Studies at the University of Western Australia and is a writer for the Australian Ballet. She is the author of *Cultural Afterlives and Screen Adaptations of Classic Literature: Wuthering Heights and Company* (forthcoming). She has essays in three books: *Gilbert and Gubar's the Madwoman in the Attic After Thirty Years* (University of Missouri Press, 2009), *Neo-Victorian Families: Gender, Sexual and Cultural Politics* (Rodopi, 2011) and *The Blackwell Companion to Historical Film* (Blackwell, 2012). She is researching literary biopics and post-feminism.

Angela Tenga is a graduate of Purdue University and an assistant professor at the Florida Institute of Technology, where her courses focus on literature, history, writing, and popular culture. Her research interests include early English literature, the literary monstrous, and the virtual self. The *Twilight* series took her by surprise when one of her students convinced her to read the novels. She has visited Forks twice.

Anne Torkelson is a graduate student studying English, publishing and print culture at the University of Minnesota Duluth. She devoured the *Twilight* saga in a weekend and believes there is much we can learn by examining children's and young adult literature.

Sarah Wakefield received her M.A. and Ph.D. degrees in English from the University of Texas at Austin, where she focused on 18th- and 19th-century British literature. She currently works at Prairie View A&M University as an associate professor of English. Her publications include a book on folklore in British women's fiction as well as work on fan culture, Victorian children's literature, and film adaptations of Jane Austen's novels. After years of analyzing evil fairies, mermaids, and vampires in literature, she found the *Twilight* saga irresistible.

Natalie Wilson is the author of *Seduced by Twilight* (McFarland, 2011) and pens one of the few academic blogs dedicated to the series at *www.seducedbytwilight.wordpress.com*. She teaches at Cal State San Marcos in the Department of Literature and Writing and in the Women's Studies Program. She has presented papers at numerous *Twilight* conferences and other public forums. Her essay in *Bitten by Twilight* was one of the first to examine the racialized implications of the saga, especially in relation to white privilege. She is also author of the blog *Professor, what if...?* and writes regularly for *Ms. Magazine Blog, Girl with Pen,* and *Womanist Musings*. Her homepage is at *www.nataliewilsonphd.wordpress.com*.

Index